To my parents

Proust's Additions

I

Proust's Additions

The Making of 'A la recherche du temps perdu'

I Text

ALISON WINTON

Fellow of Churchill College, Cambridge

Cambridge University Press

Cambridge

London . New York . Melbourne

Published by the Syndics of the Cambridge University Press
The Pitt Building, Trumpington Street, Cambridge CB2 1RP
Bentley House, 200 Euston Road, London NW1 2DB
32 East 57th Street, New York, NY 10022, USA
296 Beaconsfield Parade, Middle Park, Melbourne 3206, Australia

First published 1977

Printed in Great Britain by
Redwood Burn Limited
Trowbridge & Esher

Library of Congress Cataloguing in Publication Data

Winton, Alison, 1948-
Proust's additions.

Includes bibliographies and index.
CONTENTS: v. 1. Text. - v. 2. Table of additions.
1. Proust, Marcel, 1871-1922 - Technique. I. Title.
PQ2631.R63Z984 843'.9'12 76-58869

ISBN 0 521 21610 9 Volume I
ISBN 0 521 21611 7 Volume II
ISBN 0 521 21612 5 set of two volumes

Contents

PART I TEXT

Acknowledgements

I wish particularly to record my gratitude to Professor L.J. Austin, who supervised the thesis on which this book is based, for the unfailing help and encouragement he has given me, and for his invaluable advice at the most important stages of my research; to Professor J.M. Cocking, Dr. T.G.S. Combe, Professor A.A.B. Fairlie and Professor M.M. Bowie, for their discussion of the thesis and for their most helpful suggestions; to M. Michel Raimond; to Mme Suzy Mante-Proust, for giving me permission to publish the results of my research and to quote from the Proust manuscripts; to the Bibliothèque Nationale, Paris, for permission to reproduce photographs of manuscript pages; to the staff of the Département des Manuscrits at the Bibliothèque Nationale; and to Mrs. J. Ashman, who typed the book.

Abbreviations

DCS	*Du Côté de chez Swann*
JF	*A l'ombre des jeunes filles en fleurs*
CG	*Le Côté de Guermantes*
SG	*Sodome et Gomorrhe*
La P	*La Prisonnière*
La F	*La Fugitive*
TR	*Le Temps retrouvé*
BSAMP	*Bulletin de la Société des Amis de Marcel Proust et des Amis de Combray*
PRAN	*Proust Research Association Newsletter*
BN	Bibliothèque Nationale
Pl.	Pléiade edition
MS	manuscript
TS	typescript
n.a.fr. 16714:1 (e.g.)	page 1 (Bibliothèque Nationale pagination) of volume currently catalogued in Fonds Marcel Proust as nouvelles acquisitions françaises 16714
n.a.fr. 16761:29i (e.g.)	first page of galley-sheet 29 (there are eight pages to a galley-sheet) of volume currently catalogued in Fonds Marcel Proust as nouvelles acquisitions françaises 16761

(I.e. number before colon = volume number;
number after colon = page number.)

Note: All references to *A la recherche du temps perdu* are taken from the Bibliothèque de la Pléiade edition (3 vols., [Paris], 1954).

Introduction

It is well-known by now that the First World War interrupted the publication of A la recherche du temps perdu, and that as a result it had time to grow from its original 1500 pages to its present 3000.[1] This book, within given limits, describes the development of Proust's great novel after 1914, showing how the volumes from A l'ombre des jeunes filles en fleurs onwards were expanded (Du Côté de chez Swann had, of course, appeared already in 1913). The sources of this study are the near-definitive manuscripts, typescripts and proofs of the 1914-22 period which form part of the Proust manuscript material acquired in 1962 by the Bibliothèque Nationale, Paris; it is these documents that show not only the conception, but the final stages, of A la recherche du temps perdu.

---

1 Proust's 1911-13 estimates of the length of his then three-volume novel (e.g. his letter in Louis de Robert, Comment débuta Marcel Proust, re-edition ([Paris], 1969), pp.58-59) have been summarised many times. The clearest recapitulation is probably that given by G. Painter, in Marcel Proust: A Biography (2 vols., London, 1959 & 1965), vol. II, pp.234-35. From here on, only the first reference to a book will give full bibliographical details; succeeding ones will use simply the title, or the name of the author, unless confusion could arise. References to articles will normally be similarly abbreviated. Complete details may always be found in the bibliography at the end of Part I.

The procedure adopted in most of the book is to let the reader see which passages in the present novel were not in the near-definitive drafts. The first chapter of Part I, the text, does, however, summarise the 'base' narrative of each volume before further episodes or themes were added. The rest of Part I then describes the most significant of the late insertions, surveying their general effects (comic ones, for example), and going on to give a more detailed picture of the additions made to the speech of the characters and to the figure of Morel; those elaborating moral characteristics, and situations of uncertainty; those tracing social change and physical decline; and those which extend the rôles of the artists Vinteuil and Elstir.

Some late passages mentioned in Chapter 1 do not figure in the subsequent discussion: given such a wide field, there had to be at least a little selection. I have covered those additions which seemed to me certainly most striking, and revealing consistent pre-occupations, but individual researchers might pick out and emphasise different trends. My approach is, on the whole, thematic, in that I normally group the additions according to similar content, not according to the point in the narrative at which they appear, and not in an attempt to define, for example, the development of single characters (with a few exceptions).

The text of the book makes constant reference to Part II, the second volume. This gives, in table form, the additions to be found in the documents I studied, and their precise location (preceded by a brief description of the research method adopted). These tables, although not, as I shall shortly explain, exhaustive to the smallest detail, are nevertheless very comprehensive. To work continuously through *A la recherche* with them would be arduous; however, they might be used in the following more feasible ways. A reader might wish to study a small section of the novel, such as the death of the grand-mother, or even only a page or two. He could look at the tables to discover the stages of composition of phrases, sentences or paragraphs in that section. Another reader might be writing an article on, say, the Dreyfus Affair in the novel, or on animal imagery; he would already have all his page-references, and could then consult the tables to see which passages were comparatively early and which late. A researcher could gain a fairly accurate impression of the contents of a given Bibliothèque Nationale MS volume - let us say n.a.fr.[1] 16714, the last part of the *Sodome et Gomorrhe* MS - by seeing, from the right-hand column of the tables, what was added to the MS, and what must have been missing from that MS, as it was added only on the typescript - n.a.fr. 16741 in this case. Finally, these tables may be of some help in the preparation of any critical edition, and will perhaps be useful to the research team projecting a study of the early Cahiers, since this team is

---

1 I.e. 'nouvelles acquisitions françaises', the Bibliothèque Nationale classification.

to proceed by finding all the versions of separate 'units' in the novel:[1] the tables show exactly where the final few stages of each 'unit' are to be found.

In the material I used, there is room for at least three other studies than mine. First, except in a brief general paragraph in Chapter 1,[2] I have not tried to date individual pages or volumes. Someone more observant may find pointers which I simply missed; but I saw very little which enabled me to place the sections on which I was working, except according to the inner order of composition. Rather than confuse the issue with speculation, I have therefore left the subject for a more complete examination than I could give it, that is, an examination which would correlate the paper of sheets added to the MS with pages of letters, with the paper of the rough Cahiers, etc., and which would deduce chronology on internal evidence. J. Theodore Johnson Jr. suggests that such a correlation could and should be made,[3] and some of George Painter's work might help researchers with the dating.[4]

I have also, generally, left aside the excised material in these documents, reproducing it or referring to it only occasionally. Some of it is most interesting, although perhaps less rich

---

1 See the Proust Research Association Newsletter, no. 6, Fall 1971, p. 25.

2 Below, pp. 18-19.

3 In PRAN no. 2, Summer 1969, p. 26.

4 See his Marcel Proust: A Biography, vol. II, e.g. pp. 303-305, 321.

than that from the pre-1914 period cited by Maurice Bardèche in his Marcel Proust romancier.[1] At any rate, this again would be a subject for a separate, and long, book.

Finally, related to this second aspect, I felt it was the work of a complete critical edition rather than of this study to provide all minor variants of words or phrases, and to point out the movement of certain passages from their original positions to new ones. Thus, for example, the tables tend not to note the attribution of one speech in turn to different characters. This kind of transfer may be less important in a writer like Proust than in others; as we first knew from André Maurois, some features recorded in Proust's Cahiers are there to be worked in, not necessarily to be attached to one specific figure in the entire gallery.[2]

All conclusions in the following pages must to a certain extent be regarded as conditional on future research on the rough Cahiers, which may, for example, reveal that episodes that according to my material looked late were 'salvaged' from a much earlier series of compositions.

---

1 (2 vols., Paris, 1971)

2 See A. Maurois, A la recherche de Marcel Proust, re-edition ([Paris], 1970), p. 150; also G. Brée, 'Les Manuscrits de Marcel Proust', The French Review, XXXVII (1963), pp. 182-87 (p. 185). Bardèche confirms it too in Marcel Proust romancier, vol. I, p. 344 n.1; vol. II, pp. 80, 124.

I Documentary Material

The material for A la recherche du temps perdu in the Bibliothèque Nationale Fonds Marcel Proust falls into two sections. In the first, there are sixty-two 'cahiers' and four narrow 'carnets', giving drafts and re-workings from the time of Contre Sainte-Beuve to, probably, the end of Proust's life. In the second, with which this book is concerned, are numerous near-definitive manuscripts, typescripts and proofs: by far the greater number of these documents are post-1914. To make a rough division, the material in the first section could therefore be thought of as that of the genesis of the novel, and in the second, that of its later refinement or expansion. The Bibliothèque Nationale manuscript department itself has separated the documents in this manner, grouping the unbound Cahiers apart from the rest, which are bound.[1]

---

1 J. Theodore Johnson Jr. gives the list of the Fonds Marcel Proust current to August 1971 (under its previous provisional numbering) in PRAN no.7, Spring 1972, pp.15-23, and supplements it with another list of the more recently released volumes in PRAN no.12, Fall 1974, pp. 22-29. These, between them, record the complete holdings of the collection, now under its final classification: nouvelles acquisitions françaises 16611-16781 (hereafter n.a.fr., followed by the relevant volume number).

Since the BN's acquisition of the Proust collection in May 1962,[1] and the early articles describing it with interest and excitement,[2] most of the research projected or completed on the manuscripts for A la recherche du temps perdu has been concentrated on the first section. One of the main tasks of the recently-formed Équipe Proust in Paris is to work through the rough drafts of A la recherche, 'spécialement les Cahiers et les Carnets', towards an eventual critical edition.[3] The thorough and useful reports on the MSS provided by the Proust Research Association Newsletter have not on the whole focussed on the post-1914 material.[4] Individual articles written since 1962 have reviewed, or made use of, the rough Cahiers rather than the

---

1 'Chronique des bibliothèques françaises: Département des manuscrits: Acquisition des manuscrits de Marcel Proust', Bulletin des Bibliothèques de France, no. 7 (1962), pp.380-81.

2 G. Brée, 'Les Manuscrits de Marcel Proust', The French Review, XXXVII (1963), pp. 182-87; Anon, 'Les manuscrits de Marcel Proust à la Bibliothèque Nationale', BSAMP, no.13 (1963), pp. 70-74.

3 See PRAN, no.6, Fall 1971, pp. 25-26; the Équipe Proust, Centre d'Histoire et d'Analyse des Manuscrits Modernes, was then the Centre d'Études Proustiennes. Its reorganisation, and other activities, are outlined in PRAN no. 12, Fall 1974, pp. 7, 11-13, and no. 13, Spring 1975, pp. 15-16.

4 Except in PRAN no. 2, Summer 1969, pp. 23, 24, 26-28, and in the lists mentioned above in PRAN nos. 7 and 12.

near-definitive MSS.[1] And by far the most important single account, up to the present date, of the BN MSS, that given *passim* in Maurice Bardèche's two-volume *Marcel Proust romancier*, has drawn almost solely on the Cahiers and Carnets.[2]

Fragmentary information about the second section *is* coming to light, in isolated references in a few articles.[3] Jean-Yves

---

1 Three of the most valuable of these are: E.R.Jackson, 'The Crystallisation of "A la recherche du temps perdu" 1908-1909', *The French Review*, XXXVIII (1964), pp.157-66; A. Barnes, 'Le retour des thèmes dans la *Recherche du Temps perdu* et l'art de Proust', *Australian Journal of French Studies*, VI (1969), pp. 26-54; H. Bonnet, 'Esquisse pour une "Prisonnière"', *Le Figaro Littéraire*, 1-7 février 1971, pp.10-12.
See also 'Portrait de Françoise: texte inédit publié par J.-Y. Tadié', *Revue d'Histoire Littéraire de la France*, 71e année, nos.5-6 (1971), pp.753-64; the contributions of H. Bonnet, J. Theodore Johnson Jr., G. Tupinier and C. Quémar in *Études Proustiennes I*, published by Gallimard ([Paris], 1973), and that of C. Quémar in *Études Proustiennes II* ([Paris], 1975); and Anon, 'Un verso de cahier', *BSAMP*, no.25 (1975), pp.5-6.

2 Bardèche covers or discusses, of course, parts of the significant material published some 20 years previously by A. Maurois in his *A la recherche de Marcel Proust*, principally pp.141-56, 208-14. See *Marcel Proust romancier*, vol. I, pp.152*n*.1, 153, 154, 215, 275*n*.2, 397-402; vol. II, pp.151*n*.3, 183.
Amongst other books which have made stimulating use of the earlier MS material are H. Bonnet, *Marcel Proust de 1907 à 1914* (Paris, 1971), pp.20-21, 64-69, 75, 93, 98-101, 110, 125-26, 197-99; G. Brée, *The World of Marcel Proust* (London, 1967), pp.110-12; J.-Y. Tadié, *Proust et le roman* (Paris, 1971), pp.17, 20, 28, 30*n*.3, 47, 56, 64*n*.1, 65, 79, 82, 98, 185-86, 204-5, 223, 224*n*.7, 228, 280*n*.6, 370, 377, 387, 393.

3 A. Barnes, 'Le retour des thèmes dans la *Recherche du Temps perdu* et l'art de Proust' (pp.44-48), 'Le Jardin de Marcel Proust: pour le cinquantenaire des "Jeunes Filles en Fleurs"', *The Modern Language Review*, LXIV (1969), pp.546-54 (pp.549*n*.2, 552 - here, incidentally, A. Barnes's findings do not tally with mine), and 'A propos d'un paragraphe du *Temps retrouvé*: Proust et le tragique', *BSAMP*, no.23 (1973), pp.1609-13 (p. 1610); J. Theodore Johnson Jr., '"La Lanterne magique": Proust's Metaphorical Toy', *L'Esprit Créateur*, XI (1971), pp.17-31 (pp. 20-21*n*.3), 'Proust, Ruskin et la petite figure au portail des Libraires à la Cathédrale de Rouen', *BSAMP*, no.23 (1973), pp. 1721-36 (p. 1734), and in *Études Proustiennes I*, pp.173-76; J. Milly, 'Le Pastiche Goncourt dans "Le Temps retrouvé"', *Revue d'Histoire Littéraire de la France*, 71e année, nos.5-6 (1971), pp.815-35 (p.831); C. Quémar, in *Études Proustiennes I*, pp. 280-81, 284-89, 291-92, 322-35 (for *DCS* only).

Tadié makes incidental mention of the post-1914 drafts in his Proust et le roman,[1] and Maurice Bardèche devotes some space to dating and to description of the later documents, with a particularly helpful summary of the state of Proust's typescripts and proofs at the beginning of 1914.[2] None the less, the fact remains that the most complete information on the post-1914 material is still that provided by work done before the acquisition of the relevant documents by the BN, and it is to this that we must continue to turn for an impression of the way Proust's novel developed during the war and until the end of his life. Excised passages from the galley-proofs of Le Côté de Guermantes, the original beginning of Sodome et Gomorrhe I, expansions of the La Prisonnière manuscripts and typescripts, variants on the stay in Venice, the contents of a long rough insertion to be found in the MS of Le Temps retrouvé, and snippets given in an article on punctuation by one of the Pléiade editors, are all in issues of BSAMP published no later than

---

1 Almost all these mentions refer to information already provided by issues of BSAMP or by the Pléiade edition: those which perhaps do not are on pp. 140n.2, 399.

2 Bardèche, vol. II, appendix I, pp. 371-74. The most important other references are in vol. I, pp. 196, 238-39, 244; vol. II, pp. 71-72, 75-77, 92-93, 147, 149, 161-63, 170, 207, 210, 213, 274, 279-82. See also vol. II, pp. 259-260, for some noteworthy general remarks on Proust in the post-1914 period. (Bardèche refers to the bound, later, volumes as the Dossier Proust: see p. 7 of vols. I and II.)

1962.[1] The Pléiade edition, of course, used many of these later documents, but here, indications in notes of reworkings and additions must inevitably be only ad hoc, and one of the editors has himself expressed hope of a full critical edition.[2] Anthony Pugh's unpublished thesis offers a fuller exposition of variants and structural shifts during the post-1914 period; nevertheless, both he and M. Suzuki, the author of the BSAMP articles on La Prisonnière, were hampered by their necessary dependence on

---

1 These articles are, respectively: For CG, P. Clarac, 'Les "croyances intellectuelles" de Marcel Proust', BSAMP, no. 8 (1958), pp. 460-68 (pp. 465-68).
For SG, 'Première version du début de "Sodome et Gomorrhe I", présentée par André Ferré', BSAMP, no. 6 (1956), pp. 165-70.
For La P, M. Suzuki, 'Le "Je" Proustien', BSAMP, no. 9 (1959), pp. 69-82 (pp. 69-74), and 'Le comique chez Marcel Proust', BSAMP, no. 11 (1961), pp. 377-91, 'Le comique chez Marcel Proust (II)', BSAMP, no. 12 (1962), pp. 572-86.
For the stay in Venice, La F, A.R. Pugh, 'Le séjour à Venise, propos sur le texte de "La Fugitive"', BSAMP, no. 9 (1959), pp. 29-43.
For TR, 'Un inédit de Proust en marge du "Temps retrouvé", présenté par André Ferré', BSAMP, no. 5 (1955), pp. 9-16.
The article on punctuation is A. Ferré, 'La ponctuation de Marcel Proust', BSAMP, no. 7 (1957), pp. 310-29. (See also A. Ferré, 'Quelques fautes de ponctuation dans les éditions de Marcel Proust', Revue d'Histoire Littéraire de la France, 54e année (1954), pp. 213-18; and there are too some preliminary remarks in L. Pierre-Quint's Comment Travaillait Proust (Paris, 1928), pp. 13-15.)

2 P. Clarac, 'Les "croyances intellectuelles" de Marcel Proust', BSAMP, no. 8 (1958), pp. 460-68 (p. 468).
For the editors' descriptions of some of the relevant documents, see vol. I of the Pléiade edition, pp. xxiv-xxxvi, and particularly p. xxxiii (cp. my own description below, pp.19-21).
In Part II, pp.12-13, I describe a few seeming discrepancies between my documents and the Pléiade editors'.

microfilms, on sometimes merely briefly-glimpsed documents, and, in Pugh's case, on incomplete material.[1]

The disparate items of information released by these scholars have been valuable and tantalising, but simply because of their brevity, or their summary nature, it is still Albert Feuillerat's Comment Marcel Proust a composé son roman which is the most comprehensive published attempt at a general synthesis; and even he was examining only two volumes, central though these were, of the many now available. Any study of the post-1914 MSS must acknowledge indebtedness to confirmatory points provided by the other books and articles; but it is undoubtedly Feuillerat's often competent, but often contentious, work which has pioneered research into the documentary history of A la recherche from 1914 to 1922, and which continues to be referred to and discussed as the standard exploration in this field.

Feuillerat's method of presentation - an outline of a given section or personality as it was in the 1914 galleys, and then a summary of the subsequent changes made to that section or character, progressing through the volumes concerned - is clear,

---

1 Anthony R. Pugh, 'The Composition of Marcel Proust's A la Recherche du Temps Perdu' (unpublished Ph.D. thesis, University of Cambridge, 1959): see his preface for a summary of his documents, and also pp. 277-77a, 286, 288, 304, 323n.30, 333(?), 344(?), 358, 376, 382, 384-85, 417, 422-25, 495, 498-501. (It is occasionally unclear exactly which documents Pugh has seen himself, or to which he is referring, for JF, CG, and SG.) For M. Suzuki's thought-provoking discoveries, see the last footnote but one.

well-organised and interesting. His reconstruction of the original third volume need not concern us in detail, since it is based on hypothesis, and in any case deals with a stage earlier than that which I study. As far as I can tell from my material, there are some astonishingly accurate guesses in this reconstruction, such as the claim that the whole Amanien d'Osmond episode was a late one;[1] others would appear to be quite wrong, for example the assumption that the passages about the princesse de Parme's _dame d'honneur_ were in the original version,[2] or that the lines on the Voices in _La Prisonnière_ formed part of the first draft.[3] However, since the whole 1914 _Recherche_ has not been found, and perhaps never will be,[4] Feuillerat's broad outlines seem a reasonably plausible conjecture, and are backed at many points by Bardèche's research.[5]

---

1 A. Feuillerat, _Comment Marcel Proust a composé son roman_ (New Haven, 1934), pp. 157-58, and _n_.15. See below, Ch. 5, p.219.

2 Feuillerat, p. 157. See below, p. 35, and Ch. 6, pp. 257-58.

3 Feuillerat, p. 198. See below, Ch. 2, p.98 _n_.1.

4 The MS of the third 'Grasset volume' seems to have been lost or destroyed. See G. Painter, _Marcel Proust: A Biography_, vol. II, p. 237, J.-Y. Tadié, _Proust et le roman_, p. 27, _n_.8, and H. Bonnet, 'Les souvenirs de Céleste', _BSAMP_, no. 24 (1974), pp. 1827-38 (pp. 1834-36); we know from the fragment of the letter published in G. Cattaui's _L'Amitié de Proust_ (Paris, 1935), p. 184, that Proust burned some of his MSS on leaving boulevard Haussmann, and M. Bardèche remarks on the dearth of existing Cahier material for this hypothetical third volume: see his vol. I, pp. 242-44, 300-301; vol. II, pp. 162-64, 208-10. However, H. Bonnet, in the article just cited, says that the Cahier of _Le Temps retrouvé_ seems _not_ to have been burned (p. 1835); and Plate 1 in _PRAN_ no. 2, Summer 1969 (between pp. 20 and 21), giving contents of the Cahiers, does show a not insubstantial documentation for _Sodome et Gomorrhe_ on.

5 Such as the fact that the _Sodome et Gomorrhe_ Verdurin dinners were originally to take place in or near Paris: Feuillerat, pp. 170-71; see Bardèche, vol. II, pp. 153-55, 159, 162, and also Painter's conclusions, vol. II, p. 238.

Feuillerat's means of organising his material tends to lead to an anecdotal or episodic approach which stresses the spoiling of the first structure of the novel,[1] and, above all, to a lack of any but a rather sweeping connection between the separate additions described. Certainly, much debate has been provoked by his conclusions: that Proust, in these years, was becoming more cerebral, and making his hero so, as his own youthful lyricism inclined to leave him; that he had grown more misanthropic - partly because of the war, partly as the result of a deepening susceptibility and the solitude in which he increasingly lived - and hence was denigrating his characters; and that he was using his novel as a kind of latter-day diary, pouring into it everything he thought of, and determined, as his life drew to a close, to let none of his current observations and experiences slip into oblivion.[2] On some points, such as the growing

1 Much of A. Pugh's thesis, too, implicitly or explicitly criticises Proust for spoiling his original structure in moments of excess or even, it is suggested, panic. (See, e.g., his pp. 281, 294, 312, 331a, b, 352, 535-37.)

2 Pugh also sees this third drive as a fundamental one in the 1914-22 period: pp. 252, 273, 486, 529-30, 532.
These conclusions, and others, of Feuillerat's are to be found on pp. 108-132, 253-70. (Feuillerat seems to have been unaware of the Agostinelli affair: for descriptions of this, see Painter, vol. II, chapters 9 and 10; R. Vigneron, 'Genèse de Swann', Revue d'Histoire de la Philosophie, 5e année (1937), pp. 67-115 (pp. 96-115).)
One of the most germane and original discussions of Feuillerat's main thesis is J.M. Cocking's, in '"Jean Santeuil" et "A la Recherche du Temps perdu"', BSAMP, no. 6 (1956), pp. 181-97; see also, e.g., H. Bonnet, Le Progrès spirituel dans l'oeuvre de Marcel Proust (2 vols., Paris, 1946 & 1949), vol. II, pp. 144-52; P. Costil, 'La construction musicale de la "Recherche du Temps perdu" (I)', BSAMP, no. 8 (1958), pp. 469-89; M. Raimond, 'Note sur la structure du "Côté de Guermantes"', Revue d'Histoire Littéraire de la France, 71e année, nos. 5-6 (1971), pp. 854-74 (pp. 854-55).

intellectualisation of Marcel's universe, it is possible to agree; but one can attribute this, where it happens, to a deliberate plan on Proust's part, and one which was always fundamental to the pattern of the novel, rather than to the drying-up of his stylistic gifts. As I shall show, some of the 'lyrical' passages in the last half of the novel are in fact very probably late ones. As for the misanthropy, there are some misapprehensions in Feuillerat's interpretations: he does not see, for example, that Proust is not attacking Françoise for her linguistic errors,[1] nor that many of the 'denigratory' additions are directed less at individual characters than at some wider leitmotif, often one related to the Marcel-Albertine affair, or else one that elaborates, by apposition or contrast, the implications of Le Temps retrouvé. This is especially true of the expansions made to the characters' spoken language, which account for a large number of the changes to Norpois, Françoise and M. de Guermantes discussed by Feuillerat. And the belief that Proust simply 'put into' his novel everything that interested him, quite apart from the facile view it betrays of complex references within A la recherche, must be modified by the publication of post-1914 rough drafts and fragments which did not find their way into the novel as we now have it.[2]

---

1 See below, Ch. 3, pp. 131-32.

2 See, e.g., the Cahier extracts in 'Notes en marge du "Temps perdu", présentées par André Ferré', BSAMP, no. 6 (1956), pp. 158-64, probably, from the subject-matter, written after 1914; Bardèche, vol. II, pp. 280, n.2, 400-402; and especially the passages given passim in the Pléiade edition notes, e.g. II 708n.1.

I hope that my grouping of expansions under thematic headings rather than episodic ones will, by clarifying the careful links between many of the revisions, go some way towards rectifying the image of arbitrary or even spiteful motivation on Proust's part which is often implied in Feuillerat's study. As far as the research material itself is concerned, I provide, for Le Côté de Guermantes I, a fuller picture of the stages of enlargement than Feuillerat was able to, and for the rest will draw on documents he again did not have, and which may be the nearest to a primary whole version, subsequently expanded, that can be studied.[1]

These documents are as follows:-[2]

For A l'ombre des jeunes filles en fleurs:

n.a.fr.16732	First typescript
n.a.fr.16735	Second typescript
n.a.fr.16754	1913 Grasset galleys, uncorrected
n.a.fr.16753	1913 Grasset galleys, corrected
n.a.fr.16761	1914 Grasset galleys, virtually uncorrected (Feuillerat's first document)

1 It would be impossible to acknowledge in notes every point on which my research coincides with that of Feuillerat (and Pugh, etc.), but I do draw attention to the most important. Pugh, in any case, was researching from a different angle, and states specifically that his study is not concerned with the content of the additions (p. 277e).

2 (Volume numbering and pagination in this study are always those of the BN.)

For _Le Côté de Guermantes_:

n.a.fr.16736	Typescript, up to II 296
n.a.fr.16760	1914 Grasset galleys (Feuillerat's second document[1])
n.a.fr.16705-16707	Manuscript, from II 345
n.a.fr.16762, 16763	First Gallimard galleys
n.a.fr.16765	Third Gallimard galleys

For _Sodome et Gomorrhe_:

n.a.fr.16708-16714	Manuscript
n.a.fr.16739-16741	Typescript, _Sodome et Gomorrhe II_
n.a.fr.16766	Proofs, _Sodome et Gomorrhe II_

For _La Prisonnière_:

n.a.fr.16715-16719	Manuscript
n.a.fr.16742, 16743	First typescript
n.a.fr.16744	Second typescript
n.a.fr.16745-16747	Third typescript
n.a.fr.16767	Galleys (posthumous)

For _La Fugitive_:

n.a.fr.16719-16722	Manuscript
n.a.fr.16749	Typescript[2]

---

1 His copy, however, was apparently uncorrected (see his pp. 7, 21), whereas these are extensively worked on by Proust.

2 Probably posthumous.

For Le Temps retrouvé:

n.a.fr.16722-16727 Manuscript

n.a.fr.16750, 16751 Typescript[1]

A more detailed description of these volumes, and of any special difficulties they present, is given in Part II, under Notes and Descriptions for each A la recherche volume. The dating of many of them must be conjectural; however, there are some facts of which it is possible to be fairly sure.

---

1 Posthumous.
There is also a manuscript volume of 86 pages in the Fonds Marcel Proust (n.a.fr. 16704) which gives part of A l'ombre (from I 704 to roughly I 953 §1). It is written in pencil in, according to the BN, Albert Nahmias's hand; since there are no corrections by Proust, and the 1911-12 typescripts copy it exactly, I do not refer to it.
Incidental reference is also made in this book to n.a.fr. 16703, some MS fragments from DCS; n.a.fr. 16730 and 16755, respectively part of the typescript, and the second page-proofs, of DCS; n.a.fr. 16768, more posthumous proofs of La P; n.a.fr. 16737, typescripts of the grandmother's death. These last two volumes were not available when I was doing my research (mainly 1970-71); neither were n.a.fr. 16738, typescripts of part of SG, n.a.fr. 16764, the second Gallimard galleys (incomplete) of CG, nor n.a.fr. 16748, the first half of the La Fugitive typescript, to name the only three other important documents subsequently released that are relevant to this area of research. Both n.a.fr. 16764 and 16748 are uncorrected, and probably not of substantial value; the two major gaps in the documents for this study are therefore n.a.fr. 16737 and 16738. (There are several volumes in this section of the Fonds Marcel Proust for DCS too, but I do not of course cover these.)
Also released since 1971 is n.a.fr. 16729, classified as 'Reliquat manuscrit de la Recherche'; this collects, inter alia, some drafts of additions, and some sheets which must originally have been attached, in the form of additions, to the MSS covered here.

The typescripts of _A l'ombre_ are, of course, a continuation of those of _Du Côté de chez Swann_, and were made in 1911-12.[1] The typescript of _Le Côté de Guermantes_ (the first half of the volume) was also made before the publication of _Du Côté de chez Swann_, since Charlus appears in it as Fleurus.[2] All the manuscripts (n.a.fr. 16705-16727) were written _after_ the appearance of Albertine, since she is in the main text of the documents; they were thus, presumably, composed no earlier than about late 1914-early 1915, since rough drafts would be made first, and they may well be considerably later. This possibility applies particularly to the MS of _Le Temps retrouvé_, whose main text actually comprises the war-chapter.[3] The first Gallimard galleys for _Le Côté de Guermantes_ can be dated between 1918 and 1920.[4] Painter's correlation of dates indicates that the typescripts of _Sodome et Gomorrhe_, and corrections on them, were made between January and April 1921;[5] and, as is well-known,

---

1 Painter, vol. II, pp. 172, 174, 183.

2 Bardèche (vol. II, pp. 71-72, 75) says it was made in the second half of 1913.
Since this and the typescripts of _A l'ombre_ are pre-1914, I refer to them only rarely in my text, but have given details of them in the tables in Part II.

3 This dating seems to be confirmed by H. Bonnet's important article 'Esquisse pour une "Prisonnière"', _Le Figaro Littéraire_, 1-7 février 1971, pp.10-12, which would place all the 'definitive' MSS from _La P_ to _TR_ well after March 1915, since the working-out was not done before this stage (pp. 10, 11).

4 That is, between the first publication of _JF_ and the publication of _CG_.

5 Painter, vol. II, pp. 311-312, 324.

the first typescript of _La Prisonnière_ was made in the first half of 1922, and was subsequently partially retyped twice between mid-August and late October 1922.[1]

The narrative of the MS volumes, which are swollen exercise-books, is written on the recto face of the page: some of these pages were clearly cut out of other exercise-books and inserted. The narrative itself is, practically without exception, in Proust's writing;[2] this handwriting is large, clear and firm, and the difference between it and the crabbed and very small 1910-11 hand might help in approximate dating of rough drafts in the earlier Cahiers.[3] Anything on verso faces is usually a rough working-out; from the end of the _La_

---

1 Painter, vol. II, p. 354; his account of the number of retypings is confusing. The BN has three typescripts, as did the Pléiade editors: III 1057-58.
Some clues as to dating may be found in Proust's correspondence with Gaston Gallimard and Jacques Rivière, where there is much general reference to changes and additions; but in the letters to Rivière, it is largely extracts appearing in the _Nouvelle Revue Française_ that are discussed, and in any case, letters to both Rivière and Gallimard do not specify precisely which additions are being made. All in all, the correspondence provides little really detailed information about the successive states of the MSS, etc.; but readers who wish to glance at Proust's day-to-day exchanges with his editors about the vicissitudes of production and his own habits of composition could refer to _Marcel Proust et Jacques Rivière: Correspondance 1914-22_, présentée et annotée par P. Kolb (Paris, 1955), principally pp. 7, 27-28, 31-32, 36, 47, 159-60, 166, 169-70, 174, 204; and _Lettres à la NRF_ (Paris, 1932), principally pp. 113, 115-16, 119, 121, 137, 144-49, 153, 171, 177, 182, 185, 194, 204-5, 224, 246, 255-56, 273.

2 Where there is copying in another hand, it is usually the same one, probably Céleste Albaret's.

3 The earlier handwriting, tight and often almost illegible, is to be seen in n.a.fr. 16703, a collection of fragments giving a rough version of _DCS_.

Prisonnière MS onwards,[1] these versos coincide more and more with their final version, and are often copied straight on to the opposite recto page. And, as can be gathered from the Pléiade edition notes, there is considerable reworking on almost all the late volumes. Handwritten pages are inserted into the typescripts; here and there, glued into the manuscripts, are some fragments that are evidently older than anything else in the exercise-book.[2] Many passages are simply excised: others are crossed out, then to be taken up again, sometimes almost verbatim, sometimes with new elements worked in, in a margin or layer addition.

These features, and others, could in themselves each repay close attention;[3] but undoubtedly the most striking aspect of all this material is the new additions, appearing, when they are inserted on the MS, in different ink and slightly different handwriting from the main narrative, and, on MSS, typescripts and proofs, written into margins, between the lines, and in those famous concertina-like extra sheets of paper, attached to the page, that range from comparatively small - an inch or two - to huge - over three feet long![4] These extra sheets, which I shall call 'layers', are nearly all on unlined, heavy, creamy-white

---

1 About n.a.fr. 16718:132.

2 This is true of *CG*, *La F*, and *TR*. See *Notes and Descriptions* for these, Part II.

3 I give some examples of them in Part II, pp.5-12, 15-19.

4 The one on n.a.fr. 16714:1 is about 39" in length: this gives most of II 1101-8.

paper: sometimes still newer layers are glued on to them, and again, small layers may be glued into margins in order further to illustrate an already expanded point. There can be two individual and clearly chronologically separate additions in one margin; or a layer may itself be composed of different sections, subsequently glued together. I have given a picture of as many of these features as possible in the tables, and it is the content of the additions,[1] where they are linked by a given common factor, that I shall try to describe in this part of the study.

If so much was added, what was there at first? For reasons of space, any account of this is bound to be sketchy; but I shall now attempt a brief outline of what is to be found in the earliest complete version of each volume during the 1914-22 period, and the principal episodes missing from these versions. For A l'ombre and for Le Côté de Guermantes up to II 296, this base document is the 1914 Grasset galleys; for the death of the grandmother it is the first Gallimard galleys; and for the rest of the novel, from II 345 on, it is the manuscript.[2]

---

1 (Including, normally, the handwritten pages inserted into the typescripts, mentioned just above.)

2 All statements on the following pages may be verified from the tables in Part II, and a number of them will be elaborated, with specific details and references, in succeeding chapters.

A L'OMBRE DES JEUNES FILLES EN FLEURS

The substance of the 1914 version of this volume has already been described by Feuillerat. To recapitulate:

The early version starts on what is now I 434, with 'Le Marquis de Norpois[1] avait été ministre plénipotentiaire [...]', thus not giving the first three-and-a-half pages about Swann and Cottard[2] (although some discussion of Swann's new social attitudes does appear about thirty-six galley pages later[3]). The dinner, and the visit to the theatre, take place as they do now, but without a number of the references to Françoise's cooking (I 445-46, 484-86), and especially without a great many of Norpois's phrases (e.g. I 461-63), his advice about the investment of Tante Léonie's fortune, now inherited by Marcel (I 454-55), and Marcel's melancholy over his father's judgement that 'il n'est plus un enfant' (I 481-83). Marcel falls ill, as at present, but there is no consultation with Cottard (I 497-99); and although the visits to the Swanns are central in the 1914 version, Albertine's name, as we know from Feuillerat,[4]

---

1 Corrected from 'M. de Norpois'.

2 n.a.fr. 16761:29i.

3 On n.a.fr. 16761:33v-vi; see under I 431-34a in Part II.

4 Feuillerat, p. 42.

is not mentioned (I 512, 598); considerable portions, too, of the discussion of Swann's lowered social tastes, and of Odette's position in society, are not to be found (I 513-15, 516-23, 599-603, 605-6). The galleys relate without a break the Swanns' doubly flattering habit of consulting Marcel's preferences as to their excursions (I 526) and talking openly with him of Gilberte's virtues (I 536); the passages about Marcel's bemused state (I 527-28), and Vinteuil's music (I 529-34), thus do not yet figure.[1] Bergotte's appearance and conversation, substantially the same in 1914 as now, are not for the moment, however, elaborated with the page on his phrases about his own work ('cela peut être utile', 'c'est doux') (I 556-57), nor with his medical advice to Marcel (I 570-73). Mme Swann takes her walks in the Bois in the 1914 version, but without the final two pages or so which dwell on her provisional exclusion from the Faubourg Saint-Germain (I 638-40). Other elements not yet in the 'Autour de Mme Swann' section are the meeting with the princesse Mathilde (I 541-43, 543-44), the gift of Léonie's furniture which Marcel makes to the brothel, and subsequently regrets (I 577-79), and the lines on Odette's 'cocotte' taste for flowers (I 593-94). However, the largest single unit absent from this section is certainly that now occupied by Marcel's deeper love for Gilberte. The 1914 version of this love, and the ways in which it was later expanded, have

---

1 See I 509-11, 546-47 for other descriptions of Marcel's rapt state not yet in the novel.

been thoroughly described by Feuillerat, so I shall not go into detail here.[1]

To calculate merely from the Gilberte and these other principal passages alone, therefore, at least 85 of the present 210 pages for this first part of A l'ombre did not appear in 1914.

Proust was also to make a few interesting excisions: the 1914 narrative had provided more detail about Swann's feelings for Odette, and even gave him a speculation as to her possible criminality;[2] it furthermore made Charlus the source of much of Marcel's information about Swann's emotions, the source, too, of a statement that the anguish aroused by the second woman Swann fell in love with caused his death![3] And it is worth noticing that the experience of involuntary memory in the WC does not appear in these proofs: it was at first placed much earlier, about thirty pages before the dinner with Norpois.[4]

Marcel of course departs for Balbec in the 1914 version, but since there is no reference to Gilberte, and since the passage about trains and stations originally came rather later,[5] the second part starts simply 'Quand nous partîmes cette année-là pour Balbec, mon corps [...]', followed by the

---

1 Feuillerat, pp. 36-41, 118-22. The principal passages about Gilberte not in the 1914 galleys are in I 500-502, 528-29, 565-66, 581-92, 597, 607-15, 621-35.

2 n.a.fr. 16761:32vi-33vi.

3 n.a.fr. 16761:37vii-viii. Cp. I 524-25.

4 In the 1913 galleys, n.a.fr. 16753:54viii-55ii.

5 On about the equivalent of II 648; n.a.fr. 16761:44viii-45i.

description of Marcel's malaises (I 645 on).[1] The comic evocation of his drunkenness in the train is substantially shorter in this early version, and does not comprise the reading of Mme de Sévigné (I 652-54); on the other hand, there was a description, eventually excised, of Marcel's desire to see Bayeux Cathedral and simultaneous anguish at the thought that to do so he would have to leave his grandmother.[2] The arrival at Balbec and the depiction of the inhabitants of the hotel were largely as they are now, but without Marcel's reactions to the intimidating general manager (I 691-92), or Françoise's inconvenient friendships with the hotel staff (I 692-94) and her attitudes to masters and to the aristocracy (I 694-96). The personnel is, as yet, lacking the plant-like hotel-boy (I 706-7); and, although the rides with Mme de Villeparisis and the meeting with Saint-Loup remained almost unmodified between 1914 and publication, one long elucidation of Saint-Loup's 'intellectual' nature is not in the early version (I 733-34). As for Charlus's visit, in the 1914 galleys it is not he who issues the invitation to tea (with the subsequent pretence that he has not), but Mme de Villeparisis.[3]

---

1 n.a.fr. 16761:44iv-v.

2 At the equivalent of I 652; n.a.fr. 16761:45vi. Mentioned briefly by Feuillerat, p. 44.

3 See I 758, 759-60.

So far, then, the original stay in Balbec is broadly similar to the present one; but from this point, many of the most striking events as we now have them are missing. Proust did describe, in 1914, Rachel's behaviour with Saint-Loup and the Rivebelle dinners (without some of the developments about the waiters and guests, and about Marcel's drunkenness and his sleep on returning: I 810-11, 813-14, 816-17, 819-23). But the 'plus pittoresque qu'agréable' Jewish colony (I 738-39), the humorous general meditation on faults of character, provoked by Bloch's bad manners, the dinner with the Bloch family, and Bloch's insistence that he at any rate is going to accept Saint-Loup's invitation to Doncières, do not appear at all in this version (I 740-48, 768-79, 867-68). The visit to Elstir's studio occupies only nine galley pages,[1] as compared with its present 25 or so (I 833-40, 842-43, 847-54, 860-64 were not initially there).[2] And, most important of all, the well-known fact that the 'jeunes filles' do not appear in the 1914 first visit to Balbec means that the Grasset galleys lack not only some 30 pages now between I 787 and I 866,[3] but also the enormous section from I 870 to I 951; neither are the manager's

---

1 n.a.fr. 16761:63viii-65i.

2 For a full description of this first Elstir, see Feuillerat, pp. 54-65, and my Ch. 8, pp. 345-50.

3 I 787-98, 800-802, 806-8, 823-25, 828-33, 844-47, 855-60.

feelings about the empty hotel to be found (I 951); so that the galleys ran simply as follows, after 'les inflexions de la voix' (I 869):

> Mais nous restâmes peu de temps à Briquebec après le départ de Montargis[1] dans l'hôtel qui n'allait pas tarder à fermer et n'avait jamais été si agréable,[2] où parfois la pluie nous retenait[3]

etc.[4]

As we know from Feuillerat, who gives a detailed account of, and some quotation from, the 1914 ending,[5] the volume was also to finish quite differently; the passage now concluding it came, at first, just before the rides with Mme de Villeparisis,[6] and Proust finally fragmented his original ending, probably to his own regret.[7]

One important transfer eventually to take place was that of the evocation of the 'rural sea'; now in Sodome et Gomorrhe (II 783-84), it had come in the first Balbec stay, after 'sa molle palpitation' (I 705).[8] There was, too, a fuller and considerably more idyllic description of Marcel's attitude to

---

1 These names for Balbec and Saint-Loup still sometimes appear in the 1914 galleys.

2 See I 951.

3 See I 952.

4 n.a.fr. 16761:65iii.

5 Feuillerat, pp. 65-67.

6 After 'quelques promenades en voiture', I 704: n.a.fr. 16761:52i-ii, v.

7 He praises it in a letter to L. de Robert (Comment débuta Marcel Proust, p. 65; see also p. 57).

8 n.a.fr. 16761:52iv-v.

his grandmother than the present one (on I 727).[1] And, very shortly before Charlus's arrival at Balbec, these galleys contained a passage about a certain Mlle Claremonde, a cousin of Saint-Loup's and supposedly 'd'une vertu revêche', who makes signs to Marcel when he is out for a walk;[2] this was, presumably, meant as a preparation for the kind of surprises Charlus's behaviour is to exemplify.

Of the three hundred pages now recounting the journey to Balbec, and the stay there, at least 170, then, were not in the 1914 version.[3]

---

1 n.a.fr. 16761:56ii.

2 n.a.fr. 16761:58vi-viii.

3 A few difficulties arise in the discussion of late A l'ombre passages. To begin with, since the Fonds Marcel Proust has for this volume no document later than the 1914 galleys, it is not possible, as it is for the other volumes, to trace the stages of addition of large episodes like the Bloch dinner. Second, and considerably more important, it is common knowledge that although the 'jeunes filles' sections do not appear here in 1914, there was always to be a 'jeunes filles' chapter in the 1912-13 version, as can be seen from those chapter-headings for the next volumes that were printed opposite the title-page of DCS in 1913 (Painter, e.g., quotes these in his vol. II, p. 235). Thus, evidently, large parts of, for example, the section from I 870 to I 951 cannot be post-1914; but which, my material does not show. I have drawn on these sections as cautiously as possible in my discussion (often reminding the reader of the problem), and normally only where a theme or character appearing in them is consistently late elsewhere.

LE CÔTÉ DE GUERMANTES

The first half of Le Côté de Guermantes (II 9-296) is the last section of the novel for which a definitive 1914 version survives, since the Grasset galleys end with Charlus's jumping into the carriage 'qui partit au grand trot' (II 296).[1] Again, Feuillerat has described these galleys in some detail; I give therefore simply a rapid survey:

The new flat, the picture of Françoise and the servants, the visit to the Opéra, and the pursuit of Mme de Guermantes are in this version; so are the trip to Doncières, the return to Paris, the meeting with Rachel, and the visits to the theatre and to Mme de Villeparisis's, followed by the walk with Charlus.

However, as is well-known, the volume started not with 'Le pépiement matinal des oiseaux semblait insipide à Françoise', but with 'A l'âge où les Noms' (II 10), and many other minor and major actions or attitudes of Françoise's are not in these galleys (e.g. on II 23-24, 64-65, 147-48). Jupien too is a

1 n.a.fr. 16760:28iii.

relatively pale figure, without, as yet, the close commentary on his personality (II 20-21); and Marcel's infatuation for Mme de Guermantes does not, in this version, bear the stamp of his memories of Gilberte and Albertine (II 60-61).

Again, the visit to Doncières lacks not only some important touches to the portrait of Saint-Loup - such as his extreme pride in Marcel, and the anxious self-questioning provoked by Rachel's silence (II 103-4, 121-23)[1] - but also some of the now famous descriptive passages, such as those on the 'Demoiselles du téléphone' (II 133-34),[2] on the mingling impressions of the shape of the hill, the fog, and the hot chocolate (II 80-82), on the nature of an Edenic world of silence (II 75-78), and on sleep and dreams (II 86-88, 91-92). And the huge interpolation about the techniques of military strategy does not appear in 1914 at all (II 108-117). Absent from the 1914 meeting with Rachel are three memorable scenes: that in which the two 'poules' greet her, giving Saint-Loup a glimpse of what her real life might be (II 161-64), the laughing off stage of the timid actress (II 173-74),[3] and the accosting of Saint-Loup by an invert whom he 'punishes' (II 182-83). As for the 1914 matinée at Mme de Villeparisis's,

---

1 See also II 281-83 for a passage on Saint-Loup and Rachel not there in 1914.

2 An old passage, of course, now to be found in Contre Sainte-Beuve, précédé de Pastiches et mélanges et suivi de Essais et articles, Bibliothèque de la Pléiade ([Paris], 1971), pp. 527-28.

3 The subsequent discussion of Rachel's charm (II 174-76) is also not to be found.

Bloch, Norpois, Mme de Marsantes, M. and Mme de Guermantes and Charlus are all there; but Bloch's oriental appearance is barely mentioned,[1] he offers no anecdotes and makes no enquiries about Saint-Loup (II 218-19), and he escapes, as yet, M. de Châtellerault's insolence and the supposedly subtle dismissal by Mme de Villeparisis (II 247-49); Norpois does not converse with Marcel about his father's candidature (II 225-26),[2] and his exchanges with Bloch are unadorned by much of their present rhetoric (e.g. II 245-46); Mme de Marsantes is unequivocally saintly;[3] M. de Guermantes's use of the phrase 'quand on s'appelle' receives no commentary as yet (II 235-36), and Mme de Guermantes's attitude to writers of her acquaintance is not described (II 206-209). The 'trois Parques' and, most important, Odette, are not at the matinée (II 195-98, 252-53, 263-64, 267-68); there is no mention of Morel (II 264-67); and, although Charlus himself is present, the story of his brush with Mme de Villeparisis over the wired money, his later 'mots affreux et presque fous' about the Bloch family, and his information about the lowly origins of the name Villeparisis, are all missing (II 268-69, 287-91, 293-95).

---

1 Compare the present II 190-92.

2 (See the relevant preparation on II 150-51, also not in these galleys.)

3 See Feuillerat, pp. 94-97. The main missing passages are on II 251-53, 283.

Two excisions are particularly thought-provoking: at Doncières, Marcel originally spent a little time considering the energy of the military life all around him, and trying to analyse its charm: 'Swann, on l'a vu, moi, on le verra plus tard, ne crûmes-nous pas aimer pour elle-même la vie qu'on menait dans le salon de (sic) Verdurin et dans le casino de Balbec?'.[1] And at the matinée, one passage brought Bloch's artistic imagination into play: he was not merely 'confus et ravi' at the suggestion that he might travel with M. de Châtellerault (II 221), but saw this latter as a 'fleur animée', and wondered if he himself was perhaps 'le jouet d'un songe d'une fin d'après-midi de printemps'.[2]

Unfortunately the BN did not, at the time I was working on the Fonds Marcel Proust, have an earlier base version for the illness and death of the grandmother than the first Gallimard galleys. None the less, even at this late stage some interesting elements remain to be woven in by Proust. Certain visits, and marks of attention for the grandmother, are either absent, such as those of Mme Cottard, the grand-duc héritier de Luxembourg, and Saint-Loup (II 329-30, 338-39), or else are only briefly sketched out, such as Bergotte's.[3] And, most

---

1 n.a.fr. 16760:10vi.

2 n.a.fr. 16760:22viii-23i. See too the noteworthy development reproduced in P. Clarac's 'Les "croyances intellectuelles" de Marcel Proust', BSAMP, no. 8 (pp. 465-66), about the irritating faults, mispronunciations, etc., of the loved one; added in margins, n.a.fr. 16760:22i-ii.

3 On the equivalent of II 325 and II 328-29.

important, a number of the often satirical depictions of the doctors themselves are not in this version: missing are the lines on Du Boulbon's susceptibility (II 303-4), the entire consultation with Professor E... (II 313-14, 317-18), the visit of the nose-specialist X (II 324-25), and the summoning and sudden arrival of Dieulafoy (II 337, 342-43).

From now until the end of the novel, the base document giving completed versions of the volumes is in manuscript; I shall summarise what appears in this main MS, before additions were made to it.

The MS for the remainder of Le Côté de Guermantes narrates Albertine's visit, the abortive invitation to Mme de Stermaria, the evening of the fog and the meal at the restaurant, the Guermantes dinner, Marcel's 'interview' with Charlus, and the call he pays on the duc and duchesse; and it culminates, as now, with the revelation of Swann's imminent death. But more than ninety pages of the present 250-page text do not appear in the main MS version at all: I can describe here only the larger sections Proust was still to work in.

The main MS has no sign of the changes in Albertine's vocabulary which encourage Marcel (II 354-57); and missing from Marcel's brief visit to Mme de Villeparisis's are two developments about Charlus, one giving Mme de Guermantes's conversation with Marcel about the baron, the other recounting the latter's strange behaviour with Bloch (II 378-80, 381-82). The journey to the restaurant in the fog does not yet start with Marcel's involuntary memory (II 397-98), nor include Saint-Loup's disconcerting revelation that he has told Bloch 'que tu ne l'aimais pas du tout tant que ça' (II 399); at the restaurant, the prince de Foix appears in the MS, but the extensive observations on the insolence and the financial troubles of his group, and on the tastes of a smaller coterie to which he belongs, do not (II 402-5).

The early Guermantes dinner itself has most of its present components: the MS describes Marcel's disappointment with the Guermantes, Mme de Guermantes's arbitrary judgements and the duc's custom of setting her wit in relief, as well as the princesse de Parme's bemused state; and much of the talk we now read is in the MS too, such as the discussion about Elstir, the remarks on Victor Hugo and on Zola as poet, and the information that the Chinese eat rotten eggs. Nevertheless, for those familiar with the final text, there are some unexpected gaps. For example, the long conversation about the Iénas and their furniture is absent (II 518-23). So are the 'petit imbroglio' at the very beginning with the princesse de Parme,[1] the description of her at-home evenings, and her final departure and pleasant words about Marcel (II 424-26, 454-56, 544-45). Two of the substantial comparisons between the envious Courvoisiers and the successful Guermantes are still to be

1 The only trace of this in the MS is a brief passage commenting on her great friendliness (n.a.fr. 16705: 98-99).

inserted (II 442-46, 447-49). The unintelligent and stubborn *dame d'honneur*, the ambassadress of Turkey, and the malicious stories about the grand-duc héritier de Luxembourg do not figure in this version (e.g. II 498-99, 533-35, 537-40). As for the duchesse's distinctive traits, she almost wholly lacks her closeness to old or 'peasant' France (II 494-96, 502-503, 550-51), and as yet shows no sign of arbitrary behaviour with her luckless footman (II 483-84). Most odd, the exchanges about the orchid, so important for the beginning of *Sodome et Gomorrhe*, appear not in the main MS but on layers glued together and inserted into it (II 515-17): this sequence may simply have been composed separately, and always intended for incorporation, but one cannot know at present.[1] And some experiences more closely Marcel's are not to be found, such as his discovery that Norpois likes him after all (II 528-29),[2] and his involuntary recollection of the rue de Saintrailles (II 531-32).

Missing from the MS version of the interview with Charlus are a number of the more extreme manifestations of pride on the baron's part, and, surprisingly, Marcel's stamping on the top-hat: the MS gives, instead of this action:

---

1 Bardèche does, in fact, say that there is no plant metaphor in an early version of *SG I* (vol. II, p. 160, *n*.1).

2 (The earlier information from Odette about Norpois's uncomplimentary remarks was not in the 1914 galleys either: see I 563-64; II 271-73.)

> Hélas je ne puis me rappeler sans honte que ce fut par les lieux communs les plus vulgaires [des (?) la (?) imbéciles offenses (sic) outragés] tels que "je n'ai pas l'habitude de m'entendre parler sur ce ton" que je répondis à ces paroles [...].[1]

And the MS for the closing of the volume does not yet have the warnings given to M. de Guermantes about his dying cousin (II 574-76, 588-89), the description of the influence of Dreyfusism on Swann (II 582-83), the duchesse's final thwarting of her footman's plans (II 587-88), and the entire by-play around Swann's photograph and the huge envelope that Mme de Guermantes sends to Mme Molé (e.g. II 590-91, 593-94).

One excision and one change show that Proust was still defining his treatment of Swann's character with revisions more fundamental than might have been supposed; first, there was a comparison in the margin of the MS between Swann and Charlus which discussed the influence they had had on each other: '[...] Encore eut-il (sic) fallu les avoir connu (sic) dans leur jeunesse pour savoir lequel avait le plus pris de l'autre. Swann était évidemment supérieur [...]';[2] and second, the photograph which Swann brings to show the duchesse appears to have been originally a photograph of a Ver Meer painting on which he had written an article, not one of the coins of the Order of Malta.[3]

---

1 n.a.fr. 16707:53. Words in brackets crossed out; those underlined, in margin.

2 n.a.fr. 16706:43.

3 n.a.fr. 16707:90 and 93, crossed out or covered over, in additions in margins.

SODOME ET GOMORRHE

The beginnings of the first three Cahiers of the manuscript (which comprises seven in all), and some of the central part of the second and third, vary considerably from the text we now have.

The opening of the first (n.a.fr. 16708) has been reproduced in BSAMP;[1] the Cahier then proceeds roughly as does the final text, but, finishing at the equivalent of II 630, does not give the end of Sodome et Gomorrhe I.[2] The second (n.a.fr. 16709) presents more extended difficulties. The main narrative thread of the soirée - Marcel's attempt to be introduced to the prince - is solidly in the MS, as are the Hubert Robert fountain, Charlus's loud monotone greetings, the duc de Guermantes's mistresses, and Swann's story about the prince's Dreyfusism.[3] But, although the manuscript does recount the major events of the first part of the soirée,[4] these are in an order so different from the present one that it is virtually impossible to correlate them consistently with the text. This would be a very

---

1 'Première version du début de "Sodome et Gomorrhe I"', BSAMP, no. 6 (1956), pp. 165-70.

2 From 'Au reste j'exagérais' (II 630) to the end (II 632).

3 This last, which is on older paper, seems at first to have been written as a whole, and then cut up and divided (on, e.g., n.a.fr. 16709:60, 79, 82, 83).

4 I.e. approximately II 633-91.

interesting section of the MS to publish verbatim: it was the excised or re-arranged material in the drafts of Sodome et Gomorrhe that most made me regret the limitations I had had to set myself.[1] The ending of the soirée, Albertine's visit to Marcel, and his further explorations of society, are generally the same in the MS as they are now; however, the last page of the section, describing Marcel's impressions of the salons (II 750), is a contraction of sequences which in the MS originally elaborated on these impressions in considerably more detail,[2] and such sequences, combined with the very beginning of the early volume[3] and with the absence, as yet, of a certain amount of comic or social observation, made the MS draft focus more than the present text on Marcel's own responses, both bemused and receptive, and the often comic order he tries to impose on them.

The return to Balbec, the involuntary memory about the grandmother, and Cottard's remarks in the Casino are again in the main MS, together with some of the incidents provoking

---

1 A. Pugh has given a rough account of the proofs version of this soirée, with some reference to the MS and TS, in his thesis (pp. 384-99). He too comments elsewhere on the richness of the excised material in SG (p. 520).

2 n.a.fr. 16710:87-90, 16710:102-104.

3 (The eventually excised one given in BSAMP, no. 6.)

Marcel's jealousy, such as the behaviour of Bloch's sister and cousin, and that of Albertine with Andrée. The Cambremers come to visit; and amongst the eventually excised passages in this section is the tale of a journey Marcel makes to see Mme Bontemps and of a subsequent asthma attack; there is some question, too, of a fishing expedition on which, the next day, Albertine is to go with her friends, who have themselves just returned from one.[1] In the MS, this was originally immediately followed by Cottard's remarks in the Casino, which would have come rather later than they do at present.[2]

The MS now continues with Charlus's meeting with Morel (Santois in the MS), and with the evening at La Raspelière. The 'fidèles' are portrayed with, sketchily, most of their principal characteristics; Dechambre's death is announced and swept to one side by M. Verdurin; and Santois/Morel merely plays cards at the dinner.

The MS version of the penultimate section of <u>Sodome et Gomorrhe</u> (Chapter III, II 979-1112) astonishingly lacks about eighty pages of the present 130. This early narrative gives a very short paragraph on sleep (II 980, §2), then moves straight

---

1 Coming at about II 798; n.a.fr. 16711:75-78. Anthony Pugh mentions this (pp. 404-5). And Bardèche briefly informs us that in an early draft of <u>La Fugitive</u>, Albertine 'fait la ménade' with, amongst others, 'des pêcheuses' (vol. II, p.74).

2 (Some five pages later.)
Also eventually excised was a passage in which Marcel contemplates suicide over Albertine: margin and layer, n.a.fr. 16712:1.

to the rides with Albertine (II 993), the description of the aeroplane (II 1028-29), the 'fidèles' on the little train (II 1035), Charlus's pretended duel (II 1064), and some of the incidents now supposedly recalled to mind by the stations on the railway-line, for example the meeting with Odette's former husband (II 1082 ff.) and the intrigue of the Cambremers to attract Charlus and Morel (II 1087).

The MS for this stay in Balbec had originally contained a nightmarish dream of Marcel's about his grandmother not coming away with him on a train;[1] and it had struck a rather incongruous note by making Legrandin appear at the Cambremers' and give Marcel pleasure by reminding him of Combray.[2] Especially notable is a third MS development, reduced, in the end, to simply two additions: one in which Brichot murmurs that he cannot understand Charlus's interest in genealogies, clothes or gardens (II 1055-56), and one in which Marcel ponders on Brichot's type of intelligence (II 971-72). The original MS, however, gave a long comparison between Brichot and Swann; it remarked on the former's over-willing use of 'toutes <u>les expressions,</u> les citations, <u>même toutes les plaisanteries,</u> que Swann eût omises, parce qu'elles [traînaient] étaient un peu

---

1 n.a.fr. 16712:131-138 (the end of the Cahier), 16713:1-5. This to some extent 'stood in', in the early MS, for the long passages on sleep which came only later: see below, pp. 42-43, and Ch. 2, p. 102 n.2.

2 Margin, n.a.fr. 16713:104. Mentioned by Pugh (p. 522).

trop courantes'; nevertheless, '[on pouvait goûter avec lui sinon la délicatesse d'un goût sévère, au moins le plaisir d'apprendre]'.[1] Here followed a discussion on the ease with which verbal fashions are adopted: the fact that Cottard, for example, had often heard or read an expression 'était pour lui non un obstacle mais un encouragement à l'employer', and one must reckon also with 'l'expérience et même les sympathies, et les habitudes familiales de chacun, [qui fait] tout ce qui fait que telle chose ne leur semble pas une banalité, [et qu'ils en (illeg.) une autre] qui pour un autre en semblerait une, par distraction, ou par manque d'antipathie personnelle'.[2]

The MS for the rest of Sodome et Gomorrhe - Albertine's revelation in the train - differs little from the final version. (It is a curious fact that the description of the dawn (II 1128-30) originally appeared in the early version of the first journey to Balbec, shortly before Marcel sees the coffee-girl;[3]

---

1 Here and below, words underlined are above- or below-line additions; those in brackets are crossed out or disappear under a layer. This passage is also mentioned very briefly by Pugh (p. 526).

2 This is on unnumbered pages, joined to form a layer, between n.a.fr. 16713:65 and 66.

3 At roughly the equivalent of I 655. On the typescript (n.a.fr. 16732:179 and 16735:186) and the corrected 1914 proofs (n.a.fr. 16761:45viii-46i). Understandably, this version does not however have the phrase 'renouvellement solennellement célébré à chaque aurore de mon chagrin quotidien et du sang de ma plaie' (II 1128).

the reader of the present text might easily assume that it had been composed 'for' this moment of Sodome et Gomorrhe, so well-suited is it to Marcel's mood, with its initial rather violent movement, its use of words conveying heaviness ('coagulation', 'figé'), its solemn purple colour, and its evocation of a 'scène imaginaire, grelottante et déserte'.)

All this, then, is in the MS of Sodome et Gomorrhe; what, more precisely, is not? Proust was still to work in not only large sequences, but lesser, if important, characters and episodes. Professor E..., Mme de Citri, and the ambassadress of Turkey do not appear at the soirée (II 640-42, 687-88, 659-61); M. de Guermantes does not yet present Swann's Dreyfusism as a betrayal of the friendship extended to him by the Faubourg Saint-Germain (II 677-80).[1] The news of M. d'Osmond's continuing illness and eventual death (II 662, 725), and much of the by-play round Dechambre's death too (II 896, 900), are not in the MS; and numerous small touches to the personalities and habits of, for example, the duc de Guermantes (II 739-40), Françoise (II 726-28, 736-37), the lift-boy (II 791-93, 826-27, 1025-26), Ski (II 873-74), the princesse Sherbatoff (II 879, 1045-46), Cottard (II 880, 960-61, 976), and Mme Verdurin (II 906, 969-72) are yet to be incorporated. The MS does not have the passages on sleep and dreams (II 980-

---

1 It is also possible that the story of Marcel's much-praised reticence in front of the Queen of England was not part of the early version (II 662-63).

86), the manager's malapropisms (e.g. II 751-52, 755, 1125), most of the descriptions of La Raspelière and the countryside round it (II 895, 897-99, 904-6, 917-18, 944-45, 975, 997-1006), nor the humorous comments on the hotel-boys and on the resemblance of the Grand-Hôtel to Solomon's temple (e.g. II 772-75). The unfortunate Saniette is less frequently the object of ill-treatment than now.[1] As for even more considerable elements missing from the MS of <u>Sodome et Gomorrhe</u>, absent are some of the most memorable descriptions of the Cambremers, such as the dowager's salivary peculiarities (II 808, 817-18), Mme de Cambremer-Legrandin's more extreme manifestations of snobbery (II 810, 811-13, 922-24, 928-29, 978), and M. de Cambremer's nose and eyes, as well as his satisfaction over Marcel's choking fits (II 912-14, 978-79, 1096-97); the great majority of Brichot's etymologies (II 887-91, 925-26, 1099-1100); Céleste and Marie (II 846-50, 1125); numbers of the jealous suspicions of Albertine and her lies (II 798-802, 838-41, 850-54, 1015-16, 1097); and, linked with this, a notable proportion of the present elaboration on the theme of homosexuality. Thus Charlus himself does not, as yet, deliver his long monologue to Jupien in <u>Sodome et Gomorrhe I</u> (II 610-13); nor does he show interest in Bloch (II 1101-1107), dine at the Grand-Hôtel with Mme de Chevregny's footman, nor write his letter to Aimé (II 986-93).[2]

---

1 Missing, e.g., are II 872-73, 900-901, 930, 937; also II 1022-24.

2 A number of passages showing his more maniacal side are also lacking, for the moment: II 1069-70, 1073-74.

The discovery Marcel makes shortly before coming to the Guermantes soirée was originally, it seems, to be centrally illustrated only by Charlus, since Vaugoubert and all the incidents arising from his presence are not in the main MS but in a very much shorter rough version on two inserted layers (II 642-47, 664-66, 674-75, 676),[1] and the duc de Châtellerault and his usher do not appear at all (II 633-34, 636-37). There is no trace of Nissim Bernard (II 842-45, 848, 854-55); above all, the great majority of the anecdotes about, and developments round the character of, Morel are lacking.[2]

LA PRISONNIÈRE

From here on, the manuscript becomes generally clearer to work with than it is in the case of _Le Côté de Guermantes_ and _Sodome et Gomorrhe_, although it still presents many complications for the first part of _La Prisonnière_.[3]

At least 110 pages of the final 180 describing life with Albertine, the street-cries and the death of Bergotte (III 9-192) appear as additions either to the MS or to the typescripts.

---

1 n.a.fr. 16709:54 and 61.

2 Page-references would here be too numerous: a detailed account of the early Morel's rôle in _SG_ is given in Ch.4, pp. 173-80.

3 See the descriptions given by the Pléiade editors, III 1057-58.

Entirely missing from the main MS are almost all of the present suspicious incidents focussing on Albertine, such as the confusion about the seringas and the meeting with Gisèle (III 54-55, 177-80):[1] although this version shows Marcel questioning Andrée (III 58-59, 62), the first real doubt in the MS is that which forms in his mind as he remembers a phrase of Aimé's about Albertine, and decides to write to him (III 84-86).[2] The passages on Albertine's sleep (III 69-75, 113-16), those on the street-cries (III 116-19, 126-28, 136-38), and the account of Bergotte's death (III 182-88) are not in the MS; and none of the descriptions - some very substantial - of Morel's activities appear at all (III 44-54, 66-67, 162-64). Instead, the basic seventy pages of the MS 'life with Albertine' seem, without the weight of these later pieces, to centre, far more than the text we now have, on Marcel's calmness, and his enjoyment of the world outside, perceived from his room: where Albertine herself is concerned, lies are almost non-existent, suspicions are relatively few, though disturbing when they do occur, and proportionately more space towards the end of the section is

---

1 See below, Ch. 6, pp. 267-83, for a full description of such added incidents.

2 The MS also contains, a little later, Albertine's intention to visit the Verdurins, and Marcel's attempts to thwart this (III 88, 91, 99-102, 106-110), as well as the discovery that Léa is performing at the Trocadéro (III 144, 148-49, 151-52).

devoted to Marcel's desire for other girls and for Venice.[1]

The Verdurin soirée, the performance of Vinteuil's Septet, and the rupture of Charlus and Morel now occupy 140 pages in the text: at least sixty-five of these were additions. In its original form, the MS contained nearly all the familiar elements of this section, including the revelation that Mlle Vinteuil was to be present at the soirée, and Charlus's conversation on homosexuality with Brichot; but once more, nearly all were less dense in the MS than they are at present, lacking explanation or illustration. Again, much of the material about Morel is missing (III 193-98, 214-19, 311-12); and the lines on Swann's death do not appear in the MS (III 199-201). Neither does a substantial part of the explanation for Mme Verdurin's desire to break up Morel's and Charlus's relationship (III 228-30, 230-38, 276-77, 277-79). Such characters as Saniette (III 228, 265-66 n.) and the Queen of Naples (III 246, 247, 274-75, 321-22) are not so prominent in the MS as they were later to be,[2]

---

1 See III 165-72, 174, 175-76, without the additions given in Part II for these pages. Also lacking at this stage are some important smaller touches, such as much of the conversation at the duchesse's (III 38-43), and some of the fine general passages on love, like the address to the 'jeunes filles' and their 'interminable et toujours déconcertante arrivée' (III 64-66). (Others missing on love are III 91-98, III 142-43, III 172-74, III 191-92.) Albertine's description of the ice-cream (III 128-31), which H. March takes to be a self-parody by Proust (The Two Worlds of Marcel Proust (London, 1948), p. 236), is not yet in either.

2 It was not originally the Queen who was the only guest to show politeness to Mme Verdurin, but a certain Duchesse de St Herem (?) (n.a.fr. 16717:12).

certain important emphases are comparatively subdued in the evocation of the Septet,[1] and a number of the comic pictures of Mme Verdurin's appearance and actions are still to come (III 240-41, 248, 251, 280-81, 314-16). The MS lacks as yet many aspects of, or monologues from, Charlus (III 204-7, 208-10 *n.*, 212, 213-14, 276-77, 290-91, 293-94); surprisingly, the cursory, but apparently crucial, information about the telegram from Mlle Vinteuil and her friend, saying they cannot attend, does not seem to be in the main MS (III 241-42); and the lengthy description of the guests leaving (III 266-73), Charlus's illness (III 322-24), and the Verdurins' sudden kindness to Saniette (III 324-27), are all absent from this version.

About thirty pages of the remaining eighty-five which close *La Prisonnière* were not in the original MS. This first narrative gave a short quarrel with Albertine, the pretended separation and the reconciliation, the resumption of life together, minor revelations and accusations,[2] Marcel's increasing boredom, and the final decision to leave for Venice, followed by the announcement of Albertine's departure. Not to be found, however, are a substantial discussion of Marcel's behaviour (III 343-48), another on his conclusions and misgivings about Albertine's

---

1 The main MS does not have most of III 257, 258-59, 263, and the mention on III 277.

2 From Mme Bontemps, to the effect that Albertine may have left Balbec when she did because of Andrée (III 389, 392); from Marcel, accusations about Andrée (III 395-96, 397).

character (III 390-91), and the episode with the 'pâtissière' (III 408-10). The flinging open of the window was mentioned only briefly in the MS;[1] the important passage in which Marcel sees the sleeping Albertine as 'une morte' is not there (III 359-60); and also missing, besides some of the later interrogations and suspicions about Léa and Mlle Vinteuil (III 349-51, 356-57 *n.*, 396), are a full eight pages of detailed interrogation and disclosure from the quarrel scene (III 333-41).

The MS of *La Prisonnière* reveals, besides these gaps, eventually excised passages which it is to be hoped may one day be published in full: there was at first a much lengthier and more lyrical version of the passage now beginning 'La décroissance du jour [...]' (III 30, §2), which recalled Rivebelle, the night of the refusal by Mlle de Kermaria (*sic*), and the arrival at Balbec;[2] and Proust had written, at this stage, a long description of the profusion of flowers which Marcel admires at Mme de Guermantes's and believes to be '*disposées* là dans un ordre secret'.[3] There is, too, in the MS a startling, if rapid, reference by Charlus to the fact, unknown to Swann, that Odette

---

1 Compare the present III 401-2.

2 n.a.fr. 16715:18-19.

3 n.a.fr. 16715:22-23 ('disposées' above-line, 16715:22). These two pages are largely made up of paper with a double red margin, which seems to be that of the *DCS* period, as it appears in n.a.fr. 16703, the collection of MS fragments of *DCS*.

was the natural daughter of the German Ambassador.[1] And Proust crossed out another passage which no doubt provides some explanation for the additions on military strategy at Doncières: it occurs in the MS account of the pretended separation from Albertine:

> Je me rappelais une conversation de St Loup [d'après] à Doncières, d'après laquelle à partir d'un certain moment, Napoléon jugea que les attaques qui n'étaient que des feintes ne [devaient] pouvaient pas pour réussir, se contenter d'une simulation superficielle, [mais] et devaient être poussées à fond. [Comme] Mais [alors elles] ces feintes où l'on engage des forces réelles coûtent presque aussi cher que de[s] [attaques véritables] vraies actions.[2]

Finally, after the words 'Françoise, ayant entendu mon coup de sonnette, entra' (on the morning of Albertine's departure: III 414), Proust wrote in the margin of the third typescript: 'assez inquiète de la façon dont je prendrais ses paroles et sa conduite':[3] this, omitted from the present text, should almost certainly be in any edition of La Prisonnière, since it does then appear actually in the typed page which the Pléiade editors mention and according to which they prepared the last page of the volume.[4]

---

1 n.a.fr. 16718:5.

2 At about III 341; n.a.fr. 16718:51. Words in brackets crossed out (before general crossing-out); those underlined, aboveline. Punctuation is Proust's.

3 n.a.fr. 16747:238.

4 This page is n.a.fr. 16747:239. See III 415 n.1. The extra phrase appears also in the posthumous Gallimard galleys and proofs (n.a.fr. 16768:72iv, 16768:310 verso).

LA FUGITIVE

Up to the first sight of Mlle de Forcheville (III 562), the MS for La Fugitive is probably the neatest of all, containing long sequences to which Proust made almost no changes, or into which he inserted additions clearly and with little reworking. Nevertheless, of these first 140 pages, over thirty had still not been incorporated into the main MS.

The original plot gives the attempts to make Albertine return, partly through correspondence, partly with the help of Saint-Loup; Albertine's death; the subsequent meditations on love; Aimé's investigations; the gradual forgetfulness; and Andrée's allegations that she had no relations with Albertine. However, a number of powerfully dramatic actions do not yet appear: for example, Albertine's taking wrapping-paper the day before her departure and forcibly returning money she owes Marcel (III 427-28), his offer to her of a yacht as well as a car, his plan for eventual suicide in order to spend as much money on her as possible (III 455-56, 465-66 n.), and his final telegram begging her to come back, just before the news of her death (III 476). Marcel's summons to the police-station for supposed abduction of minors, and Bloch's tactless comments to M. Bontemps, are not yet in the MS (III 432 n., 442-44, 446-47);

neither are a number of the comparisons with the Gilberte affair, including Marcel's five-page protracted speculation as to whether he could have loved anyone, not just Albertine (III 501-7).[1] And entirely absent from the main MS are the discoveries - made with the all-too-willing help of Françoise - about Albertine's rings (III 462-65), the slip that results in Françoise unexpectedly bringing back the letter which Marcel has asked her to post to Albertine, the immediately following lengthy and important comparison with Phèdre (III 458-61), and the scene in which Marcel overhears Saint-Loup's 'paroles machiavéliques et cruelles' as he tells one servant how to engineer the dismissal of another (III 470-71).

Excisions in this section show that Proust had contemplated both extending his narrator's insights into his own character, and allowing him to take refuge in a certain type of cliché: in one rough working, to be found near the final draft of Mme Bontemps's telegram, Marcel observed that he now understood, 'après les avoir trouvé (sic) si ridicules', Baudelaire's lines on 'le viol, le poison, le poignard, l'incendie';[2] and, some thirty pages later, Proust, in a crossed-out note to himself, wrote that he must see whether he had thought of using, on Albertine's departure, Norpois's expressions or quotations: 'Ce

---

1 See also, for Gilberte, III 429 and 456.

2 Crossed out, together with a note in the margin on the placing of these lines, n.a.fr. 16719:73. Compare with III 379 (where the reference is an addition).

serait à celui qui saurait tenir' and 'celui qui saurait souffrir un quart d'heure de plus (?) que l'autre [...]'.[1]

The next section of MS was expanded relatively little once the base version had been written; this narrated the Mlle de Forcheville intrigue, the by-play around the _Figaro_ article, and two of Andrée's revelations: that she did after all have physical relations with Albertine, and that a marriage between the latter and the Verdurins' nephew had been under consideration. (The mistake about Mlle de Forcheville belongs definitely to an early version of the novel, since some of the episode appears, with much reworking, on paper with a double red margin, and a few names used in drafts on this paper are older ones: Montargis for Saint-Loup,[2] and, for Mlle de Forcheville herself, Mlle d'Ossencourt and later Mlle d'Ablancourt.[3])

The main MS does not, however, include such minor incidents as the visit of Charlus to Marcel, in the company of Morel (III 597-98), and that of the princesse de Parme to Marcel's mother (III 612-13);[4] nor does Marcel receive, as yet, the two letters of congratulation on his article (III 589-91).[5] And some of

---

1 Layer, n.a.fr. 16719:125; on about the equivalent of III 504. (See Part II for I 461-63.)

2 n.a.fr. 16720:112 verso.

3 Respectively on n.a.fr. 16720:112 verso, and 16721:11 (see III 579 _n._2).

4 However, the prelude to this - III 596-97 - is _in_ the MS.

5 See III 701 _n._, also an addition.

Andrée's disclosures are still to come: the information that Albertine's inconsistency could be attributed merely to a past attack of typhoid (III 619-20); the lie about the visit to the aviation field; what really did happen on the evening of the seringas; and, most startling of all, Albertine's relations and arrangements with Morel (III 599-601, 611-12).[1]

The final section of La Fugitive too is almost exactly the same now as in the MS, which recounts the stay in Venice, the telegram from Gilberte, Marcel's show of defiance towards his mother, the news of the marriages, and Saint-Loup's homosexuality. It is true that a long commentary on these marriages, and on the sadness they give Marcel, is missing (III 661 n.-664); Bloch in the restaurant, Saint-Loup's eyes flickering over the waiter, Gilberte's jealousy of Rachel, and the financial gains accruing to Odette as she smooths out 'telle ou telle difficulté' between her daughter and son-in-law (III 680-81, 683-84) - none of this figures in the main MS; neither do the lines on the girl whom Marcel is now keeping (III 677 n.). But the only really substantial description not in the base narrative is that of Norpois and Mme de Villeparisis in Venice (the Pléiade edition gives both the first version of this addition, III 1051-54, and the second longer one[2]). As for suppressions, the

1 Andrée's visits, now two, were at first only one (see Part II for III 612-14). Pugh mentions this (p. 468).

2 III 1051-54 and III 630-39 respectively.

versos of two MS pages, interestingly enough, provide what is apparently both a continuation, and a rough draft, of the excised dream about the grandmother which came partially in *Sodome et Gomorrhe*.[1] This dream seems to have occurred on the train-journey back from Venice, since a reference to the return to Paris appears immediately after it.[2]

LE TEMPS RETROUVÉ

As the Pléiade editors tell us, there is no precise division in the MS between *La Fugitive* and *Le Temps retrouvé*.[3] However, from the point at which they place the beginning of *Le Temps retrouvé*, the number of additions is proportionately larger, and these additions are less well integrated into the main MS, than for any other section, especially in the case of the last matinée.

Meanwhile, of the 160 pages giving the stay at Tansonville, the Goncourt pastiche, the war-chapter, the visit to the brothel and Saint-Loup's death, over fifty appear only as additions.

---

1 (See above, p.40.) n.a.fr. 16722:11-12 versos, at the equivalent of III 652. A fragment also appears crossed out on n.a.fr. 16722:16.

2 n.a.fr. 16722:11 verso.

3 III 688*n*.1; see too III 1118-19 for comments similar to those that follow.

The MS stay at Tansonville is neatly balanced on first, Marcel's discoveries about the two ways and Gilberte's former desires for him, and second, the effect of Saint-Loup's inversion on his marriage; it ends with Marcel's making a few mechanical general enquiries of Gilberte about Albertine, with the reference to La Fille aux yeux d'Or, and with the Goncourt pastiche (which originally came after most of the comments on it[1]). The war-chapter of the MS is also proportioned much as it is now, if more meagre in substance. The war-time fashions and changes in society, some description of Paris by night, the opposition of Saint-Loup's patriotism to Bloch's cowardice, and the way in which the maître d'hôtel plays upon Françoise's feelings, all appear in the MSS; the rest is built around the correspondence with Gilberte and Saint-Loup, the meeting and conversation with Charlus (very much shorter than at present), the brothel, the continuing friction between Françoise and the maître d'hôtel, and Saint-Loup's death. The chapter would probably have ended at 'je pense au peu de chose que c'est qu'une grande amitié dans le monde' (III 852), since the next two pages, up to 'La nouvelle maison de santé dans laquelle je me retirai', were added après coup.

The huge rough-draft layer about artistic problems connected with the war, reproduced in BSAMP, comes just before

---

1 At about III 723. The pastiche started on n.a.fr. 16722:99, the conclusions on n.a.fr. 16722:88.

the conclusion of the war-chapter;[1] and in one passage which did not, for some reason, find its way into the Pléiade text, the lift-boy told Marcel that not only was the rich young man of Balbec an invert, but that, contrary to Charlus's affirmations (III 297 n.; III 307), his three friends were too: his mistress's task was to 'lever les jeunes gens'. The lift-boy himself had been approached, and Marcel remembers 'l'invitation que l'ami noble de l'homme riche m'avait adressée q.q. (sic) jours avant (?) son départ de Balbec. Mais cela n'avait sans doute aucun rapport et était dicté par la seule amabilité'.[2]

When Proust returned to these sections, he extended Marcel's enquiries of Gilberte, and, further, made their object not only Albertine but (sometimes with contradictions) Léa (III 694-96, 695 n., 707-8). Taking up a development which came later in *La Fugitive* too,[3] he was to add Gilberte's imitation of Rachel (III 702-3); and Saint-Loup's rôle was also temporarily incomplete. Not in the MS are his behaviour 'dans le monde', the claim that inversion usually makes for happy marriages (III 703-5), much of the war-time conversation with Marcel on military strategy, and his transformation into 'le

---

1 At about the equivalent of III 851: n.a.fr. 16725:87. See 'Un inédit de Proust en marge du "Temps retrouvé", présenté par André Ferré', *BSAMP*, no. 5 (1955), pp. 9-16.

2 16724:18 (a layer given separate pagination by the BN). At about the equivalent of III 747.

3 See above, p. 53.

discoureur, le doctrinaire qui ne cessait de jouer avec les mots' (III 758-62). Françoise, although, as we have seen, in the MS, does not yet praise 'protectors' like Legrandin, nor betray such new 'faults' as dissimulated curiosity and the adoption of slang and incorrect pronunciation from her daughter and the maître d'hôtel (III 700-701, 748-50).[1] Proust was still to develop the account of social or fashionable responses to the war, devoting another four pages to Brichot's articles (III 789-93), and elaborating especially the portrait of Mme Verdurin, inserting, for example, the reaction her resumption of croissants induces on the morning of the news about the _Lusitania_ (III 730-34, 768-69, 772-73). The pages on Jupien's brothel lack a few vignettes (III 816-17, 826-27, 830-31) and some of the clients, such as the député of the Action Libérale and the elder prince de Foix (III 816, 827-28); and for the moment, there are no comparisons between Pompeii and the ending of Paris (III 806-7, 833-35, 837 _n._). But undoubtedly the most noticeable gap in the MS is the absence of numerous passages about Charlus and Morel, ranging from small aspects of Saint-Loup's relationship with the latter[2] to detailed descriptions of the violinist's actions during the war (III 730, 768-69), his mimicry of Bergotte (III 767-68 _n._), his return to hetero-sexuality (III 780-81), Charlus's plan to kill him (III 803-6),

---

1 See also III 844-45.

2 On, e.g., III 705.

and his arrest, as a result of which he contrives in his turn the detention of Charlus and d'Argencourt (III 852-53).[1] Not in the MS are substantial sections of Charlus's exposé - part sensible and part flippant - of the follies of war-time attitudes (III 784-88, 794-95, 797-98); and, to anticipate, the later meeting with the baron does not include the duchesse de Létourville's embarrassment at his state, nor that list of deceased acquaintances which he recites 'avec une dureté presque triomphale' (III 862-63).

The discouragement in the train and the flood of involuntary memories are almost identical in the early and final versions; and, again, the aesthetic meditation, once it had been written, received comparatively little expansion of major importance, although it is interesting that the reflections on 'cette muse nocturne' (III 911-12, 914) and two developments on popular and modern art do not yet appear (III 888-89, 893-95), and that four considerable discussions of the usefulness for the writer of suffering and jealousy in love are not in the main MS (III 903-5, 905-7, 908-10, 916-17). Nor does this version have the well-known exhortation the narrator gives himself: to cease believing in 'l'objectivité de ce qu'on a élaboré soi-même', and to restore 'aux moindres signes qui m'entouraient [...] leur sens que l'habitude leur avait fait

1 See III 779 for the preparation for this.

perdre pour moi' (III 896-97).[1]

However, it is the 'bal costumé' which reveals the greatest difference of scale between former and present state. Originally about forty or forty-five pages, it is now 130! I shall try to give some close account of the basic structure as it was in the MS.[2]

The entry into the matinée is introduced, as now, as a 'coup de théâtre' which raises grave objection to the completion of the projected work (III 920). Marcel does not understand why those present seem to have changed so much; astonished at his difficulties in recognising his host and M. de Châtellerault, he none the less instinctively feels he must hide his hesitation, and then realises, for the first time in his life, that the metamorphoses in these people have taken place also in him; he is addressed, too, as 'un vieux Parisien' (III 927). This discovery of the 'action destructrice du Temps', at the very moment when he wants to create 'des réalités extra-temporelles' in the work of art, distresses him (III 930); but

---

1 A substantial layer in n.a.fr. 16726 is formed of some old fragments of DCS period (see Part II, under III 883-89a); and attached to n.a.fr. 16726:17 are two sheets of old MS paper, with what appears to be a comparatively early aesthetic discussion, much along the lines of the Contre Sainte-Beuve argument.

2 Bardèche gives a most important description of the draft which may have immediately preceded this one (vol. II, pp. 274-77).

it will, he sees, help him in 'la matière même' of his book (III 932). Time has altered the guests in a variety of ways - the prince d'Agrigente, for example, has grown more handsome, and others resemble eighteen-year-olds 'extrêmement fanés' (III 935-36). The degree of whiteness of the hair indicates, it seems, the depth of time lived through; the faces of the women have evolved like geological formations; Odette, however, appears not to have aged (III 940, 946-48, 950). The predominant imagery in this section is theatre imagery.[1]

The Faubourg Saint-Germain has undergone deep change, its previous composition being remembered by only a few. Marcel is introduced to an elegant lady (a new-comer and a friend of Bloch's): the conversation they have, although agreeable, is made difficult by the discrepancy between the social 'vocabulary' and knowledge of each. Marcel feels he can 'extraire des vérités importantes' from the modifications betokened by this - modifications which, he appreciates, take place in all periods (III 967); and he remembers the separate and fluctuating aspects many of the guests have presented to him in the past. A 'grosse dame' who is, in fact, Gilberte greets him and talks to him about Robert (III 980-85); Marcel thinks of the retired life he is about to lead; now comes Rachel's controversial poetry-reading, some illustration of the duchesse's declining wit (III 1004-5), an almost casual, and evidently not final, mention of the fact

1 See, e.g., III 921, 923, 938, 947.

that it is Mme Verdurin who is the new princesse de Guermantes (III 1012),[1] and the account of the duc's final liaison with Odette, in whose home he is always to be found and who, unlike Mme de Guermantes, pays no attention to his disapproving but near-senile glares. Marcel is reminded of Charlus's assertion that Mme de Guermantes was not as irreproachable as she had always been thought to be, and, recalling the look she gave him, Marcel, in the Combray church, he speculates about the truth of the matter (III 1023). Finally, meeting Mlle de Saint-Loup, he ponders on all the connecting links in his life, and the novel ends, as now, with the idea of Time as an 'aiguillon' (III 1032), the fear of an accident or an illness, the wondering about the number of nights needed to complete the task, and the sudden inspiration to mark the work above all with 'la forme [...] du Temps' (III 1044-45). The stilt image is used in the finale, and the word 'Fin' indeed appears at the end of the MS, after a few last pages of extreme confusion, whose nature can be gathered to some extent from the Pléiade editors' notes (for III 1048).

It is hardly feasible to summarise in any detail here the content of the late eighty pages or so which came to swell this early structure.[2] Generally speaking, Marcel now sees far more

1 See also III 940 §2, another very meagre indication _in_ the MS.

2 For fuller descriptions, see below, Ch. 2, pp. 118-21, and Ch. 7, pp. 301-4, 305-7, 323-25, 328-30.

people, a large number of them anonymous or invented solely for the purposes of the demonstration, who show him the destructive effects of time, its 'perspective déformante', and the emergence of heredity; a great deal of the imagery, no longer that of the theatre, is drawn from snow-similes and above all from sculpture; and the forgetfulness of this new society about its own origins is thoroughly discussed. Many facets of Bloch - the nature of his transformation, his questions about high society, his parvenu status (III 952-56, 965-67, 968-70) - do not appear in the base version; nor does Marcel's mistaken notion that Rachel (whom he does not recognise) is trying to flirt with him (III 1000-1001). The entire La Berma episode is missing (III 995-99, 1013-15), as are both the account of Odette's eventual senility and the conversation with Marcel in which she divulges the multifarious incidents of her love-career (III 951-52, 1020-23). There is almost no stress on illness in the MS, and nothing of the specific final illnesses of Marcel himself and the process whereby the idea of death 's'installa définitivement en moi comme fait un amour' (III 1039-43). As for the novel-to-be itself, the remarks about the incomprehension of the first sketches which 'je pus montrer' are absent (III 1041); and Proust had yet to add not only the affirmation that life seemed even more worthwhile than in the 'brefs éclairs' Marcel had hitherto experienced, now that 'elle me semblait pouvoir être éclaircie, elle qu'on vit dans les ténèbres', but also the rest of this fine passage, which compares the writing of the work with other difficult yet creative actions, claims that its readers will be 'les propres lecteurs d'eux-mêmes',[1] and talks of the help that Françoise will be able to give (III 1032-35).

No doubt many of the features of A la recherche which Proust chose to accentuate in the revision of his drafts were, as this outline shows, already central in the MS, such as the temporarily fruitless involuntary memories,[2] and the brittle conversation of 'le monde'.[3] None the less, it is already possible, even without a close study, to see either new emphases emerging, or themes that were at first relatively subdued now being steadily elaborated. We can see, for example, that the MS held much less about Albertine's lies, and Marcel's suspicions of her, than the present novel does.[4] Careful attention seems to have been devoted to Charlus in the gradual expansion;[5] and the subject of homosexuality itself

---

1 See also III 910-11 for a very similar late passage.

2 See above, for CG, pp. 33-34, 35.

3 See above, for CG, p. 34.

4 See above, for La P, the summary of 'life with Albertine', pp. 44-46; also for SG, p. 43, and TR, pp. 55-56.

5 See above, for JF, p. 25, CG, pp. 33, 35, SG, p. 43, and TR, pp. 57-58.

is inevitably brought into a more prominent position with the development of characters like M. de Châtellerault and Vaugoubert, and the creation of others like Nissim Bernard.[1] Morel too, it is clear, was far more shadowy in the base versions than in the later ones. New areas of interest are opening up in military strategy, in etymologies, and in sleep and dreams.[2] The 1914 A l'ombre galleys give less consideration to Odette's social position than does the finished volume.[3] The linguistic habits of such characters as the duc de Guermantes, Norpois, Françoise and, of course, Albertine would appear to be attracting Proust's further efforts;[4] the rôles of other characters like Elstir and Saniette are still evidently to be expanded;[5] and themes of old age, illness and death do not have the weight in the drafts that Proust later gave them.[6]

It is not at present possible to be completely certain whether all the additions to be found in these MSS, typescripts

---

1 See above, respectively p. 44 and pp. 26, 44.

2 See above, pp. 30, 42-43.

3 See above, for JF, p. 23. Also for CG, p. 31.

4 See above, for CG, p. 31 (the duc de Guermantes); for JF, p. 22, and CG, p. 31 (Norpois); for CG, p. 29, and TR, p. 57 (Françoise); and for CG, p. 33 (Albertine).

5 See above, for JF, p. 26(Elstir); and for SG, p. 43, and La P, p. 46 (Saniette).

6 See especially the 'bal costumé', just above (under TR, pp. 59-62); but also Swann's and Bergotte's deaths, La P, above, pp. 45, 46.

and proofs are really late. Some of them may have been 'rescued' by Proust from writings of a much earlier period, such as the flight on the 'Demoiselles du téléphone';[1] others may simply have been worked out 'to one side', at the same time as the main MS was being written but at a moment when Proust had not decided exactly where to put them. It seems, for example, improbable in the extreme that the near-definitive version of the 'bal costumé' was intended to mention merely _en passant_ Mme Verdurin's rise to princesse de Guermantes,[2] and that it should have occurred to Proust only on revision to make this the 'coup de théâtre' it now is.[3] As Pugh suggests, Proust perhaps actually composed by means of a ground-plan with, as it were, 'simultaneous' additions.[4] Such problems would be for investigations of the rough Cahiers to solve; meanwhile, although these caveats should be borne in mind, and although it should also be remembered that a number of passages at first destined for inclusion in the novel were excised, making some space for the expansions, evidently the additions already mentioned, and the smaller ones to be described, must account for a great many of the post-1914 1500 pages.[5] Instead of having to characterise

---

1 See above, for _CG_, p. 30 (and _n_.2).

2 See above, for _TR_, pp. 60-61.

3 See III 954-56, part of a layer glued on to the MS of _TR_. (Bardèche does, however, confirm the late conception of this idea: vol. II, pp. 276-77.)

4 Pugh, pp. 246, 348.

5 See above, p. 1 (and _n_.1).

the doubling in size of the projected 1914 novel in general terms such as 'rich' or 'monstrous',[1] we shall at last be able to know in some measure what it was that appeared on the supposedly definitive versions to make them so much fuller than they initially were.

In this chapter, I have principally considered missing passages now occupying at least one page; but of course there were numerous short but telling late additions, of anything between a few words and half-a-page, many of them echoing the major insertions, but some representing in their own way a consistently new *leitmotif*, less obtrusive, but firmly built up; and in the following chapters I count these as introducing further elements into the work nearly as significantly as the more obvious late blocks elsewhere.

---

1 See, e.g., A. Maurois on the expanded novel: 'ce caractère monstrueux et cette surabondance qui font son unicité' (*A la recherche de Marcel Proust*, p. 273); similar remarks are made by, for instance, G. Picon (*Lecture de Proust* (Paris, 1963), p. 20) and R. Shattuck (*Proust's Binoculars* (London, 1964), pp. 103-5).

2 The Additions: General Effects

The revisions Proust worked into his drafts should not, of course, be seen simply as a large-scale elaboration of themes which were now to appear and re-appear throughout the novel. A number of additions, dramatic, comic or metaphorical, were clearly made with a view to heightening a given scene, or increasing suspense about an episode already in the earlier version; and this care over individual sequences shows equally in the more substantial insertions, both in their particular placing in the novel and in their wider bearing on the dramatic pattern of the work, that of the gradual and often qualified descent downwards after Combray, capped by the final illumination. This chapter will try to suggest the immediate impact of the expansions.

DRAMATIC EFFECTS

On the most superficial level, a survey of the drafts reveals numerous small additions whose function is purely explanatory. Thus, the 1914 galleys of *Le Côté de Guermantes*, showing the duc about to highlight the witticism his wife has just made at Mme de Cambremer-Legrandin's expense, read as follows:

> Il savait que la verve de sa femme avait besoin d'être stimulée par la contradiction (c'est ainsi que Mme de Guermantes, enchérissant sur une première image, était souvent arrivée à produire ses plus jolis mots);

but the Gallimard galleys make a further clarifying note, referring back to the witticism itself, so that the final text reads:

> Il savait que la verve de sa femme avait besoin d'être stimulée par la contradiction, la contradiction du bon sens qui proteste que, par exemple, on ne peut pas prendre une femme pour une vache (c'est ainsi que Mme de Guermantes, enchérissant sur une première image, était souvent arrivée à produire ses plus jolis mots) (II 232a).[1]

More important, Proust will slip in additions contrived almost solely to prepare for the drama of a scene to come. Revising *Le Côté de Guermantes*, he inserted or elaborated, at more than seven junctures, passages which make the reader pause to wonder what exactly is going to happen at Charlus's after

---

1 Underlined words not in n.a.fr. 16760:23vii; in n.a.fr. 16762:19iii-iv.
From here on, I shall not give close reference in footnotes to the exact document-page location of individual additions, but shall refer the reader to the passage-numbering (as above, II 232a) in Part II, where precise details are given. Unless a noteworthy variant is specifically indicated, all additions are quoted exactly as they now appear in the Pléiade text.
For two other examples of this kind of addition, see III 288c and III 331a.

the Guermantes dinner: the occasions on which Mme de Guermantes tells Marcel that Charlus has implied he does not know him, Marcel then wants to ask Saint-Loup the explanation for this, and Saint-Loup himself informs Marcel that Charlus has something to say to him, were all added _après coup_ to the MS (II 378-80a; II 410a; II 412a). Not content with this, Proust then inserted, in the margin of the third Gallimard galleys, the sentence in which Saint-Loup actually passes on the message that Charlus would prefer Marcel not to go to the dinner at all (II 412c). And other additions to the Guermantes dinner itself, made on revision of both the MS and the first Gallimard galleys, constantly refer the reader to the fact that Marcel has to be at Charlus's at eleven o'clock (II 422a; II 486a; II 510a).[1]

The longer additions, which can be subdivided into separate elements that extend the underlying structural _leitmotive_, may similarly be seen to consolidate, by contrast or by renewed emphasis, the stage of the narrative into which Proust inserted them. For example, powerful though the original beginning of _Le Côté de Guermantes_ was ('A l'âge où les Noms [...]'), the new one - the interpolated page-and-a-half about Françoise[2] -

1 Such references were in the MS, now crossed out, covered over, or eventually excised (on n.a.fr. 16706:108, 16707:5, 37, 39 - at about the equivalent of II 508, 543: see II 543 _n_.2, and also the reference on II 541, not an addition), but they were considerably weaker, often amounting only to a mention _en passant_. See also, for similar additions about Charlus, II 283b; II 284a; II 380a; II 381-82a; II 412d; II 506b.

2 See above, Ch. 1, p. 29: II 9-10a and indented additions.

matches it, both as a more vigorous recapitulation of some of the major themes of the previous two volumes and as an introduction to conflicts and moments of pleasure that are to come. Unifying the growing novel, it provides not merely an unobtrusive foreshadowing of the opening of La Prisonnière and the descriptions of the street-noises, with its reference to the attention Françoise pays to sounds outside;[1] it even takes up themes suggested in the overture of Du Côté de chez Swann, but here demonstrated in Françoise and others, as well as in Marcel: the power of habit and the emotions of the journey, with both its delights (the footman's reactions) and its anguish. This post-1914 opening recalls, too, the antagonism between the hero and Françoise, and the way in which they administer shocks and rebuffs to each other's sensibility, important at Combray, where he seemed to her to be insensitive to Léonie's death,[2] and destined to recur not only throughout this volume and Sodome et Gomorrhe[3] but especially during Albertine's stay. This antagonism is finally resolved in Le Temps retrouvé, as Jane Robertson interestingly remarks.[4] If, however, the second

---

1 See II 9, first fourteen lines.

2 I 153-54.

3 See, e.g., II 736-37, where Françoise's use of language annoys Marcel (discussed below, in Ch. 3, pp. 131-32).

4 'The Relationship between the Hero and Françoise in A la Recherche du Temps Perdu', French Studies, XXV (1971), pp. 437-41 (pp. 440-41) (on p. 438 is a discussion of this particular passage, to which I am indebted for the remarks above on reactions to a new place, and to the article in general for some points mentioned in this paragraph).

opening resumes the central *leitmotif* of the blunting of what was initially unassimilable, it does so in a different manner from that of the overture: here, we are moving on a more burlesque and social plane, apposite to our coming introduction in this volume to high society, and preparing us for the ironic perspectives through which it will be shown. (Indeed, to direct the reader's attention to servants on the very first page of a volume which will be largely concerned with the aristocracy is an appropriate counterbalance to the scenes which will follow.) To sum up, the important second period of the narrator's explorations is now initiated with a robustness called for by the tone of the volume, the age the hero has reached, and the structural needs of the whole novel; these narrative requirements could not have been met by the gently progressing discovery of the nature of Marcel's dreams which was at first the sole beginning.[1]

The long passage which describes Charlus's parting conversations with his guests, added on a layer to the MS of *La Prisonnière* (III 266-72a; III 271-72a), can also profitably be considered in its immediate setting. In wide terms, the fact that a large part of the talk is about music brings out the superficial approach of 'le monde' to art; it reiterates in

---

1 M. Raimond refers to the added passages on Françoise as a realistic counterpoint to the development on Names, in 'Note sur la structure du "Côté de Guermantes"', *Revue d'Histoire Littéraire de la France*, 71e année, nos. 5-6 (1971), pp. 854-74 (p. 854).

submerged form the reader's impression of the careless attention which most of the guests have just bestowed upon the Septet, and implicitly sets in relief the seriousness of Marcel's listening, thereby looking forward to the last opposition of all in the novel, that between 'le monde' and art. But these late pages also have here a particularly dramatic function. The humility with which Mme de Mortemart, for example, converses with the baron contrasts with the 'execution' the reader knows will take place, and stresses the point that Charlus may be master in one world but not in another. The discussion about who shall and who shall not be asked to given functions introduces not only intimations of exclusion from private groupings, especially in the person of the 'jeune Péruvien', who wrongly imagines he is not going to be invited by Mme de Mortemart; it brings in the idea of revenge for such exclusion, with this Peruvian's private resolution to 'lui faire mille mauvaises farces' (III 271), each element thus reminding us of Marcel's reactions to Albertine in _La Prisonnière_ and, of course, of Mme Verdurin, who feels particularly 'left out' this evening and will involve Charlus in a 'mauvaise farce'. Above all, the new passage amplifies convincingly the picture of the intolerable treatment being meted out to the Patronne: these guests are queuing up for Charlus, waiting indefinitely with 'une épuisante patience' (III 268), yet will not address a word to Mme Verdurin. This is a most skilful elaboration of the simple MS paragraph beginning 'Les invitées de M. de Charlus s'en allèrent assez rapidement' (III 273), which originally merely sketched out, albeit with telling strokes, the final departure, and made it a speedy one at that. Furthermore - and this could be made as a general comment on the 'lengthening' effect of all the late additions - given the actual time the passage takes to read, the reader is kept waiting for the final dénouement, yet is constantly aware that this is to take place; the longer pause alone would be enough to direct suspense on the figure of Mme Verdurin in the background, growing more and more impatient and furious.

Doubtless almost all of the additions to be described could be shown to build on the base narrative as successfully as these two: many make so important a contribution to central contrasts in the novel, and to the clarity of outline of individual characters, that it is difficult to believe they were not always included in the plan. And many of those which I shall discuss according to theme comprise, or consist of, concretely dramatic dialogues or confrontations. The additions to the 'bal costumé' and those describing Marcel's illnesses heighten the tension about the book that is to be written, while at the same time letting the reader compare what Marcel has actually achieved with the generally declining, rigid world he left behind in order to achieve it.[1] Morel's newly violent and contradictory character

1 See above, Ch. 1, pp. 59-63, and below, pp. 118-21, and Ch. 7, pp. 305-7, 323-25, 328-30.

gives rise to theatrical scenes, such as those in which Charlus spies on him at Maineville (II 1075-81a) and Marcel overhears him abusing his fiancée (III 162-64a, pp. 163-64).[1] The inserted sequences showing characters trying to restrain themselves from a given action but then, in spite of themselves, losing control are comically tense;[2] and the expansion of Albertine's lies and Marcel's interrogations provides numerous further exchanges in the course of which the pair 'spring' disagreeable surprises on each other.[3] Such added sub-stories as that of the duc's reactions to the illness and death of M. d'Osmond show that, contrary to Feuillerat's assertion, some of Proust's most striking post-1914 effects belong quite as much to the dramatically imaginative as to the psychologically generalising.[4] And most of those additions I discuss later portraying menace, tyranny and interference are brought alive by their staging of arbitrary behaviour or shocked responses, as when the Guermantes footman is abruptly deprived of his outings by a mistress who seems to be kind.[5]

Besides these, many of the insertions to be described in this book, as well as depicting the sudden eruption of

---

1 See below, pp. 114-15, and Ch. 4, pp. 187-88, 198.

2 See below, Ch. 7, pp. 309-13.

3 See above, Ch. 1, e.g. pp. 43, 48, and below, Ch. 5, pp. 211-13; Ch. 6, pp. 270-83.

4 See Feuillerat, pp. 124-29.

5 See below, Ch. 5, pp. 228-30.

undesirable traits, go further in confirming the sense of two-sidedness always apparent in the novel; thus Proust starts to show open interest in the extent to which the victim is partly to blame for his own victimisation, or observes that Rachel's sadism is not indicative of her true feelings for Saint-Loup.[1] One of the series of additions does bring out specifically this aspect of character, and, of the consistently elaborated themes, is that which, the most straightforwardly, draws attention to dramatic contrasts.

Thus in several insertions, most of them comic, Proust now dwells on the emergence of odd sides of personality, on faults, eccentricities and minor madnesses. Françoise's stubborn refusal to use the telephone ('Les progrès de la civilisation permettent à chacun de manifester des qualités insoupçonnées ou de nouveaux vices') and her inability to tell the time ('c'était chez Françoise un de ces défauts particuliers, permanents, inguérissables, que nous appelons maladies') were added to the MS of Sodome et Gomorrhe (II 730a) and to the MS and typescript of La Prisonnière (III 155a, b; III 155-56a; III 156a). A number of the passages in which Charlus is said to be 'un peu fou', and, more particularly, that citing his letter to Aimé as an example of 'folie unilatérale chez un homme intelligent', were also late insertions (II 379-80a; II 991a).[2]

1 II 179d. See Ch. 5, p. 225 n.1, for fuller remarks on Rachel's new sadism.

2 See also III 299a; III 305b; III 318-19a.

And the attribution to both Bloch and his father of a special fault, 'par conséquent le défaut dont il[1] ne s'apercevait pas', comes in two long additions to A l'ombre (I 740-48a, pp. 740-41; I 767-79a, p. 776). But above all, the substantial general commentaries on character-defects as 'une maladie intermittente de l'esprit' (II 1090b),[2] on the cross-breeding of faults, with the hereditary building-up of 'réflexes vicieux' (III 156a) and 'égoïsmes accumulés' (III 585-86a), and the three-and-a-half-page humorous discussion à la La Bruyère of the fact that 'Dans l'humanité, la fréquence des vertus identiques pour tous n'est pas plus merveilleuse que la multiplicité des défauts particuliers à chacun' (I 740-48a, pp. 741-44), - all these are late.[3]

In the revision, Proust however developed still more widely his new examples of 'maladies intermittentes de l'esprit', and added long further sections illustrating the volte-face and the

---

1 Bloch here.

2 See II 940-41a, p. 941, for a very similar idea.

3 For other general added passages on faults, see II 692-93a; III 108a; III 110-11a. The chapter on Morel (Ch. 4, pp.197, 199-200) also shows at work this concept of 'faultiness' of character; and see III 181-82a for an addition on both Morel's and Albertine's madness. For 'les défauts d'Andrée', see III 59-61a; also III 62b and III 604a.
For other additions about annoying traits, flaws of personality, and madness, see: II 204b; II 789a; II 791-93a; II 792-93a; II 793a; II 920-21a, p. 921; III 204-7a, pp. 206-7; III 823a; III 970a.

completely unexpected characteristic. This was of course always part of the original plan,[1] but it is, none the less, interesting that some of the most startling metamorphoses in the novel were incorporated only after 1914. As we have seen, Marcel now receives contradictory reports about Norpois's attitude to him.[2] The fine meditation about the 'interminable et toujours déconcertante arrivée' of the 'jeunes filles' and about the way in which a tender and 'rose' girl will, on a subsequent meeting, utter 'les propos d'une lubrique Furie', was actually not worked in until after the first typescript of La Prisonnière had been made, in other words in the last year of Proust's life (III 64-67a). The attribution of arbitrary and incomprehensible ill-humour to Rachel and to Jupien is post-1918, inserted only after the printing of the first Gallimard galleys (II 121a; II 142a).[3] Legrandin's 'voix rageuse et vulgaire que je ne lui soupçonnais pas' appears for the first time in the margin of the 1914 galleys (II 204a). And with the revision of La Prisonnière come two glimpses of an equally unlooked-for kindness, albeit a temporary one: Proust added to the MS both the passage in which Legrandin himself proves so

---

1 See R.M. Birn's good discussion, 'The Theoretical Background for Proust's Personnages "préparés"', L'Esprit Créateur, XI, no. 1 (1971), pp. 42-51 (particularly p. 48).

2 See above, Ch. 1, p. 35: I 561-64a, pp. 563-64; II 271-73a; II 528-30a.

3 For Jupien, see also II 20d; II 21 a, b, c.

firm a support for Marcel's dying great-aunt (III 14c), and, most important of all, that in which the Verdurins decide to rescue Saniette from penury - thus, for M. Verdurin at any rate, presenting 'une face nouvelle insoupçonnée' (III 324-27a; III 326a).

However, the most consistent centre for the expansion of this theme is Saint-Loup. In almost all cases, the later aspects tend towards the unpleasantly surprising.[1] The 1914 version already contained the scenes in which Saint-Loup coldly drives past Marcel, and then supposedly explains this (II 138, 176); but Françoise's assertion that 'il n'y avait qu'à le voir quand il était en colère après son cocher' (I 779-80a; I 780a), Marcel's sudden impression that his strength is 'menaçante' (II 106a,n.), and the letter informing Marcel that he will never forgive him (II 307-8a; also II 338-39a, p. 338),[2] are all additions. Particularly noteworthy, Saint-Loup's complacent recital to the stupefied Marcel of his words to Bloch ('que tu ne l'aimais pas du tout tant que ça') (II 399a), and his advice to the servant as to the best means of contriving the dismissal of a co-worker, were both late expansions ('ce ne pouvait être en son nom qu'il parlait [...] ma confiance en lui était

---

1 A more positive one is that showing the change wrought in Saint-Loup by the war, which has made him wittier, even 'éblouissant' - and his rapid word-play is certainly not a talent the reader had associated with the, if anything, earnest young man of Balbec and Doncières (III 760-62a. See also III 846-47a).

2 Explained, in another addition, as the result of Rachel's stories: II 348b.

ébranlée depuis que je venais de l'entendre tellement différent de ce que je le connaissais') (III 470-71a). And Proust came back yet again to the Côté de Guermantes passage about Bloch, adding in the margin of the first Gallimard galleys the lines on Saint-Loup's expression: 'Du reste sa figure était stigmatisée, pendant qu'il me disait ces paroles vulgaires, par une affreuse sinuosité que je ne lui ai vue qu'une fois ou deux dans la vie [...]' (II 399b).[1]

---

1 For Saint-Loup, see also I 731a; I 731-32a; I 732a; I 735a; I 869a. Proust added to the MS of Sodome et Gomorrhe another example of Saint-Loup's indiscretion, but finally decided to excise it. The two friends are taking a walk through Doncières, and Marcel mentions Charlus. Here Saint-Loup says: '"[...] je lui ai fait une scène sur la sortie qu'il t'a faite chez lui le soir de ton 1er dîner chez ma tante Guermantes"', and the addition continues with Marcel's protest: '"Mais je t'avais défendu de lui en parler!" "Ça m'est égal, je l'ai fait exprès, ce n'est pas mauvais de lui donner des leçons de temps en temps" "Mais ce n'est pas bien de ta part pour moi" "Enfin que veux-tu, c'est ainsi. J'ai tenu à le dire, je l'ai dit, et je recommencerais si c'était à refaire". Je me rappelai aussitôt ce qu'il avait déjà répété à Bloch, [...] et qu'il m'avait avoué avec le même air de satisfaction. C'était décidément [...] quelque chose à quoi (?) une fois par hasard il fallait s'attendre avec St Loup, quelque chose d'absolument excentrique (?) à son caractère, qui était peut'etre (sic) en lui le caractère d'un parent dont il tenait comme on a le nez d'un oncle, peut'être une violence momentanée et qu'ensuite il essayait de fonder en raison comme il était plus intellectuel qu'intelligent, due à q.q. état de l'estomac ou des nerfs.' [Punctuation as Proust's.] (In a layer, n.a.fr. 16712:11; at about the equivalent of II 859.)
Germaine Brée makes some interesting remarks on the way in which Saint-Loup changes in The World of Marcel Proust, pp. 207-8.
For some additions about Charlus's brusque and 'incomprehensible' changes, including those in which he issues the invitation to evening tea, see I 758c; I 759a; I 759-60a; II 268-69a; II 269a; II 381-82a, II 381c; II 557a.
For other additions about changeability or 'intermittences', see particularly II 756d, which contains the famous 'Car aux troubles de la mémoire sont liées les intermittences du coeur', and I 869-951a, p. 895; III 80a; III 377-78a, p. 377; III 619-20a. Also: I 565-66a; I 754c; II 174-75a; II 264-67a and II 273a; II 364-65a; II 365a, II 372-73a; II 1021b; III 692b; III 797-98a.

COMIC EFFECTS

A number of the expansions are also most comic:[1] self-deception and pretence, and the unveiling of real motives, are a consistent source of humour in Proust and are exploited just as much in the late passages as in any of the 1913-14 writings.[2] Where the characters are showing a new self-assertiveness, it is often in contexts which make them ridiculous.[3] The additions to the interview scene with Charlus, and many other insertions, render the baron's grandiose self-exaggeration even more absurd than before.[4] Françoise's fresh distortions of the language, the post-1914 comparison of her feverish culinary activity to Michaelangelo's sculpture, and Norpois's added ponderous yet mechanical phrases, are among the principal springs of comedy for the dinner at the beginning of _A l'ombre_.[5] And nearly all

---

1 M. Suzuki, in fact, sees the bent towards the comic as emerging far more in the additions than it does in the MS (see the articles in _BSAMP_, no.9 (1959), p. 72; no.11 (1961), pp. 385-91; no.12 (1962), pp. 572-75, 578-79, 585-86). Bardèche appears to confirm this briefly (although it is unclear whether he is referring to the whole novel) (vol. I, p. 352, _n_.2).

2 See, e.g., below, Ch. 5, pp. 237-38.

3 See below, Ch. 5, pp. 238-41.

4 See below, Ch. 5, pp. 244, 246-50.

5 See I 445-46a, I 458c, for the cooking; for the others, see below, Ch. 3, pp. 131, 158-59.

the additions about bisexuality and inversion are comic, such as the introduction of the homosexual embassy staff into the soirée in Sodome et Gomorrhe (II 674-75a) and the tales about Nissim Bernard;[1] sometimes the humour is rather grim, as in late discussions of the co-existence of homosexuality and marriage.[2]

Most of the added themes, in fact, are illustrated by some or many humorous examples: almost uniformly entertaining, for instance, are the inserted abuses of spoken language, which are often accompanied by a wry comment: '"les montagnes, disait la fille de Françoise en donnant à *intéressant* un sens affreux et nouveau, ce n'est guère intéressant"' (II 147-48a).[3] Even the additions about illness[4] have their comic elaborations: Nissim Bernard is a hypochondriac (II 842-45a, p 845), and M. de Cambremer delightedly remarks on the similarities or differences between his sister's choking-fits and Marcel's.[5] Indeed, many apparently bleak subjects, such as degeneration,[6] are set in an ironic or amusing perspective, either directly, by the tone of the narrative, or else obliquely: the additions demonstrating Marcel's lack of willpower or his attitude to bisexuality are certainly not humorous,[7] but those echoing these features in

---

1 See below, Ch. 6, pp. 290-91.

2 See below, Ch. 6, pp. 292-94.

3 See Ch. 3, *passim*. Germaine Brée even states that comedy in Proust is always accompanied by the comedy of language (*Du Temps perdu au temps retrouvé* (Paris, 1950), p. 128).

4 See below, Ch. 7, pp. 320-30.

5 See below, Ch. 5, p. 218.

6 See below, Ch. 7, pp. 314-17.

7 See below, Ch. 7, pp. 308-9, and Ch. 6, pp. 272-83.

other characters are. The lack of willpower is balanced by the newly-elaborated picture of Mme Verdurin's vain efforts not to succumb to her desire to tell Morel that Charlus has called him 'mon domestique';[1] and Marcel's shocks about Albertine, and his speculations as to whether or not she is lesbian, are paralleled by Nissim Bernard's experiences with the tomato-faced twins.[2]

These are the broad aspects; but Proust did work in some more purely enjoyable scenes during the post-1914 period. Emphasising his hero's social naïvety, he added the incident in which Marcel, not knowing what to do with the envelope handed to him at the Swanns', discovers only later that it contained the name of the lady he was to take in to dinner (I 546-47a; I 549b; I 575b), as well as those accounts of his blunders (and not only his) about the top-hats at Mme de Villeparisis's matinée (II 221a; II 222-23a, p. 222; II 271a; II 277b; II 277-78a; II 278b).[3] And, as I have already mentioned, Marcel's outburst of temper during the 'interview' with Charlus, and his destruction of his host's top-hat, were added, added in fact quite late, since they appear for the first time in the third Gallimard galleys (II 553b; II 558-59a).[4]

---

1 III 314a, b; see below, pp. 90-91, and Ch. 7, p. 313.

2 II 854-55a and indented additions; II 855b. (See below, Ch. 6, p. 290.)

3 This latter by-play is noted (only as regards Marcel) by Feuillerat, pp. 103-4.

4 See above, Ch. 1, pp. 35-36.
This action was once performed by Proust himself, according to Painter (vol. I, p. 309).
There is clearly a connection between these passages added to Le Côté de Guermantes, in that they focus on top-hats: II 212-13a, a TS addition, also does.

Proust began, too, to exploit more fully a _topos_ comic since Molière and earlier, inserting into his drafts several passages about doctors.[1] Three lesser professionals are introduced: the Brazilian doctor who 'prétendait guérir les étouffements du genre de ceux que j'avais, par d'absurdes inhalations d'essences de plantes' appears for the first time in a margin and layer addition to the first Gallimard galleys (II 226-27a,_n._); and Proust worked into, respectively, the later Gallimard galleys and the _Sodome et Gomorrhe_ typescript the specialist X..., who gives the whole family colds (II 324-25a), and the 'célébrité des maladies nerveuses', who is 'rouge, jovial' and whose athlete's arms are of use in eventually helping his patients into the strait-jacket (II 796-97a, p. 797).[2] However, it is the entirely new character Professor E... to whom Proust devotes the most loving attention, taking him to task for his use of language (II 640-42a, pp. 641-42),[3] illustrating his obsession about lifts, exposing his lack of

---

1 Some of these are favourable: du Boulbon is promoted in one addition from 'intellectuel' to 'artiste' (II 458a; II 458-59a; see also II 301a, b; II 302a), and in another Proust writes that it would be madness to believe in medicine if it were not a greater madness not to! (II 298-99a). A few others are unequivocally unfavourable, and here this later preoccupation joins that with illness (see below, Ch. 7, pp. 321, 324); but the majority are satirical - such as, tending now to deflate du Boulbon, II 303-4a, II 304a.

2 The addition about X... comes on only a _second_ version of the grandmother's death; it seems that all these additions may have been made at roughly the same period.

3 The two other passages in which doctors are rebuked for their linguistic habits are also late additions: II 408a and II 900b.

feeling for the grandmother (II 313-14a, II 317-18a), and finally giving him credit for not betraying an excess of satisfaction on learning that his diagnosis was correct and the grandmother did die after all: and here also, part of this last addition and provoked by Professor E...'s reactions, is the suggestion that if the ill man were left to himself, he would get better or at least survive, but 'le médecin, salué par lui avenue de l'Opéra quand il le croyait depuis longtemps au Père-Lachaise, verra dans ce coup de chapeau un geste de narquoise insolence' (II 640-42a).[1]

Equally late were a number of those passages describing inscrutable ceremonial, mainly in connexion with inversion, and ironically applying lines from _Esther_ and _Athalie_ to 'choruses' of young men. These additions reinforce on a comic level the Jew/homosexual analogy initiated in _Sodome et Gomorrhe I_. For example, Vaugoubert's enchantment at Charlus's revelations about embassy staff-members appears on a layer in the MS of _Sodome et Gomorrhe_ - these are

> révélations rapides, pareilles à celles qui dans les tragédies de Racine apprennent à Athalie et à Abner que Joas est de la race de David, qu'Esther "dans la pourpre assise" a des parents "youpins" (II 664-66a)

---

1 As noted above (Ch. 1, p. 33), Dieulafoy too is added: II 337a; II 342-43a; II 343a. For additions about Cottard, more especially about his responses to M. de Cambremer's remarks to him, see: II 900a; II 960-62a; II 962-63a; II 975-76a, p. 976; II 976c, d, e, f, g, h; II 1096-97a, p. 1097. See also Charlus on medicine and doctors: II 290-91a, p. 291; II 291a.

- and Proust came back to the passage and elaborated the comparison further on the typescript (II 665-66a).[1] Above all, a large number of the tableaux of the Grand-Hôtel 'chasseurs' are new ones. The interest in these hotel-boys, only fully developed in the revision of Sodome et Gomorrhe, is however hinted at with an insertion at the end of A l'ombre in which the manager tells Marcel that 'les chasseurs laissaient un peu à désirer; vous verrez l'année prochaine quelle phalange je saurai réunir' (I 951a).[2] And Proust does add to Sodome et Gomorrhe some substantial passages fulfilling this promise, such as that in which Marcel remarks that 'ce grand palace' was 'dressé comme un théâtre, et une nombreuse figuration l'animait jusque dans les cintres', describes the costumes of the personnel, and continues:

> En bas, c'était l'élément masculin qui dominait et faisait de cet hôtel, à cause de l'extrême et oisive jeunesse des serviteurs, comme une sorte de tragédie judéo-chrétienne ayant pris corps et perpétuellement représentée [...]dès le hall, [...] "un peuple florissant" de jeunes chasseurs se tenait, surtout à l'heure du goûter, comme les jeunes Israélites des choeurs de Racine. Mais je ne crois pas qu'un seul eût pu fournir même la vague réponse que Joas trouve pour Athalie quand celle-ci demande au prince enfant:

1 See too II 666b. (The later reference back to this scene is also an addition: II 774d.)

2 See too I 706-7a, which also mentions the hotel-employees and prepares for the SG expansions.

> "Quel est donc votre emploi?" car ils n'en avaient aucun. Tout au plus, si l'on avait demandé à n'importe lequel d'entre eux, comme la vieille Reine:
>
> "Mais tout ce peuple enfermé dans ce lieu,
> A quoi s'occupe-t-il?
>
> aurait-il pu dire:
>
> Je vois l'ordre pompeux de ces cérémonies
>
> et j'y contribue."

It is this scene that makes Marcel wonder whether he is in the Grand-Hôtel or in Solomon's temple (II 772-75a, II 774b-h, II 775a, b). The elderly invert Nissim Bernard, too, now 'se plaisait singulièrement, qu'elle fût juive ou catholique, à la cérémonie racinienne [...]' (II 842-45a; see also II 843a; II 845-50a, p. 845): both this and the story of Charlus's dinner with Mme de Chevregny's footman, when once more the hotel is likened to a temple and the hotel-boys to a Racinian chorus (II 986-87a), were added to the typescript of Sodome et Gomorrhe.[1]

Finally, some of Proust's most extreme and memorable sketches of physical curiosities belong to the post-1914 period.

---

1 For other additions about hotel-boys or about the 'cérémonie racinienne ', see II 610-13a, pp. 612-13; II 755a; II 854b; also II 826a. A few more additions give similar fanciful scenarios and spectacles, portraying mainly waiters: I 810-11a; II 99a, b; II 165b; II 168b.
To digress slightly, some less comic passages mentioning Racine are also additions, such as Albertine's remarks about Marcel/Assuérus's anger (III 395a), or Marcel's long comparison between himself and Phèdre (mentioned above, Ch. 1, p. 51: III 458-60a; traced back to its origins in DCS by J.M. Cocking, Proust (London, 1956), pp. 48-49, 51).
As well as to Racine, who according to V. Graham is Proust's most frequently-quoted author (The Imagery of Proust (Oxford, 1966), p. 153), there is increased reference to Mme de Sévigné in the post-1914 period. (This equally adds to the theme of hereditary resemblance between the mother and grandmother, an expansion noted below, Ch. 7, p. 330 n.2.) See I 646-47a; I 649a; I 650b; I 652-54a; I 694b; I 696-97a; I 762-63a; II 23e; II 301c; II 312a; II 329-30a, p. 330; III 140-41a; III 363-64a.

His comic descriptions had often veered in the direction of the cartoon, as witness some of the Du Côté de chez Swann depictions of Mme Verdurin,[1] but it is not, I think, tendentious to maintain that his relish for the exaggerated lines of the caricature does grow during these last years.

For example, the assertion that M. de Cambremer's eyelids are too thick to let any intelligence through, and the description of his nose, were added to the MS of Sodome et Gomorrhe, and Proust came back to this passage and worked it still further on the typescript and afterwards:

> [...] Aussi, décontenancé par la minceur de ce regard bleu, se reportait-on au grand nez de travers. Par une transposition de sens, M. de Cambremer vous regardait avec son nez.[2] Ce nez de M. de Cambremer n'était pas laid, plutôt un peu trop beau, trop fort, trop fier de son importance. Busqué, astiqué, luisant, flambant neuf, il était tout disposé à compenser l'insuffisance du regard; malheureusement [...] le nez est généralement l'organe où s'étale le plus aisément la bêtise
> (II 912-14a; II 912-13a; II 912d; II 913a).

And Proust also added to the typescript M. de Cambremer's custom of looking at victims of his wife's impertinent jokes, and laughing:

> Comme le marquis était louche - ce qui donne une intention d'esprit à la gaîté même des imbéciles - l'effet de ce rire était de ramener un peu de pupille sur le blanc, sans cela complet, de l'oeil. Ainsi une éclaircie met un peu de bleu dans un ciel ouaté de nuages. Le monocle protégeait, du reste, comme un verre sur un tableau précieux, cette opération délicate [...];

once Mme de Cambremer's whim has run its course,

---

1 E.g. I 205.

2 Sentences underlined were not in the MS addition.

> M. de Cambremer cessait de rire, la prunelle momentanée disparaissait, et comme on avait perdu depuis quelques minutes l'habitude de l'oeil tout blanc, il donnait à ce rouge Normand quelque chose à la fois d'exsangue et d'extatique, comme si le marquis venait d'être opéré ou s'il implorait du Ciel, sous son monocle, les palmes du martyre (II 978-79a).

His mother emerges from the additions as little more appealing. Her tendency to excessive salivation is mentioned in the MS of Sodome et Gomorrhe (II 1088),[1] but Proust now incorporates the series of passages explaining and illustrating this propensity. Those lines in which, 'dans un dernier mâchonnement enthousiaste', she tells Marcel that her daughter-in-law is 'si hartthhisstte!' were added to the MS (II 824a),[2] but all the other developments were inserted on the typescript or later, such as that in which, in a delirium of delight over the newly-imparted information that Chopin is Debussy's favourite musician, she gives vent to cries of enthusiasm:

> Et sa voix était aussi caillouteuse que si, pour m'exprimer son ardeur pour Chopin, elle eût, imitant Démosthène, rempli sa bouche avec tous les galets de la plage. Enfin le reflux vint, atteignant jusqu'à la voilette qu'elle n'eut pas le temps de mettre à l'abri et qui fut transpercée, enfin la marquise essuya avec son mouchoir brodé la bave d'écume dont le souvenir de Chopin venait de tremper ses moustaches (II 817-18a; II 818a, b).[3]

---

1 On very clean paper, however; it might be late (n.a.fr. 16713:93).

2 Together with a brief mention of her 'voix qui sembla alors soulevée par une vague rouler des galets' and of the 'imperfection [...] du ratelier (sic)' (margin, n.a.fr. 16711:110).

3 See also II 808b; II 809a; II 810-11a; II 823b.

As for Mme Verdurin's forehead, all descriptions of this are late ones.[1] Proust started to provide details of its appearance in an addition to the MS of *Sodome et Gomorrhe*, and elaborated further on the typescript. He now tells us that Mme Verdurin is no longer what she was in the days of Swann and Odette, for the exhausted air of admiration she then wore during the playing of music has finally incorporated itself into her very face:

> Sous l'action des innombrables névralgies que la musique de Bach, de Wagner, de Vinteuil, de Debussy lui avait occasionnées, le front de Mme Verdurin avait pris des proportions énormes, comme les membres qu'un rhumatisme finit par déformer. Ses tempes, pareilles à deux belles sphères brûlantes, endolories et laiteuses, *où roule immortellement l'Harmonie,*[2] rejetaient, de chaque côté, des mèches argentées, et proclamaient, pour le compte de la Patronne, sans que celle-ci eût besoin de parler: "Je sais ce qui m'attend ce soir." [...]
> (II 906a, b, c).

Subsequent variations come as additions to the typescript: when, praising Cottard, Mme Verdurin raises her hand, it is now 'vers les deux sphères aux mèches blanches de ses tempes musicales' (II 962a); and, already trying to persuade Marcel to abandon Rivebelle and come to her instead, Mme Verdurin further informs him that the Rivebelle 'galettes' carried off a seventeen-year-old girl with peritonitis:

---

1 Although her 'front bombé' was mentioned in 'Un Amour de Swann' and the MS of *Le Temps retrouvé*, its comic potential was not by any means fully realised (I 258, III 940 §2).

2 Underlined words not added until the typescript.

> C'est triste pour sa pauvre mère, ajouta Mme Verdurin, d'un air mélancolique sous les sphères de ses tempes chargées d'expérience et de douleur (II 970a).

This striking new aspect of Mme Verdurin's face continues to be noted in additions almost to the end of La Prisonnière; Proust inserted on the MS the lines in which, agitated by the thought of a fresh and brilliant recruit to the clan,

> la Patronne, tout en faisant semblant de n'avoir rien entendu et en conservant à son beau regard, cerné par l'habitude de Debussy plus que n'aurait fait celle de la cocaïne, l'air exténué que lui donnaient les seules ivresses de la musique, n'en roulait pas moins, sous son beau front, bombé par tant de quatuors et les migraines consécutives, des pensées qui n'étaient pas exclusivement polyphoniques [...]
> (III 228-30a; III 229a, b, c).[1]

And one of the other passages must be very late indeed, since it was added only on the third typescript of La Prisonnière:[2] it is that in which the forehead reappears at the point of Mme Verdurin's laying the final heavy touch on Morel's discomfiture with the report that Charlus has called him 'mon domestique':

> A ce moment s'agitait sous le front bombé de la Déesse musicienne la seule chose que certaines personnes ne peuvent pas conserver pour elles, un mot qu'il est non seulement abject, mais imprudent de répéter. Mais le besoin de le répéter est plus fort que l'honneur, que la prudence. C'est à ce besoin que, après quelques

---

1 Underlined words added or reworked on third typescript.

2 (As was the reworking just above, III 229a, b, c.)

> légers mouvements convulsifs du front sphérique et chagrin, céda la Patronne (III 314a).[1]

THE NARRATOR'S INTELLECTUAL AND SENSORY INTERESTS

More specifically than these dramatic or comic ones, a number of additions bring to the reader's attention the vision of Marcel himself, and may even explore relatively untried intellectual or sensory fields.

Intellectual enthusiasms

Erudite interests, important but unostentatious in the base versions, were, in two cases at least, extended so greatly during the post-1914 revision that the most casual reader could not miss them. These two, already mentioned,[2] are etymologies and military strategy. Etymologies did appear in Du Côté de chez

---

1 For Mme Verdurin's forehead, see also III 248a; III 251a; and for a more general comic passage, III 240-41a. Similar expansions are the passage about the ogre-like appearance of the prince Von (II 510a, b), and the odd punning late paragraph, not one of Proust's more successful additions, about the Paris editor who has 'quelque chose de tranchant. Il avait l'air d'un couteau à papier en ébène' (II 904b). See also perhaps II 217-18a, on Mme de Villeparisis; II 654a, b, II 655a and III 42-44a, p. 42, on Bréauté; and on Mme de Cambremer-Legrandin, II 811b, c, and II 914-15a.

2 Ch. 1, pp. 30, 43, 64.

Swann, where the curé was knowledgeable about them,[1] and there were some in the main MS of Sodome et Gomorrhe, but they did not obtrude in this early narrative, their presence being apparently accounted for as an illustration of the generalising and classification of 'ce qui m'avait paru particulier' - here, proper names (II 1098).[2] Again, Marcel's interest in military affairs was mentioned in the typescript of Le Côté de Guermantes, although limited to his anxiety to classify generals in order of merit (II 128); and by the time Proust wrote the main MSS for La Prisonnière and Le Temps retrouvé, he was incorporating some reference to military strategy into the body of these Cahiers.[3] However, he returned to this foundation and built on it enormously in proportion to the indications already there.

Marcel's very interest emerges from the expansion substantially emphasised: it is he who now asks for the exposition about

---

1 I 103-6, 146. The Du Côté de chez Swann documents show, however, that even these, and the references to them, were relatively late; they were inserted on the second page-proofs, i.e. only in 1913 (margins, n.a.fr. 16755, pp.64 verso, 65, 65 verso, 67, 91).

2 On II 921-25, 929-31, 932-33, 936-38, 1098-99, 1110. See also II 1014.

3 Such as the excised passage given above, Ch. 1, p.49, and on III 752 (evidently written after the CG additions discussed below). See also II 112-113a, not a true addition; and II 509, where, in the MS, Mme de Guermantes accuses Robert of believing 'qu'il a inventé la stratégie'.

military strategy in the first place,[1] and an addition to Le Temps retrouvé stresses his curiosity as to its application;[2] as for the etymologies, the enthusiasm is still more noticeable. Where in the MS it was Albertine who was interested,[3] now not only does Marcel constantly return to Brichot, asking him privately to talk about place-names to the Verdurins' guests, 'parmi lesquels je lui avais dit qu'il était sûr d'en intéresser au moins un' (II 922a, II 929b), and saying 'je brûlais d'interroger [Brichot] sur bien d'autres noms' (II 894e); he actually makes himself almost as comically absent-minded as Brichot, so absorbed in the etymologies that he does not realise M. Verdurin is being ironical about the professor's erudition (II 902a, b, c).[4]

This eagerness to learn, significant in itself, is a sound narrative device, allowing Proust to proceed to add to the etymological theme first, sheer bulk of verbatim illustration, mostly in Sodome et Gomorrhe, and second, the curé's little book on Normandy place-names and the thorough exposures by Brichot of all the mistakes the 'brave ecclésiastique'[5] has

---

1 II 108-117a, p. 108, where he would like details, and p.109, where he presses for examples.

2 III 752a; cp. III 752 without the addition.

3 II 1014, 1098-99.

4 The MS does briefly give such comedy at Marcel's expense, but in only subdued manner (II 949). See also II 894-95a for his new enthusiasm.

5 II 887-91a, p. 888.

made.[1] (It is thought-provoking that in a number of cases the mild countryside interpretation of the curé gives way, in the true derivation, to a more bleak, even pagan, landscape, opening up often to water and the sea.[2]) Marcel's questions, in similar fashion, lead directly to the addition of the great majority of references to military strategy in the novel, ranging from the huge passage inserted into _Le Côté de Guermantes_ (II 108-117a) and later expanded even further,[3] to the gradual tracing of Saint-Loup's mistaken prophecies and 'livresques' arguments[4] (II 412e, f; II 607-9a, p. 608; III 744a; III 982-83a).[5]

These two interests do have some points in common. They are both activities of the 'reason',[6] and Proust implies at the

---

1 These are the additions giving etymologies or discussion of them: those mentioning the curé are underlined: II 179a; II 706-7a; _II 809-10a_; _II 887-91a_; _II 888a_; _II 888-89a_; II 889a; _II 889-90a_; II 893-94a; II 894e; II 898b; II 912-14a, p.913; II 913_c_,d; _II 922a_; II 922-23a; _II 925-26a_; II 930-31a; II 931b,c; II 931-32a,b (and _II 995c_); II 933b,c; II 938a,b,c,d; _II 994a_; II 997-1006a, p.1005; II 1075-81a, p.1076; II 1086a; II 1098b,c,d; II 1099-1100a; II 1100a,b,c,e; II 1101-8a, p. 1105; II 1109a; _III 982b_. Also possibly II 895-97a, p.895. Victor Graham's article, 'Proust's etymologies' (_French Studies_, XXIX (1975), pp. 300-312), provides sources, some dates for the renewed interest (1919-22), and a few general comments (see particularly pp.300, 301, 303, 308, 309).

2 See, e.g., II 887-91a, pp. 888-89, and II 888-89a.

3 II 109a; II 110a,b; II 110-11a; II 111a; II 111-12a; II 112a,b,c,e; II 112-113a; II 113a,c; II 114a; II 115a; II 116a,c,d; II 117b,c,d.

4 See III 744a.

5 Other additions about military strategy are: II 79a; II 91-92a, p.91; III 705b; III 746-47a; III 758-59a; III 759-60a; III 760a; III 980-81a; III 982a. See also II 106-7a, II 107a, which compare Marcel with the commander Duroc; III 1032-35a, p.1032, for a new use of military strategy imagery; and II 417a.

6 See, e.g., II 108-117a, p. 111, and II 1109a.

end of his novel that both need qualifying as valid modes of understanding. The etymology is used in a simile to represent a disjointed form of knowledge about bygone perceptions,[1] whereas the reader knows that the experiences of involuntary memory have allowed Marcel to feel the relationship between present and past, not simply acknowledge it; and added to the MS is the passage in which Marcel, talking with Gilberte at the last matinée about Saint-Loup's interest in military strategy, tells her that Robert had begun to see that, since war was 'humaine', strategy was probably not a science, and could not lead to as rigorous planning as might be hoped (III 982-83a).

At the same time, each of the interests bears certain analogies with the future writing of the novel. The etymologies show the growth of a language (albeit an unconscious growth), reflecting in a formal sphere the record of Françoise's linguistic distortions ('Son langage, comme la langue française elle-même, et surtout sa toponymie, était parsemé d'erreurs': II 23c); more profoundly, they harmonise with one of the basic lessons of <u>A la recherche</u> in as much as they get back to a primary truth before usage and habit warped it. And, inadequate though military strategy might be in some respects, one addition compares the general to the writer planning his work, and perhaps following a large diversion as a result of the 'ressources inattendues' here and the 'impasse' there - like Proust himself,

---

1 Already in the MS, III 970-71. (See also III 932a,<u>n</u>., for an important addition about the interest in names in general.)

one could say (III 759-60a, p. 760).

Sense-impressions

Other additions do, however, re-create more sensory responses. Proust appears to have become particularly interested in sound during the 1914-22 period. Marcel's efforts at Doncières to place the ticking of Saint-Loup's watch are in the 1914 galleys (II 74-75);[1] but a number of the other developments about sound are not. Both Saint-Loup's reference to Marcel's 'hyperesthésie auditive' (II 72a), and the mistaken location of night-time noises made by passers-by in the streets of Doncières (II 97-98a), were added only between the 1914 galleys and the composition of the first Gallimard ones. And the long meditations on the effect of ear-plugs and on the magical, Edenic nature of a world without sound -

> pour ce sourd total, comme la perte d'un sens ajoute autant de beauté au monde que ne fait son acquisition, c'est avec délices qu'il se promène maintenant sur une Terre presque édénique où le son n'a pas encore été créé

- were almost all worked in around the period of revision of the first Gallimard galleys.[2] Proust had already, in the early

---

1 Although this itself was an addition to the 1913 typescript (II 74-75a).

2 Except II 75a, II 77b and II 77-78a, which are rather earlier. The others are II 75-77a; II 75b; II 75-76a; II 76a; II 77c, d,e; II 78a,b. Painter dates this late section after May 1919 (vol. II, pp. 304-5).

typescript, endowed Doncières with 'une sorte de perpétuelle vibratilité musicale et guerrière' (II 70): doubtless this explains why he grouped these additions in the stay there.

The second main concentration of additions about sound comes shortly after the beginning of La Prisonnière. The MS sequences in which Marcel lies in bed, enjoying both the impressions filtering in from outside and his own memories,[1] do describe his joyful realisation that he has awoken to a spring day orchestrated from the street by 'des thèmes populaires finement écrits pour des instruments variés, depuis la corne du raccommodeur de porcelaine [...] jusqu'à la flûte du chevrier [...]' (III 116).[2] But the bell-chimes whose quality differs according to the weather ('un univers seulement audible pourrait être aussi varié que l'autre'), and the praise of hearing, 'ce sens délicieux', which brings us 'la compagnie de la rue, dont elle nous retrace toutes les lignes, dessine toutes les formes qui y passent, nous en montrant la couleur', were added only in margins (III 84a, III 116a,b); and the famous street-cries are not in the MS at all. The brief preparation in Le Côté de Guermantes for their later full development was not added until the third Gallimard galleys (II 371b), and the

---

1 E.g. III 82-83.

2 This dates back at least before 25th March 1913: see 'Vacances de Pâques', reproduced in Chroniques (Paris, 1927), pp. 106-13 (p.106), and there are similar phrases in the 1954 Contre Sainte-Beuve, edited by B. de Fallois (Paris, 1954), pp. 74-76.

street-cries themselves appear only in the second and third typescripts of La Prisonnière, divided between them in a state of considerable confusion, and much reworked.[1]

---

1 III 116-19a, and all indented additions; III 119b; III 120a; III 121-22a, p. 121; III 122-26a, p. 126; III 126c; III 126-28a and all indented additions; III 128-31a, p. 128; III 136c; III 136-37a; III 137b; III 137-38a, and indented additions; III 138d. It must be said that these passages may have been composed earlier than it would seem, since Proust had promised them for separate publication in the Nouvelle Revue Française by August 1922 (Marcel Proust et Jacques Rivière: Correspondance 1914-22, pp. 274-75), and may have extracted them from the MS for this purpose; the Pléiade editors, at least, had access to an MS copy (III 1058).
L. Spitzer gives a short but pertinent analysis of the function of the street-cries in La P: 'L'étymologie d'un "cri de Paris"', in Études de Style ([Paris], 1970), pp. 474-81 (pp. 474-75, 478-79).
Other additions about sound now inflict deafness on both Mme de Villeparisis's grandfather and (temporarily) Marcel's grandmother (II 192a; II 332a); describe 'l'harmonieuse et multisonore salutation de toutes les Voix' (III 101-2a) and the 'escadron volant de sons' of the telephone (III 155a); and, in the war-chapter, weave in the noise of the aeroplanes, the 'Wagnerian' siren, and the 'cri de joie' of the 'berloque', an 'invisible gamin' (III 777c; III 840c). See also II 139b; II 732a.
Florence Hier interestingly extends her discussion of music in Proust to cover sound in Proust too: La Musique dans l'oeuvre de Marcel Proust (New York, 1933), pp. 18-27.
Most of the street-cries are about food, and as an extension of this note it might be recorded that food is also the subject of other additions at this point of the novel, such as Albertine's description of the ice-cream (III 128-31a; see too III 138b,c,e). More generally, there are several additions in the post-1914 period about cooking and food, many in A l'ombre (I 445-46a; I 458c; I 484a; I 484-86a; I 506e,f,g; I 694b; I 869-951a, p. 904; II 502-3a,b, p.502; II 502a; II 901b; II 970a; II 972b; III 36a; III 462-65a, p. 463; III 1032-35a); some specifically refer to orange-juice or fruit-juice (II 513a,b,c; II 642-47a, p.645; II 738c; III 387a). These passages and some of the others are sensitively classified and often amusingly discussed by J.-P. Richard in Proust et le monde sensible (Paris, 1974), pp. 14-34 (particularly pp. 16, 19 n.2, 26-30), 39-40.

Proust's renewed interest in deviations from normal apprehension of the physical world, an interest apparent in the additions on deafness, flowed over too into such areas as perception during intoxication, or during sleep and dreams. The Rivebelle sequence, which Proust used as a centre for many of the later elaborations on drunkenness, had, in 1914, described the disappearance of Marcel's firm resolutions (I 809-10), his feeling of well-being (I 811), and his carelessness over a possible accident (I 814, 815-16); but when Proust revised this section, he actually gave Marcel more to drink (I 809f, I 810a, I 811a),[1] and, in a short separate paragraph, bestowed upon him the transitory notion that, his past and family discarded, he has become an 'homme nouveau' (I 809e) (to be taken up rather later in, again, the addition of Marcel's intoxicated glimpse of a different 'moi' in the mirror after the lunch with Rachel[2]). The already important remarks on heedlessness of danger are now reinforced by a half-page that attributes to drunkenness, as to heroism, the power to enclose its subject in the present (I 815a); and, inspired by the experiences at Rivebelle in A l'ombre and by the girls on Balbec beach in Sodome et Gomorrhe, the observations to the effect that the conquest of women seems much easier after, say, seven or eight glasses of port, are both additions: 'l'ivresse réalise pour quelques heures l'idéalisme

---

1 (The brief mention of Marcel's consumption of wine at the Guermantes dinner is also an addition: II 524a.)

2 II 171-72a.

subjectif' (I 816-17a; II 838-40a, pp. 838-39; II 838b). Finally, Marcel's dream that he is being punished 'pour une faute que je n'apercevais pas, mais qui était d'avoir bu trop de porto', and the comparison of sleep to 'les autres ivresses, que ce soit le vin qui les procure ou une convalescence', are part of a long post-1914 A l'ombre passage (I 818-25a, p. 820).[1]

Sleep and dreams

Proust, however, devoted still more attention to sleep itself during the reworking of the drafts. He had of course been interested in dreams, and their impingement on waking life, even in Les Plaisirs et les jours;[2] as for the earlier parts of A la recherche du temps perdu, Swann's dream is a climax in 'Un Amour de Swann',[3] and the MSS already give Marcel's dreams about

---

1 II 171-72a, p. 171, also makes this comparison. Other late passages about drunkenness make more comic play on Marcel's intoxication during the journey to Balbec (I 652-54a, pp. 652-53); unexpectedly imply that Saint-Loup habitually drinks too much (II 164b; also II 278c); and show the Verdurins insinuating that given 'fidèles' drink to excess (III 230a). See also II 1016-17a.

2 See 'Les regrets, rêveries couleur du temps: XVII: Rêve', Les Plaisirs et les jours, Bibliothèque de la Pléiade ([Paris], 1971), pp. 127-30. Cited by W.S. Bell in Proust's Nocturnal Muse (New York and London, 1962), pp. 25-26: see too the whole chapter 'Proust's Early Works', pp. 13-51.

3 I 378-80. J. Bellemin-Noël offers Freudian, and other, interpretations of this in '"Psychanalyser" le rêve de Swann?', Poétique, no.8 (1971), pp. 447-69; it is discussed rather more mechanically by W.S. Bell in Proust's Nocturnal Muse, pp. 55-65.

the grandmother and (in generalised form) about Albertine in Sodome et Gomorrhe and La Fugitive (II 760-62; III 538-39). None the less, a very large number of the present references in the novel to sleep and dreams, both brief statements and intricate developments, were added only after the composition of the drafts - including that affirmation that 'on ne peut bien décrire la vie des hommes si on ne la fait baigner dans le sommeil où elle plonge et qui, nuit après nuit, la contourne comme une presqu' île est cernée par la mer', written into the margin of the 1914 galleys (II 85c).

The Norwegian philosopher, for example, who brings with him controversies about sleep and memory (inter alia), is an entirely added character.[1] The comic passage in which Cottard discusses sleeping-drugs with M. de Cambremer, or rather states his opinion on them, whilst his wife struggles unsuccessfully with the overpowering need for an after-dinner nap, appears in neither the MS nor the proofs of Sodome et Gomorrhe, but in a separately-typed page in the typescript:

> sa tête [...] fut rejetée mécaniquement de gauche à droite et de bas en haut, dans le vide, comme un objet inerte, et Mme Cottard, balancée quant au chef, avait tantôt l'air d'écouter de la musique, tantôt d'être entrée dans la dernière phase de l'agonie
> (II 960-62a, p. 962).

---

1 See principally II 980-86a, pp. 984-85; he also appears, or is mentioned in, II 930-31a; II 931a; II 935a; II 975-76b; II 976a.

In the case of Marcel himself, over fifteen smaller insertions offer further examples of actual dreams, and sporadic reflections about the sleeping mind,[1] reflections to be taken up extensively in the celebrated major additions. These, often several pages long, seem for the most part to have been worked in towards the end of the revision period.[2] Strewn throughout the volumes, they culminate with the narrator's conclusions in _Le Temps retrouvé_, which were added in layers to the MS: these, to summarise, now tell the reader that Marcel had always been interested in dreams, which had convinced him of the purely mental character of reality; 'c'était peut-être aussi par le jeu formidable qu'il fait avec le Temps que le Rêve m'avait fasciné', and, in the writing of the book, 'Je ne dédaignerais pas cette seconde muse, cette muse nocturne' (III 911-12a, III 914a).

---

1 These additions are: I 621-35a, pp. 629-30; II 145-46a; II 335-36a; II 650-52a, pp. 651-52; II 757a; II 762b; III 144-47a, p. 147; III 492a; III 538-39a; III 539a; III 539-40a; III 591a; III 595-96a, p. 595; III 717a; III 819-20a; III 876c; III 973a.

2 They were added after the 1914 galleys of _A l'ombre_ (I 818-25a, pp. 819-23), on both the 1914 and first Gallimard galleys of _Le Côté de Guermantes_ and afterwards (II 84-85a; II 85a,b; II 86-88a,b; II 88a; II 91-92a; II 92a), in handwritten pages inserted into the typescript of _Sodome et Gomorrhe_, and even later (II 979-80a, p. 979; II 980-86a and indented additions); finally, the five-page passage in _La Prisonnière_ on sleep and dreams is not in the MS at all, appearing only in the second and third typescripts (III 121-22a,b; III 122-26a and indented additions, except III 126c).

There emerges from these later passages a preoccupation with rest, refreshment, and the effect of drugs on these;[1] with the potential of dreams either to bring back the freshness of desires or actually to give rise to new emotions of pity and love;[2] and with the influence - distorting or undisturbing - of external sense-impressions on sleep and dreams.[3] But more important is the newly emphatic consideration of the facts finally to be recapitulated in Le Temps retrouvé. Proust is now concerned to stress that the central characteristic of sleep and dreams is the very difficulty they present to the conscious mind, which can barely penetrate into this mysterious and different world, and gleans little information about the tasks set by 'l'autre maître au service de qui nous sommes chaque jour', however sly the attempt to look 'à peine la tâche finie' (III 717a).[4] He is demonstrating too the ambiguity of the dream-subjects,[5] the overturning of linear time so often apparently effected during sleep,[6] and the proof it might offer of a disjunctive personality, the dream self being compared to

---

1 I 818-25a, pp.819-20, 822; II 86-88b, p.86; II 86-88a, p.88; II 88a; II 91-92a; II 92a; II 980-86a, pp. 983-84, 986; III 121-22a, p. 121; III 124b,c.

2 III 124-26a, p. 125; III 876c; III 914a.

3 II 84-85a; II 85a; II 91-92a, p. 91; II 980-86a, pp. 980, 985-86; III 121-22a,b, p. 121.

4 I 818-25a, p. 820; II 86-88b, p. 87.

5 I 621-35a, pp. 629-30; II 981a.

6 I 818-25a, pp. 820-21; II 85a; II 86-88b, p.87; II 980-86a, pp. 982-83, 986; III 121-22a, p. 122; III 122-26a, p. 122.

an old 'moi' and awakening to resurrection by memory.[1]

The expansion of this particular theme is significant in terms of both what the novel was, before its expansion, and what it later became. These added passages, by reiterating at intervals the half-awake, half-sleeping shifting atmosphere already created in the overture, heighten the progress from such semi-darkness towards the final 'waking-up' and certainty in Le Temps retrouvé, where Marcel's revelation is, as Germaine Brée has pointed out, accompanied by images of illumination and light.[2] But they also echo some of the chronologically later parts of the novel, since, as has been implied and will be brought out elsewhere, A la recherche is itself, as a result of many of the additions, becoming in places increasingly dream-like, with the volte-faces and uncertainty:[3] 'La connaissance aurait-elle, réciproquement, l'irréalité du rêve?' (II 980-86a, p. 985).[4]

Style and imagery

The question of the development of Proust's style during

---

1 I 818-25a, pp. 820, 822-23; II 86-88a, p. 88; II 757a; II 981-82a; II 980-86a, pp. 984-85; III 121-22b; III 123b,c,n.; III 595-96a.

2 G. Brée, '"Vision" et création selon Proust', Australian Journal of French Studies, VI (1969), pp. 180-86 (particularly p. 182).

3 See above, pp.76-79. Also below, Ch.6, passim; Ch.8, p.356.

4 For other additions mentioning sleep or dreams, see especially Bergotte's sleep and dreams, III 184-86a; III 182-92a, p.186; and also III 11a; III 448a; III 561b. See too the passages on Albertine's sleep, all additions (below, pp.113-14).

the 1914-22 period is at present troubled. Victor Graham's statistical analysis of the images in A la recherche, and his discovery that these are more numerous in the post-1914 parts of A l'ombre and Le Côté de Guermantes than in the pre-1914, have not, as he himself recognises, disproved Feuillerat's assertion that the older Proust was writing in a less densely coloured and intricate style than the Proust of Du Côté de chez Swann.[1] More thorough correlations and contrasts than can be offered in this book might be needed to draw sensible conclusions here. However, as I said in the last chapter,[2] account should certainly be taken, pace Feuillerat, of the fact that in the later volumes some of the closely sensuous passages of the type found in Du Côté de chez Swann are actually additions. On the other hand, M. Bardèche most interestingly implies that Proust composed his 'descriptions' in fragments, and almost before any of the rest of the novel, then to be 'used' when suitable,[3] so some of the passages now in the margins of the near-definitive

---

1 See Feuillerat's rather crude discussion, pp. 1, 7, 129-32, 262, and V.E.Graham, The Imagery of Proust, pp. 6-7, 259. Pierre Clarac, talking about some of this material, does remark on the difference between 'le style amoureusement travaillé, savamment et précieusement musical, des parties anciennes', and that of the additions (in JF): 'Remarques sur le texte des Jeunes Filles en Fleurs. Projet d'une édition', BSAMP, no. 2 (1951-52), pp.32-56 (pp.34-35). See also below, Ch. 8, p. 343 n.2, for comments made by M. Bardèche and J. Milly.

2 p. 14.

3 Bardèche, vol. I, pp.206, 232-33, 269-71, 354-57. Examples of this procedure which I came across were the shifting of the description now at the end of SG (see Ch. 1, pp. 41-42), and the re-positioning of the 'rural' sea (see Ch. 8, p. 355).

versions may, in spite of appearances, have been written at an early date; but this would be for research on the Cahiers to establish.[1]

Thus, the impressions at Doncières of the hill in the fog, and Marcel's later memories of them, are additions (II 80-82a; II 346a, b; II 347a; II 390a, b; III 889-90a). So, as I mentioned above,[2] are all the major descriptions of La Raspelière, of the countryside around it, and of Marcel's admiration for both house and views; this expansion may have been made at a late stage because the Verdurin dinners of Sodome et Gomorrhe were originally to have taken place in or very near the capital.[3] The pictures of war-time Paris by night are almost all insertions on the main MS.[4] And some of those evocations of intense heat in Sodome et Gomorrhe are late ones: thus, where an MS layer describing Marcel's excursions with Albertine and her friends

---

1 See the discussion in Ch. 1 of, e.g., the 'Demoiselles du téléphone' (pp. 64-65).

2 Ch. 1, p. 43.

3 See Bardèche, vol. II, pp. 153-55, 159, 162. (Mentioned in Ch. 1, p. 12 n.5.) The additions about La Raspelière, the height at which it stands, and its environs, are: II 897-99a; II 898a; II 899a; II 904-6a; II 932a; II 942c; II 944-45a,b; II 944a; II 972c; II 977a; II 997-1006a, II 999a.

4 In the MS are brief passages on III 735, 736, 737, 763, 801, 802, 809. Added were: III 736a; III 762-63a; III 762a; III 801-2a; III 802-7a, pp. 802-3; III 808-9a; see also III 777c.

had read simply: 'je me rappelle les temps chauds qu'il faisait alors', Proust added to this in the margin of the typescript:

> où du front des garçons de ferme travaillant au soleil une goutte de sueur tombait verticale, régulière, intermittente, comme la goutte d'eau d'un réservoir, et alternait avec la chute du fruit mûr qui se détachait de l'arbre dans les "clos" voisins (II 837a);

and the passage starting 'Mais c'était la canicule' was worked out, partially and in rough, in an MS margin, to appear fully only in the typescript:

> l'air lumineux et brûlant éveillait des idées d'indolence et de rafraîchissement [...] tout en haut, dans le carré laissé vide, le ciel, dont on voyait glisser, les uns par-dessus les autres, les flots moelleux et superposés, semblait, à cause du désir qu'on avait, [...] une piscine pleine d'une eau bleue réservée aux ablutions (II 994b, c,d).[1]

The paragraph of lament, coming shortly after Albertine's death, that begins 'Que le jour est lent à mourir par ces soirs démesurés de l'été!' was also added to the MS (III 481a): this 'petit poème en prose' could almost be a pastiche of Baudelaire.[2] And the excised introduction of _Sodome et Gomorrhe I_,[3] which, although probably post-1914,[4] is written in what

---

1 For other additions to _Sodome et Gomorrhe_ conveying heat, see II 1013a; II 1014-15a; II 1034a. In _La Fugitive_, see III 478a.

2 Compare 'Que les fins de journées d'automne sont pénétrantes! Ah! pénétrantes jusqu'à la douleur!' of 'Le "confiteor" de l'artiste', _Petits poèmes en prose_ (Éditions Garnier, Paris, 1962), pp. 16-19. I am indebted for this suggestion to my research supervisor, Professor L.J. Austin.

3 The one reproduced in _BSAMP_, no. 6: see above, Ch. 1, p. 37.

4 (It mentions Albertine.)

Feuillerat would presumably describe as Proust's earlier style,[1] would repay a close comparison with the present beginning, thirty pages on, of Sodome et Gomorrhe II, which, by contrast, appears to be entirely added:

> [...] le jour d'été ne semblait pas avoir plus que moi de hâte à bouger. Bien qu'il fût plus de neuf heures, c'était lui encore qui sur la place de la Concorde donnait à l'obélisque de Louqsor un air de nougat rose. Puis il en modifia le teint et le changea en une matière si métallique que l'obélisque ne devint pas seulement plus précieux, mais sembla plus mince et presque flexible. On s'imaginait qu'on aurait pu tordre, qu'on avait peut-être déjà légèrement faussé ce bijou. La lune était maintenant dans le ciel comme un quartier d'orange pelé délicatement quoique un peu entamé. Mais elle devait quelques heures plus tard être faite de l'or le plus résistant [...]
> (II 633-34a).[2]

Other metaphors and similes in the later passages take up the jewel-symbolism of this opening. Proust drew on such imagery to depict two of his added characters: Nissim Bernard looks like 'une larve préraphaélite où des poils se seraient malproprement implantés, comme des cheveux noyés dans une opale' (II 289-90a), and Céleste's skin has 'une transparence opaline'

---

1 Painter, for example, refers to it as being 'in an earlier manner' (vol. II, p. 312).

2 Cp. a similar description in the MS (II 1019); the reference back to this one is however an addition (II 1019c).
Some of Marcel's reminiscences or involuntary memories are additions too: see above, Ch. 1, pp. 33-34, 35: II 397-98a; II 531-32a and indented additions. Also II 944a, II 949a; III 166a.
For other added lines similar to the passages so far cited, see: II 82-83a; II 385b,c; II 389a; II 392a; II 765-68a; II 1020b; II 1096a; III 176a; III 567c; III 630a,b; III 650a (cp. II 572-73a); III 697b; III 697-98a; III 697c; III 871a.

(II 845-50a, p. 850). Mme Verdurin's tarts are now 'remplies de cerises comme des perles de corail' (II 1001a), and Saniette, in his fear of not being wanted, takes on 'un visage torturé et un regard aussi indestructible qu'un émail cuit' (II 1022-24a, p. 1023).[1] And, to the famous sequence in which the narrator looks out from the train on the trees that leave him indifferent, Proust added the passage using the imagery of precious substances, or at any rate those fashioned by man, to convey Marcel's lack of interest:

> [...] j'avais fait ces diverses constatations avec la même absolue indifférence que si, me promenant dans un jardin avec une dame, j'avais vu une feuille de verre et un peu plus loin un objet d'une matière analogue à l'albâtre dont la couleur inaccoutumée ne m'aurait pas tiré du plus languissant ennui [...] (III 855-56a).[2]

More consistently, however, Proust exploits botanical and zoological imagery in his later descriptions. The assimilation of humans to plants and to animals is not new in the work, persistent as it is in both Du Côté de chez Swann and the base versions of the succeeding volumes,[3] but its use is now particularly bold.

---

1 See also II 1024a.

2 For other additions mentioning jewels, or using jewel-imagery, see: I 526-36a, p. 527; I 869-951a, p. 946; II 424-26a, p. 425; III 208-10a,n., p. 210; III 210a,n. Three separate small additions mention pearls: II 511a; III 626b; III 717c.

3 See, e.g., I 162; II 628-30.

The Temps retrouvé addition that describes Saint-Loup's behaviour 'dans le monde',[1] tracing his emerging Guermantes heredity, remarks, for example, that his colouring gave him 'comme un plumage si étrange, faisait de lui une espèce si rare, si précieuse, qu'on aurait voulu le posséder pour une collection ornithologique' (III 703-4a; III 703b; III 704a). The imagery in Céleste's speech abounds in zoological comparisons (II 845-50a, pp. 846-48; II 846c; II 847a, c);[2] and the girl briefly desired by Marcel at Balbec, whose 'figure double et légère ressemblait aux graines ailées de certains arbres', is an entirely added character (II 838-40a, p. 839). Proust inserted in the margin of the La Prisonnière MS a passage in which Charlus's silvering hair is likened to a precious bush 'que non seulement l'automne colore, mais dont on protège certaines feuilles par des enveloppements d'ouate ou des applications de plâtre' (III 226a); and the wife of the Cambremers' lawyer-friend, who appears only in additions, has a face 'ronde comme certaines fleurs de la famille des renonculacées', and

> au coin de l'oeil un assez large signe végétal. Et, les générations des hommes gardant leurs caractères comme une famille de plantes, de même que sur la figure flétrie de la mère, le même signe, qui eût

---

1 See above, Ch. 1, p. 56.

2 See also II 848c for her use of the almond as a term of comparison.

> pu aider au classement d'une variété, se gonflait sous l'oeil du fils (II 821-22a).[1]

Finally, both the appearance and the removal of the plant-like hotel-boy are of late inspiration: the 1914 galleys of _A l'ombre_ do not yet include the passage in which, 'planté comme un arbrisseau d'une espèce rare', he dreams sadly of the lot of his more fortunate brothers and 'conservait son immobilité végétale' (I 706-7a), nor that in which Marcel, returning from his rides with Mme de Villeparisis, notices that

> Seul "le chasseur", exposé au soleil dans la journée, avait été rentré, pour ne pas supporter la rigueur du soir, et emmailloté de lainages, lesquels, joints à l'éplorement orangé de sa chevelure et à la fleur curieusement rose de ses joues, faisaient, au milieu du hall vitré, penser à une plante de serre qu'on protège contre le froid (I 723b).

And the modification of the Grand-Hôtel lawn in _Sodome et Gomorrhe_ by 'l'enlèvement non seulement d'un arbuste exotique, mais du chasseur qui, la première année, décorait extérieurement l'entrée par la tige souple de sa taille et la coloration curieuse de sa chevelure', takes place only in a margin and

1 The lawyer himself may be a late character: his only appearance _in_ the MS is on very clean, comparatively new paper (II 805: n.a.fr. 16711:88), and he otherwise occurs in added passages - this one, II 806a, and II 810-11a.

layer addition to the MS (II 772-75a, p. 773).[1]

These elaborations, from the 'petits poèmes en prose' to the extended botanical metaphors, are unsurprising developments of the vision already familiar to readers of the 1913 Du Côté de chez Swann; other additions do, however, show a telling departure from the previous range of visual effects.

For example, a number of the sequences in the novel which describe states of immobility, or use death imagery allegorically, are late ones. In the most obvious context, that of the 'bal

---

1 See too, for late plant, bird and animal imagery, I 812-14a; I 869-951a, p. 887; II 62a; II 80a; II 604a; II 604-6a, p. 606; II 642-47a, pp. 645-47; II 1019d; III 217a; III 1019c,d; III 1031-32a.
Proust also, during the revision, works in a number of references to clothes (I 540c,d; I 617-18a; I 619b; I 869-951a, pp. 884-85, 898-900; II 18d; II 20b,c; II 1055a,b,c; III 37c,d; III 42-44a; III 208-10a,n.; III 369-70a, p. 370; III 399d,f; III 400a);
to eyes (I 471a; I 728b; II 177b; II 204-5a; II 224a; II 424-26a, p. 425; II 490-91a, p. 491; II 661-62a; II 851b; II 851-53a, pp. 851-52; II 912-14a, pp. 912-13; II 912d; II 912-13a; II 913a; II 919a; II 976d; II 978-79a; II 979-80a, p. 979; II 1022-24a, p. 1023; II 1024a; III 62c; III 89a; III 91-94a, pp. 91-92; III 979-80a, p. 979; III 979a,b; III 984a,n.; III 1031-32a);
and to hair: this last series evidently has a particular significance (I 493e; I 503a; I 869-951a, pp. 887, 890, 920, 930-31, 932, 945; II 127b; II 610-13a, pp. 611-12; II 620-21a; II 623-24a; II 682-84a, pp. 682-83; II 1095d; III 18-19a; III 64-67a, p. 65; III 69-72a, p. 71; III 71a; III 91-94a, p. 93 §1; III 144b; III 208-10a,n., p. 210; III 359-60a, p. 359; III 365-66a,n.; III 372a; III 383a; III 387a; III 715a).

costumé', Odette acquires the hair and stiff face of a large mechanical doll (III 948b), or indeed, 'justement parce qu'elle n'avait pas changé, elle ne semblait guère vivre. Elle avait l'air d'une rose stérilisée' (III 950a); Marcel now meets an old friend whose eyes, once strikingly mobile before his rise to power, 's'étaient immobilisés, ce qui leur donnait un regard pointu' (III 941-42a); and Bloch's face is transformed so that 'ses traits n'exprimaient plus jamais rien' (III 952-53a). Such language might be expected here; but it should also be remembered that the descriptions of Albertine's sleep appear only in layers attached to the MS of _La Prisonnière_, or else are not in it at all.[1] These tranquil yet stirring passages stress her vegetative inanimate state and her lack of volition:[2]

---

1 Mentioned more briefly in Ch. 1, p. 45.
The additions are III 69-72a; III 72-75a; III 74a,b,c; III 113-16a; III 113a,b; III 113-14a; III 114a,b; III 115b.
It is possible that III 69-72a might at first have been part of an MS layer, since it does appear in the first typescript. Again, as in the case of the street-cries (see above, p. 98 _n_.1), these had been offered to the _NRF_ by August 1922, and so may have been removed from the MS (see _Marcel Proust et Jacques Rivière: Correspondance 1914-22_, pp. 274-75, 280, 282-83, 286, 291).

2 C. Quémar's thorough and central article brings out the 'de-humanising' aspects of Marcel's love: 'Les égoïsmes de l'amour chez Proust', _Revue d'Histoire Littéraire de la France_, 71e année, nos. 5-6 (1971), pp. 887-908 (p. 906 discusses these passages); see too L. Bersani, _Marcel Proust: The Fictions of Life and of Art_ (New York, 1965), pp. 78-80.

> En le [corps] tenant sous mon regard, dans mes mains, j'avais cette impression de la posséder toute entière que je n'avais pas quand elle était réveillée. Sa vie m'était soumise [...]
> (III 69-72a, p. 70);

and the harsher statement of this power over the sleeping Albertine was late too:

> [...] je sentis ce demi-cercle immobile et vivant, où tenait toute une vie humaine [...]; je sentis qu'il était là, en ma possession dominatrice
> (III 365-66a,n., p. 366).[1]

Probably the most self-conscious of these new depictions is that, not of Albertine, but of Morel, frozen into immobility by the knowledge that Charlus is spying on him in the Maineville 'palace': this whole episode appears for the first time on a layer glued to the typescript of Sodome et Gomorrhe:

> C'était bien Morel qu'il avait devant lui, mais, comme si les mystères païens et les enchantements existaient encore, c'était plutôt l'ombre de Morel, Morel embaumé, pas même Morel ressuscité comme Lazare, une apparition de Morel [...]. Morel avait, comme après la mort, perdu toute couleur; entre ces femmes avec lesquelles il semblait qu'il eût dû s'ébattre joyeusement, livide, il restait figé dans une immobilité artificielle [...].

And Mlle Noémie talks to Charlus of Morel as she would of 'un mourant': 'Les questions des femmes se pressaient, mais Morel, inanimé, n'avait pas la force de leur répondre' (II 1075 81a,

---

1 See also, for Albertine's sleep, III 67b (in III 67n.2); III 387a; and the fragment quoted in the Pléiade notes - 'profonde Albertine que je voyais dormir et qui était morte' - which appears only as an interpolation on the MS page (III 1047n.4: III 1151a).

pp. 1080-81).[1]

Going much further than these, however, are the additions using one particular metaphor on which Proust does draw to a minor extent in his base versions, but which now, systematically exploited, not only quite outweighs in bulk any other single late image; solidly repeated again and again, it also strikes the student of the post-1914 material as being as deliberate a fresh turn as any of those more thematic or episodic additions to be discussed later, and as unquestionably deriving from a unity in Proust's intentions which is not necessarily present in the other physical descriptions so far cited. This metaphor is the likening of humans to statues.

In the MS versions, Albertine, climbing on to a hillock in order to see a marble goddess on a pedestal, had herself seemed to be a 'petite statue' (II 389); Saint-Loup was like a sculpted rider in a freize (II 414); and there were, in Le Temps retrouvé, references to the rigidity or chilling of the body (III 938; III 940 §2) and its resemblance to stone (III 946 §2; III 948 §2).[2]

---

1 Also added are the few lines just after Marcel's shock on receiving Mme de Stermaria's letter: 'Bientôt l'hiver; au coin de la fenêtre, comme sur un verre de Gallé, une veine de neige durcie [...]' (II 392b); the passage in La Prisonnière linking immobility with intense fear, again at a moment of shock (III 148a); and that in which Bergotte 'allait ainsi se refroidissant progressivement', heat leaving his body as it will one day leave the planet (III 184a). (Discussed below in more detail, Ch. 7, pp. 316-17.) See also I 526-36a, p. 533; I 691-94a, p. 691; I 869-951a, pp. 905-6; III 401a; III 430b; III 858b.

2 See also II 703; III 376; III 383; III 528; III 859; and one of the descriptions of Mme Verdurin in 'Un Amour de Swann' (I 258-59).

But now, in varied contexts, Proust takes up and renews the comparison. Mme de Villeparisis's servant, whose appearance passed without mention in the 1914 galleys, now becomes, by virtue of an addition made some years later, a man

> à l'air hardi et à la figure charmante (mais rognée si juste pour rester parfaite que le nez était un peu rouge et la peau légèrement enflammée, comme s'ils gardaient quelque trace de la récente et sculpturale incision) (II 199-200a);[1]

and the discussion in the 1914 A l'ombre of Gilberte's resemblance to her mother in terms of a painter's or wood-carver's work ran simply:

> [...] on reconnaissait en Gilberte les traits, l'expression, les mouvements de sa mère [...],

but Proust, in the revision, altered this to read as follows:

> [...] on reconnaissait en Gilberte bien des traits - par exemple le nez arrêté avec une brusque et infaillible décision par le sculpteur invisible qui travaille de son ciseau pour plusieurs générations -, l'expression, les mouvements de sa mère [...] (I 564a; see also b).

The description of the grandmother's face during her last illness as of a sculpture was not added until the margin of the first Gallimard galleys: 'Ce travail du statuaire touchait à sa fin', etc. (II 324a). And it is in additions to the 1914 galleys that the elderly Alix, her attempted 'showing-off' thoroughly quashed by Mme de Villeparisis, assumes the appearance of a park statue. On the first occasion, the reader will recall,

---

1 Cp. here the descriptions of the footmen in 'Un Amour de Swann' (I 323-26); Proust may, in part, have intended this insertion as a reminder.

> Le coup d'Alix avait raté, elle se tut, resta debout et immobile. Des couches de poudre plâtrant son visage, celui-ci avait l'air d'un visage de pierre. Et comme le profil était noble, elle semblait, sur un socle triangulaire et moussu caché par le mantelet, la déesse effritée d'un parc (II 199b);

on the second, she 'supporta le coup sans faiblir', and

> restait de marbre. Son regard était perçant et vide, son nez noblement arqué. Mais une joue s'écaillait. Des végétations légères, étranges, vertes et roses, envahissaient le menton. Peut-être un hiver de plus la jetterait bas (II 202a).[1]

Apart from these metaphors, significant already, Proust added to the La Prisonnière MS, in a margin and on a layer, the suggestive paragraph in which Marcel sees Albertine almost as a stone effigy in a tomb, just after the 'reconciliation' and at the height of tension in his relationship with her: she tells him to come to her room, but 'je m'endormirai vite après, car je suis comme une morte', and Marcel pursues:

> Ce fut une morte en effet que je vis quand j'entrai ensuite dans sa chambre. Elle s'était endormie aussitôt couchée; ses draps, roulés comme un suaire autour de son corps, avaient pris, avec leurs beaux plis, une rigidité de pierre. On eût dit, comme dans certains Jugements Derniers du moyen âge, que la tête seule surgissait hors de la tombe, attendant dans son sommeil la trompette de l'Archange. [...] Ainsi je restais, dans la pelisse que je n'avais pas encore retirée depuis mon retour de chez les Verdurin, devant ce corps tordu, cette figure allégorique de quoi? de ma mort? de mon oeuvre? [...] (III 359-60a).

---

1 As has been mentioned (Ch. 1, p.31), neither she nor her companions, the 'trois Parques', were originally present at Mme de Villeparisis's matinée; the passage introducing them was, like these two, added to the 1914 galleys (II 195-98a).

Making one of the most unfortunate few errors of the edition, the Pléiade text gives here, not 'figure allégorique de quoi? de ma mort? de mon _oeuvre_?', but 'figure allégorique de quoi? de ma mort? de mon _amour_?', thereby quite reducing the significance of the passage.[1] Marcel's anguish has deadened everything both outside and inside himself. If Albertine's resemblance to an entombed figure is an allegory for the narrator's own progress towards death and lack of creativity, this passage shows a second meaning of all the similar additions: they largely evoke old age or the gradual work of the 'sculptor' heredity, but, as well as representing the increasing stratification of the groups Marcel finds himself in, they may too denote a growing rigidity in his own vision.

However, the _Temps retrouvé_ additions using stone and statue imagery - rife here, as might be expected - have an opposite effect, serving now as a contrast to Marcel, not an allegory for him - or, at any rate, as a merely physical allegory. These additions are all in the very last

---

1 This mistake was made because the first typescript (n.a.fr. 16743:186) leaves a blank for the word, which is then filled in as 'amour', possibly by Robert Proust, on the third typescript (n.a.fr. 16747:145), whereas the MS (n.a.fr. 16718:68, addition) clearly has 'oeuvre'. S. Weber suggests that the 'corps tordu' could also refer to Marcel himself: see III 360n.1, and his article 'Le Madrépore', _Poétique_, no. 13 (1973), pp. 28-54 (pp. 48-49).

Cahier.[1]

Mlle de Saint-Loup herself is said to be 'pétrie' like a masterpiece by time (III 1031c);[2] and the comparison of her nose to Gilberte's and Odette's was a margin addition:

> Un trait aussi particulier eût fait reconnaître une statue entre des milliers, [...] et j'admirais que la nature fût revenue à point nommé pour la petite-fille, comme pour la mère, comme pour la grand'mère, donner, en grand et original sculpteur, ce puissant et décisif coup de ciseau (III 1032a,n.).

The deterioration of the vicomtesse de Saint-Fiacre is also new: 'Ses traits sculpturaux semblaient lui assurer une jeunesse éternelle', but she has become, in fact, 'une dame aux traits tellement déchiquetés que la ligne du visage

---

1 (The 'bal costumé' starts on n.a.fr. 16727:5.) Other additions to this scene use snow and ice imagery, conveying a similar effect of rigidity: the prince de Guermantes's moustaches look as if they are covered with ice and 'semblaient incommoder sa bouche raidie' (III 920c,n.), and M. d'Argencourt is a 'bonhomme de neige' (III 921-23a, p. 922). See also II 690-91a and II 698n.1: II 1182a, where the face of the ill Swann has been compared to a melting block of ice; and for other additions in TR using similar imagery, but not sculpting metaphors, see III 923-24a, III 924a; III 934-35a,n.; III 937b; III 938c; III 939-40a, p. 940; III 947a. Cp., for this scene, the early draft reproduced by Bardèche (vol. II, pp. 408-11), where there are only two sculpture images (pp. 408, 409).

2 This participle was at first 'composée', then 'sculptée'.

n'était pas restituable' (III 942-43a). It is only in layers that Proust describes Legrandin's face, which, on his abandoning the use of rouge, assumes 'l'apparence grisâtre et aussi la précision sculpturale de la pierre', or that he traces the sudden changes in women once too beautiful: 'sculptées comme un marbre aux lignes définitives duquel on ne peut plus rien changer, [elles] s'effritaient comme une statue' (respectively III 934a,n.; III 945a, b). The long insertion about La Berma observes grimly that 'Cette fois c'était bien d'un marbre de l'Erechtéion qu'elle avait l'air [...] on voyait de longs rubans sculpturaux parcourir les joues, avec une rigidité minérale' (III 995-99a, p. 998); the comparison of the duc de Guermantes's face, 'effritée comme un bloc', to 'une de ces belles têtes antiques trop abîmées', and its 'dureté sculpturale', are late elaborations (III 1017-18a; III 1017-18b); and, finally, Proust added too the paragraph in which his narrator thinks of all the ill and the dying, who no longer get up and, even among their visitors, are like 'des gisants que le mal a sculptés jusqu'au squelette dans une chair rigide et blanche comme le marbre, et étendus sur leur tombeau' (III 943b).[1]

It is evident, then, that Proust's dramatic and metaphorical imagination has not deserted him in these years, and that his comic gifts still range from gentle deflation to the parading of the visually mechanical. Humour of a certain kind derives from unhappiness and a caustic view of motivation, but it is difficult to reconcile the relaxed whimsy of the additions

---

1 For other late references to sculpture, statues and stone, see especially II 351b; II 603-4a, p. 603; II 989a; II 1078b; and also I 452-53a; I 493b; I 560f; I 712-13a, p. 713; I 787-98a, p. 791; I 818-25a, p. 819, §§ 1 and 3; I 842-54a, pp. 851-52; I 869-951a, pp. 905-6, 931, II 652a (see here II 479b; II 482b); II 669-70a, p. 670; II 686a; II 772-75a, p. 774; II 785a; II 1015-16a, p. 1016; III 30-31a; III 141-43a, p. 142; III 193-97a, p. 197; III 630n.1: III 1052-53a; III 988-89a, p. 988.
One may see a circular process at work in Proust's use of some of the images described in this chapter, in that he goes back to the metaphors of an earlier, discarded form of writing. M. Marc-Lipiansky, for example, points out that in Jean Santeuil Proust sometimes over-elaborately borrows images from precious substances (La Naissance du monde proustien dans Jean Santeuil (Paris, 1974), p. 200); and J.M. Cocking, commenting on the difference between two abandoned drafts and A la recherche itself, observes that Proust changes his flunkeys from unparticularised statues to very particularised figures in paintings ('Proust and painting', in French 19th Century Painting and Literature, edited by Ulrich Finke (Manchester, 1972), pp. 305-24 (p. 309)). The artificiality of the precious substances, and the immobility of the statues, return to serve, now, a completely controlled aim.
Quite apart from this chronological link, the later jewel-imagery conveys an impression of chiselled hardness similar to that of the statue-imagery.

about the Racinian choruses or the plant-like hotel-boy with the misanthropic disenchantment which Feuillerat attributes to Proust as the one denominator behind so many changes. And if *Marcel's* intellectual interests are emphasised, his creator cannot, as Feuillerat assumes, be judged to be retreating further and further into the cerebral or into the enunciation of 'lois générales': on the contrary, Proust maintains much interest in the sensuously equivocal nature of, for example, sleep,[1] and when he wishes to show Marcel observing a widespread process - the results of time working with heredity - he does so by means of a specific sensory image.

The attempt made in this chapter to define broadly the bent of Proust's imagination during the later years of his life thus leaves an impression, perhaps too crude, that some of his most striking post-1914 dramatic effects are those of the volte-face; that, on the comic side, his delight in physical peculiarities is growing; and that he is more noticeably attracted to the statue-metaphor than to any other.

Going on, now, to look at the *leitmotive* which Proust chose to elaborate, one should bear in mind that some violence is being done to them by abstracting them from their particular sites in the novel and grouping them according to subject-matter - although, it must be said, the student of the post-

---

1 P. Costil makes similar comments in 'La construction musicale de la "Recherche du Temps perdu" (I)', *BSAMP*, no. 8 (1958), pp. 469-89 (p. 475).

1914 material does occasionally feel that Proust has thought of the demonstration first, written the examples next, and finally inserted them where they will least inconveniently fit. This can almost certainly be put down to lack of time, since the great majority of the additions were worked in with much care over the detailed changes accordingly needed in the original text, and were also, as was implied in the first part of this chapter, determined partially, sometimes wholly, by the appositeness of the context.

3 Spoken Language

The last chapter has given some illustration of Proust's descriptive style in the post-1914 period; how did the 'style' of his own characters develop? Proust's critics, from the 1920's to the present, have commented on his interest in, and talent for recreating, the idiosyncrasies of spoken language,[1] and, as can be seen from the rough passage in the MS of <u>Sodome et Gomorrhe</u>,[2] phrases which were 'un peu trop courantes' had concerned him at an early stage. Indeed, Maurice Bardèche tells us that Proust had been accumulating 'expressions toutes faites' in his notebooks since 1908,[3] and since the culmination of the

---

1 Jacques Rivière made some acute observations on the subject to Proust himself, in a letter of 1922 (<u>Marcel Proust et Jacques Rivière: Correspondance 1914-22</u>, p. 265); more recently, J.-F. Revel has been most appreciative of this aspect of the novel, in <u>Sur Proust</u> (Paris, 1970), pp.37-39. Amongst many others, see, e.g., Bardèche, vol. I, pp. 339-42; G. Brée, <u>The World of Marcel Proust</u>, p. 145; R. Fernandez, <u>A la gloire de Proust</u> (Paris, 1944), p.113; J. Mouton, <u>Le Style de Marcel Proust</u> (Paris, 1948), pp. 184-207; L. Pierre-Quint, <u>Marcel Proust: Sa vie, son oeuvre</u> (Paris, 1925), pp. 163-71.

2 See above, Ch. 1, pp. 40-41.

3 Bardèche, vol.I, p. 339, <u>n</u>.1. See also vol.I, pp. 420-21, and vol. II, pp. 204, 280 <u>n</u>.2, for Proust's collection of expressions in his Carnets.
It was Maurois who first revealed Proust's collecting of expressions (<u>A la recherche de Marcel Proust</u>, p. 141); but he does not date this.

novel was always to be its own writing, in a form of expression which would not blunt Marcel's experiences, a record of verbal banality, or strained linguistic originality, would be an essential counterfoil to the climax of the work. So, even before the expansions, there are numerous manifestations of facile or affected speech in the drafts of the novel. Legrandin's languorous prose in Du Côté de chez Swann forever hovers on the verge of sentimental stereotype.[1] Mme Bontemps, railing against the lack of culture displayed by 'toutes ces femmes d'Excellences, qui ne savent parler que de chiffons', was already, in the 1911-12 typescripts of A l'ombre, using such easily emphatic phrases as:

> quand on entend des choses comme ça, ça vous fait bouillir. J'avais envie de la gifler. Parce que j'ai mon petit caractère, vous savez (I 605).[2]

Odette had long had a penchant for anglicisms: 'le "tub"' and 'le "footing"', indispensable adjuncts to her life, are there in the 1911-12 typescripts (I 616);[3] and Françoise inclines to grammar-mistakes and to her own curious neologisms in the manuscript of Sodome et Gomorrhe and the early typescript of Le Côté de Guermantes, such as '"Je suis été [...]"' (II 787) and 'En tous cas c'est de la même "parenthèse"' (II 22).[4]

---

1 E.g. I 130-32.

2 In n.a.fr. 16732:147 and 16735:153.

3 n.a.fr. 16732:149 and 16735:155.

4 n.a.fr. 16711:69 and 16736:13 respectively.

None the less, one of the most striking features of the post-1914 drafts of the novel is the extent to which Proust added to, and discussed, peculiarities of his characters' language. The increase is noticeable on even a quick skimming-through of the documents, since these particular additions are the most pervasive of all: only in La Fugitive is there a rallentando of insertions specifically made to introduce clichés, *idées reçues*, malapropisms, distorted pronunciation and linguistic pretensions of all sorts.[1] Furthermore, whereas previously the mechanical or fashionable phrases tended to be amalgamated with the rest of the character's speech, now they are deliberately picked out: either by Proust himself, forcing the reader to pause over them by means of quotation-marks or direct commentary, or, more surprisingly, by the actual speakers, who sometimes, with complacency, draw attention to their correct use of an expression in vogue.

Hardly any of the characters escape the widening pre-occupation with spoken language. A few emerge enhanced, as approved specimens, but the majority are more than confirmed in

---

1 This is, of course, more especially the kind of addition that may have been drawn from the established repertory in the Cahiers; Proust may simply have had more time, at a later stage of composition, to work his examples in. (I am grateful to Professor J.M. Cocking for this word of warning.) Nevertheless, the enormous growth of illustration does suggest a deeper and deeper fascination with the problems raised by cliché; character, in some cases, even changes as a result of the insertions.

their lack of genuine sympathy for language, and some, such as Saint-Loup, are unfavourably altered. New linguistic abuses of one type can be predominantly associated with an individual figure, sometimes extending his or her former mode of expression: thus the later anglicisms continue to be attributed to Odette, the Hellenisms to Bloch, and political stock-in-trade to Norpois; but other characters now become entirely new representatives of given trends - Saniette of archaisms, the hotel-manager of malapropisms, and Saint-Loup of fashionable expressions, for example.

I shall make some attempt here to give a detailed picture of this expansion; certainly, there is a wealth of examples from which to choose. The account starts with the characters who, in the insertions, use language well or without affectation; goes on to the less fortunate usages of all the others (Marcel, Swann, Charlus, Morel, Albertine, the Verdurin circle, Odette, the Blochs, the staff of the Grand-Hôtel, and M. de Guermantes); and culminates with the chief exemplars: Françoise and her daughter, Saint-Loup, and M. de Norpois.

It is Céleste and Marie, Mme de Guermantes, and, in one half of her persona, Françoise, who actually 'benefit' from Proust's upsurge of interest in spoken French.

Proust added all the Sodome et Gomorrhe passages about

Céleste and Marie to the typescript, taking up most of his long principal insertion with the documentation of the vigorous and eccentric imagery they use in their criticisms and praise alike of Marcel, who remarks:

> Je n'ai jamais connu de personnes aussi volontairement ignorantes, [...] et dont le langage eût pourtant quelque chose de si littéraire que, sans le naturel presque sauvage de leur ton, on aurait cru leurs paroles affectées (II 845-50a, p. 846).

And the passages in La Prisonnière providing a little more of Céleste's imagery, together with Marcel's comment that her language is stranger and more individual than Albertine's, were added only to the third typescript (III 17-18a; III 128-31a, p. 131). It is possible that Proust decided to bring these two sisters into his novel (doubtless elaborating on their actual use of French)[1] to serve as examples of those people who orally originate the appealing phrases that later become the type of hackneyed expression of which so many illustrations will be given in this chapter. One could imagine, say, Céleste's 'Il se tient debout, tout droit comme une évidence' (II 848e) passing into the language as a metaphor for physical straightness, and finally becoming a dead figure through over-use.[2]

---

1 Mme Albaret has stated that she did talk to some extent in this manner to Proust: see, e.g., P. Kolb's review of The Imagery of Proust (V. Graham), Modern Language Quarterly, XXIX (1968), pp. 116-20 (p. 119). Henri Bonnet gives some examples of her speech in 'Les souvenirs de Céleste', BSAMP, no. 24 (1974), pp. 1827-1838 (p. 1830).

2 For Céleste and Marie, see also all indented additions under II 845-50a; II 796-97a, p. 796; II 1125c. P. Albouy interestingly claims that Céleste, by her use of imagery, 'nous propose la vision mythique de Marcel', in 'Quelques images et structures mythiques dans "La Recherche du Temps perdu"', Revue d'Histoire Littéraire de la France, 71e année, nos.5-6 (1971), pp. 972-87 (p. 976; also 980).

As for Mme de Guermantes and Françoise, they both, as critics have pointed out, bear witness through their speech to old France,[1] their usages recalling an unchanging country tradition of proverbs and 'savoureuse' pronunciation. Proust's responsiveness to this traditional language is of comparatively early date, since examples were added to the pre-1914 Côté de Guermantes typescript for both Françoise[2] and Mme de Guermantes;[3] and as etymologies were inserted into Du Côté de chez Swann in 1913, Proust's interest in philology must have been growing at about this period.[4] None the less, almost all the distinctive, often nearly archaic, habits of speech of these two appear only after 1914, either in the course of longer additions or as the sole subject of interpolations.

Thus, Proust worked in at a late stage all Mme de Guermantes's main displays of unusual or attractive pronunciation: she now carefully chooses her words and anecdotes,

---

1 E. de Gramont puts this observation well in Marcel Proust (Paris, 1948), p. 283; see also, e.g., J. Mouton, Le Style de Marcel Proust, pp. 184-88; M. Mein, 'Fromentin, a Precursor of Proust', Forum for Modern Language Studies, VII (1971), pp. 221-36 (pp. 224-25).

2 E.g. II 16g, h, i; II 25a.

3 E.g. II 224d.

4 See above, Ch. 2, p. 92 n.1.

despite this self-awareness greatly pleasing Marcel. Very late, for instance, is the comment that, provided there was no affectation, and no attempt to 'fabriquer un langage à soi, alors cette façon de prononcer était un vrai musée d'histoire de France par la conversation' (III 35-36a).[1] And, where Proust had merely put into her mouth the words 'Elle est bête comme un (heun) oie', he now adds in the margin of the MS of Le Côté de Guermantes:

> dit d'une voix forte et enrouée Mme de Guermantes, qui, bien plus vieille France encore que le duc quand elle n'y tâchait pas, cherchait souvent à l'être, mais [...] par une sorte de prononciation presque paysanne qui avait une âpre et délicieuse saveur terrienne (II 485b).[2]

Those passages in which Françoise too is said to use 'paroles [...] inspirées d'un sentiment traditionnel et local et qui obéissaient à des règles très anciennes' (II 64-65a), or draws on old forms of the language like those of Mme de Sévigné or Saint-Simon (II 23e, II 68-69a), were also late ones.[3] But,

---

1 This was added only to the third typescript of La Prisonnière.

2 For other illustrations, see II 489b; II 494-95a,b; II 496a; II 502-3a,b; II 523a,b; II 524-26a; II 549-51a (see here II 509c); III 35a,b; III 36a; III 36-37a; III 37a,b; III 43a; III 587-88a.
(The 'peasant' pronunciation appears briefly in the early drafts on II 224, 485: '"su"' and 'eun'.)

3 For Françoise's 'old' speech and her 'langage simple et expressif' (II 1018a), see, e.g., II 24a; II 25b; II 26d,f; II 525a; II 726-28a, pp. 726, 728; II 737a; II 790-91a.

quite apart from her representative historical value, almost all the lines showing Françoise in the further rôle of somewhat dubious inventor of the language, either making grammatical errors or stubbornly forcing linguistic novelties into a mould familiar to her, are post-1914, such as her insistence on saying 'New-York' for 'York', and, furthermore, her mispronunciation of it as 'Nev'York', neither of which appear in the 1914 galleys (I 445-46a). It must be many of these insertions which Feuillerat has in mind when he assumes that Proust is trying to denigrate Françoise,[1] and the assumption may at first be understandable, since the young Marcel himself is critical of the distortions.[2] However, as well as all the mistakes, Proust adds an overt vindication of Françoise: he inserts into the MS of _Sodome et Gomorrhe_ that passage making it clear that he is trying to show in her speech the charms and oddities of an idiom fast dying out, and, simultaneously, the convolutions undergone by the French language itself in the course of its development. Françoise, waxing malicious about Albertine's clothes, has just used the word 'estoppeuse' for 'stoppeuse', whereupon Marcel makes an unkind comment on the mistake: but

---

1 He mentions largely those grouped around the beginning of _CG_: see his pp. 70, 117.

2 (It is of course always clear that Proust does not approve this attitude: see not only the example just below, but also I 154.)

> ce reproche était particulièrement stupide, car ces mots français que nous sommes si fiers de prononcer exactement ne sont eux-mêmes que des "cuirs" faits par des bouches gauloises qui prononçaient de travers le latin ou le saxon, notre langue n'étant que la prononciation défectueuse de quelques autres. Le génie linguistique à l'état vivant, l'avenir et le passé du français, voilà ce qui eût dû m'intéresser dans les fautes de Françoise (II 736-37a).[1]

However, far more numerous are the additions of words or phrases which, even if they too could be thought of as modelling the language, are less ambiguously <u>abuses</u> of language - hackneyed or fashionable expressions, slang, ostentatious or bombastic terminology, and 'fillers-in'. Even Marcel is not exempt from

---

1 Other additions thus vindicating Françoise are II 23c and III 515a,<u>n</u>. For her mistakes, her picturesque but less than correct expressions, and her obstinate mispronunciations, clustered very thickly around the beginning of <u>CG</u>, see: I 483e; I 484a; I 484-86a; I 492e; I 496a; I 691-94a, p. 693; I 697-98a; I 866-68a, p. 866; I 869-951a, pp. 896, 950-51; II 9-10a; II 10a,b,c,d; II 17b; II 18c,g; II 19a,d,e; II 20a; II 21e; II 21-22a; II 22c; II 23b,d; II 23-24a; II 23f,g; II 24b; II 25e; II 26a,b,g,h,i; II 27a; II 28b; II 34-35a; II 66a,b; II 147-48a, p. 147; II 148a; II 207a; II 334a; II 359c,d; II 729b; II 776b; II 777a,b; II 845-50a, p. 846; II 977b; II 987-93a, p. 988; III 14-16a, p. 16; III 63a; III 141b; III 182-92a, p. 190; III 364-65a; III 414a; III 568a,<u>n</u>.; III 842c; III 844b; III 846a; III 1034b,<u>n</u>.
Jupien too benefits linguistically: II 20-21a; II 21a; II 308a; III 830-31a. For a few other examples of this renewed interest, see I 509-11a, p. 510; II 18a; II 288-89a; II 429a; II 893b; II 896c.

the general change, although falling prey less to cliché than to imitation of the unusual: his repetition of the Swanns' '"commen allez-vous"', 'un incessant et voluptueux exercice' for him, was added to A l'ombre only after 1914 (I 504b).[1] The near-artists too are allocated their own lazy linguistic habits. The information that Dreyfusism has overturned Swann's 'jugements littéraires et jusqu'à la façon de les exprimer', instanced by such slangily familiar phrases as 'C'est un très grand bonhomme que le père Clemenceau', does not appear until the third Gallimard galleys (II 582-83a);[2] and, although Charlus is sometimes, in the additions, given the rôle of criticising the language of others, doubtless as much to distinguish himself as from concern for his native tongue,[3] he now acquires his own private set phrase. It is in a separate addition to the 1914 galleys that, talking to Marcel, he invokes 'l'enchaînement des circonstances':

> c'était une des expressions favorites de M. de Charlus et souvent, quand il la prononçait, il conjoignait ses deux mains [...] comme pour faire comprendre par ce complexus ces circonstances qu'il ne spécifiait pas et leur enchaînement (II 287c),

---

1 See too I 526-36a, pp. 526-27; I 546-47a; I 869-951a, p.877.

2 See further, for this side-effect of Swann's Dreyfusism, II 582b,c; II 583c,d,e; II 714a.

3 His acid comments on the 'payer le thé' of Jupien's niece were added to La Prisonnière (III 44b, III 44-45a, III 47a); see also II 610-13a for his commentaries on ordinarily-used common nouns; and II 947b; III 796d; III 826-27a.

and all subsequent appearances of this phrase, or minor variations on it, are late, including the remark that one could tell Charlus was growing old from his extensive reliance on it, as if on 'un tuteur nécessaire' (III 212b).[1]

The elaborations of Morel's and Albertine's speech contrast them further with their lovers Charlus and Marcel, and occasionally even precipitate developments in the narrative. Marcel's opinion that the expression 'payer le thé' has come to Jupien's niece from Morel himself was added (later than the expression itself) to the first typescript of La Prisonnière (III 47-49a). Such slang as 'fout'le camp' occurs only in the course of long insertions (III 51-54a, p. 51; III 193-97a, p. 195); Proust changes 'ce vieux dégoûtant [Charlus] peut bien se faire empaler si ça lui plaît' to 'ce vieux dégoûtant peut bien se faire zigouiller si ça lui plaît' on the typescript of Sodome et Gomorrhe (II 1066a); and late too are both Morel's

---

1 The others are: III 216-19a, p. 219; III 220a; III 221a; III 275b; III 293b. The subject that provokes them is normally Morel. For other additions to, or about, Charlus's speech, see II 295a,b; II 953-54a, p. 953; II 1042-43a; II 1052c; III 297b.
One addition to Sodome et Gomorrhe shows that Charlus was to have had another set phrase. He is brooding over Morel's habit of not replying punctually to his notes, and reflecting that the musician 'lui posait des lapins, [...] sans même prévenir, sans s'excuser' (cp. II 1067-68a, p.1067):

> Et M. de Charlus répétait cette phrase qui avait pris chez lui la forme automatique d'un tic, comme tel refrain de café concert ou telle phrase de la Symphonie avec Choeurs, qu'on chante sans l'entendre, dans les moments d'émotion: "C'est à ne pas croire".

(Cited with some minor corrections included. At the equivalent of II 1067; in a layer over which another was glued, n.a.fr. 16713:80.)

abuse of his fiancée - 'grand pied de grue' - and the accompanying comment that the words are 'fautives au point de vue du français' (III 162-64a, p. 164).[1] Albertine's new expressions are, like Morel's, largely slang or vulgar. The 'jeunes filles' sections in A l'ombre provide a number of her phrases, and, whilst we cannot be sure whether these really are late,[2] it may be safe, since so many of her other expressions in the novel were added, to assume that the A l'ombre ones too are post-1914, as is probably Marcel's lowered self-esteem when he recognises 'sa maîtrise dans un mode de désignations où j'avais peur qu'elle ne constatât et ne méprisât mon infériorité' (I 869-951a, pp. 876-77).[3] On firmer ground with Le Côté de Guermantes, the passages in which Marcel concludes from Albertine's new vocabulary that she will now be accessible to his advances are all additions,[4] mainly to the MS, but considerably extended on the Gallimard galleys (II 354-56a; II 355a, b, c; II 356a, b, c, d, e; II 356-57a; II 357a; II 357-58a; II 357b, c; II 358a); and Proust worked into La Prisonnière

---

1 Also pp. 162-63; and see too II 1006-9a, p. 1008; III 51-54a, p. 53.

2 See above, Ch. 1, p. 28 n.3.

3 See also I 787-98a, p. 793; I 869-951a, e.g. pp. 879-81, 882-83, 912.

4 Already mentioned in Ch. 1, pp. 33, 64. This sequence has been much commented on; it is cited by, e.g., Bardèche, vol. II, pp. 123-24; S. Beckett, Proust (London, 1931), p. 33; G. Deleuze, Proust et les signes (Paris, 1970), p. 135; J.-Y. Tadié, Proust et le roman, pp. 324-25.

the more worrying aspects of such changes, when it seems to Marcel that her 'C'est vrai?' must originally have become ingrained as a habitual response to compliments 'dès sa nubilité précoce' (III 20-21a),[1] and when it is horror, now, that is provoked by her crude 'me faire casser le pot' (III 333-39a, p. 337 - and p. 334; III 339-41a).[2]

The speech of the members of the Verdurin clan continues as might be expected in the additions, which bestow on M. Verdurin heartily elaborate phrases like 'à moins que vous ne vous éternisiez par vos jérémiades dans cette casbah ouverte à tous les vents' (II 901a),[3] and on Mme Verdurin not only slang words like 'bécasse' (II 940b)[4] and the war-time idioms 'caviarder' and 'limoger' (III 733a),[5] but also such forceful and meaningless affirmations as:

> "Mais je vous en réponds! c'est moi qui vous le dis", expression par laquelle elle cherchait à étayer une assertion jetée un peu au hasard (III 280d).[6]

---

1 Suzuki notes this addition in 'Le comique chez Marcel Proust (II)', BSAMP, no. 12 (1962), pp. 572-86 (p. 574) (referring to the document concerned as the second TS, however: it is in fact the first).
See too, here, III 121n.1: III 1076a.

2 For other jargon or slang phrases of Albertine's, see II 734a; II 780-81a; II 851-53a, p. 853; III 18c.

3 See also I 869-951a, p. 883; II 901c,d; III 228b,d.

4 See also II 583b; II 949b.

5 See also III 784-93a, p. 792.

6 And see too III 244d; III 280-82a, p. 280; III 312a.
For other additions to or about Mme Verdurin's speech, see: II 917a; II 938e,f; II 939b,c; II 943a; II 948-49a; III 764-65a, p. 764.

Brichot too, as the author of articles during the war, is given, in a more literary context, some war-time mechanical phrases: 'je veux que' (III 792a), and others.[1] As for his language in the rest of the novel, the MSS show that he was always inclined to playful Rabelaisiana, to heavily fanciful archaisms, and to supposedly elegant variations;[2] but Proust inserted further lengthy examples. The professor's 'obituary' of Dechambre in Sodome et Gomorrhe ('lui, du moins, [....] a dû mourir dans l'accomplissement du sacerdoce, en odeur de dévotion beethovénienne') appears in a long addition to the MS (II 895-97a, pp. 896-97, II 897a,b), and so, in another, do his opinions on Balzac, found most irritating by Charlus:

> au risque de contrister les âmes en mal de déférence balzacienne, sans prétendre, Dieu me damne, au rôle de gendarme de lettres et dresser procès-verbal pour fautes de grammaire, j'avoue que le copieux improvisateur dont vous me semblez surfaire singulièrement les élucubrations effarantes, m'a toujours paru un scribe insuffisamment méticuleux [...]
> (II 1050-52a, II 1050d, II 1051a).[3]

---

1 Such as III 784-93a, pp. 790-92; III 790a; III 792b.

2 See III 282-83 without the additions. (The passage M. Bardèche quotes from the Cahiers shows, however, only the barest trace of these linguistic tics in Brichot's prototype, Crochard: see Bardèche, vol. II, appendix IV, pp.397-99.)

3 See also II 876a,b; II 877a; II 887-91a; II 891a; II 894a, b,c; II 896a; II 934-35a; II 937a; II 950a; II 952b,c; II 1050c; II 1052b; III 227e; III 282e,f,g; III 283a,n.,b,c, d,e; III 296a; III 299b; III 330b; III 883-89a, p.884 (cp. I 453. Here Brichot is doubtless being confused with Norpois, as he is on other occasions: see III 781 n.2; III 783 nn.3,4,5; III 784 nn. 3,4; III 785 n.1.).

The Cottards themselves change rather more: where Mme Cottard had, in the presence of Odette's brilliant friends, stayed simply 'sur la réserve, sinon sur la défensive',[1] she is now, with explicit clarification, 'sur la réserve, sinon sur ce qu'elle appelait la "défensive", car elle employait toujours un langage noble pour les choses les plus simples' (I 596f, I 596-97a, p. 596).[2] Her husband, as we remember from Du Côté de chez Swann, was always sensitive to both fashionable and traditional idioms, but only because he was ignorant of their usage. Now, however, Proust tells the reader, in an addition to the MS of Sodome et Gomorrhe, that Cottard at last knows how to 'user comme il convenait de toutes [les expressions] que l'usage autorise, et, qu'après les avoir longtemps piochées, il possédait à fond' (II 881d). This mastery of the field - perhaps partly the result of his new professional status[3] - is demonstrated by specific additions, almost all to Sodome et Gomorrhe, in which he decorates his conversation with the imitation of banalities:

> je vais vous dire "une bonne chose", dit Cottard qui avait pris en affection cette expression utilisée dans certains milieux médicaux (II 892d),

---

1 Part of an addition to the typescript: I 596e.

2 And she is given a sprinkling of hackneyed phrases and idées reçues: see I 596d; I 596-97a, p. 597; I 599-603a, pp. 602-3; I 603-4a; I 605-6a; I 607d,e; I 607-15a, p.615; II 329b; II 922b; II 964-65a; II 965a; II 1040a; III 177-80a, p.178.

3 See below, Ch. 5, p. 251 n.1.

with irrelevant allusion:

> Os homini sublime dedit caelumque tueri", ajouta-t-il, bien que cela n'eût aucun rapport, mais parce que son stock de citations latines était assez pauvre, suffisant d'ailleurs pour émerveiller ses élèves (II 1072-73a),

and with such jocular phraseology as 'elle n'y va pas avec le dos de la cuiller' (II 881a).[1]

The revisions of Saniette, however, make him an exception in the clan: he is the only 'fidèle' whose speech is fundamentally reoriented. The base version of La Prisonnière bore no trace of his penchant for grammatical archaisms: added to the MS were his '[exaspérante familiarité] avec les formes anciennes du langage' (III 225b), and, a little later, those outmoded usages ('surveiller à', 'offusquer le sentiment général') which bring him to the tyrannical notice of M. Verdurin (III 228b, III 265-66a,n.).

Odette had always, as I have mentioned, indulged in anglicisms;[2] Du Côté de chez Swann itself showed her liking for an 'accent légèrement britannique' and the occasional English word or phrase, both in her persona as the 'dame en rose' (I 78) and at the Verdurins' (I 191, 202).[3] But after 1914 the

---

1 Cottard, like Professor E... (see above, Ch.2, p.83), also distorts the language (II 900b). See II 922-23a, II 923a,b, and II 976b for further illustration of his new confidence; and for more added half-fanciful, half-vulgar phrases, etc., see: I 497-99a; I 516-23a, p. 523; II 869a; II 875a,b,c; II 880a,b; II 881b,c; II 882a; II 893a; II 895b; II 904a; II 922b,c; II 959-60a; II 960-62a; II 963-64a, p. 964; II 964b,c; II 974-75a; II 975-76a, p. 976; II 976g; II 1071b,c; II 1072b; III 281a.

2 See above, p. 125.

3 See also 'my dear', in the MS of TR (III 950).

trait becomes one of her most distinctive. Proust did, it is true, endow her with some less individual society affectations, such as 'je suis très "honnête homme", vous savez' (II 271-73a, p. 271), or 'une bien belle histoire!', which has passed to her, via Swann, from the Guermantes (I 509-11a, pp. 510-11).[1] But it is now the adoption and skilful, if blatant, use of words like 'cake' (I 507c), 'Royalties' (I 516-23a, p. 519),[2] 'crack' (I 537b), 'tract' (I 561a), 'sweaters' (I 621-35a, p. 621), even the more easily assimilable 'good-bye' (I 607h) and 'Good morning!' (I 637b), which predominate. None of these are in the 1914 galleys of A l'ombre; neither is Odette's arrangement for Bergotte to write 'le leader article dans le Figaro. Ce sera tout à fait the right man in the right place' (I 581b), nor her enquiries about the estrangement between Marcel and Gilberte: 'Je suis contente d'être exceptée et que vous ne me "dropiez" pas tout à fait' (I 638-40a, p. 640). And the effect of the war on her language was added to Le Temps retrouvé only in the reworking of an already late passage:

---

1 Also in this addition is the remark that the expressions we have recently borrowed from others are those we most like to use (p. 510). For the Guermantes expression, see II 338a; and for other more general additions to Odette's speech, see: I 539b; I 547a; I 604-5a; II 188a (linking with I 526-36a, p. 535); III 784-93a, p. 788; III 788b; III 821c; III 950b.

2 See also I 543-44a, p. 544.

> Son langage à elle était pourtant, plus encore qu'autrefois, la trace de son admiration pour les Anglais [...]. Inutile de dire qu'elle ne se faisait pas faute de citer à tout propos l'expression de _fair play_ pour montrer les Anglais trouvant les Allemands des joueurs incorrects [...]. "Mon gendre Saint-Loup connaît maintenant l'argot de tous les braves _tommies_, il sait se faire entendre de ceux des plus lointains _dominions_ et, aussi bien qu'avec le général commandant la base, fraternise avec le plus humble _private_." (III 788-89a).[1]

A difficulty arises in consideration of the members of Bloch's family similar to that in the consideration of some of Albertine's linguistic mannerisms:[2] this family appears largely in the long interpolated _A l'ombre_ description of the dinner at which Marcel and Saint-Loup are guests (I 767-79a), and may not be late. It is, however, plausible that the speech of Bloch's sisters and father, and indeed the whole occasion itself, are post-1914. Bloch's sisters copy his Homeric epithets: 'Va prévenir notre père prudent et notre mère vénérable' (I 767-79a, p. 770), and his father incessantly repeats such facetiously familiar phrases as 'Comme c'est emberlificoté! quelle tartine!' (I 767-79a, p. 771).[3] Bloch himself, like Legrandin,

---

1 Other added anglicisms of Odette's are: I 508b,c,d,f; I 526a; I 526-36a, pp. 526-27, 534-35; I 581-92a, p. 583; I 594a; I 596-97a; I 598b; I 621-35a, p. 624; I 700d; II 273b (and see II 273 _n_.1); III 959-60a,_n_.
Her '_senza rigore_' is also an addition (I 594-95b). And the Swanns' pronunciation of 'odieux' with a short 'o' was added to the 1913 galleys (I 511a), as was their '"commen allez-vous"' (I 504a).

2 See above, p. 135.

3 See also, for Bloch's father, I 740-48a, pp. 747-48; I 767-79a, p. 776; and for his mother's pedantic language II 842-45a, p. 844.

was already revealing peculiarities of phrasing at Combray (e.g. I 90), but when Proust came to revise this pair, he paid considerably more attention to the vocabulary of the narrator's ill-bred literary friend than to that of the would-be poet.[1] Not only did he stress one tendency already in the 1914 galleys, adding to Bloch's mispronunciation of 'lift' as 'laïft' (I 738) the extra mistake '<u>Stones of Venaïce</u>' (I 738-40a, pp. 739-40, I 740a);[2] much more surprisingly, it was not until after 1914 that he added almost all of those very Hellenisms, or ornately exaggerated classical images, imitated by Bloch's sisters. The only examples to be found in the 1914 galleys or in the MSS are a reference to a 'tragédienne "aux yeux pers, belle comme Héra"' (II 217), a brief comment on Bloch's following of Leconte de Lisle in his use of the names of Greek Gods (II 836), and a word of praise from Norpois about his speech, 'sans doute à cause des quelques traces qui subsistaient dans le langage de Bloch de la mode néo-homérique qu'il avait pourtant abandonnée' (II 243).[3] Far from letting Bloch abandon it, the additions

---

1 Legrandin's speech appears comparatively little in any case after <u>DCS</u>; nevertheless, Proust adds only three minor affectations to his remarks to Marcel in <u>CG</u> (II 154a,b,c).

2 (Bloch is also given some ordinary slang phrases or affectations: I 869-951a, pp. 880-81; II 219a; II 220a,c; II 249a; III 216-19a, p. 219; III 589-91a, p. 590; III 740a; III 740-41a; III 881b.)

3 Also of course I 90 in <u>DCS</u>.

provide more profuse examples, spreading from A l'ombre to the end of Sodome et Gomorrhe, than Proust ever appears to have envisaged originally. To give only one: although Bloch's story about the encounter with Saint-Loup and the son of Sir Rufus Israëls was itself added to the 1914 galleys (II 218a), his further description of Saint-Loup's interrupted action appears on neither these galleys nor the first Gallimard ones, and must therefore be post-1918:

> [...] il allait monter sur son char aux belles jantes, après avoir passé lui-même les courroies splendides à deux chevaux nourris d'avoine et d'orge et qu'il n'est pas besoin d'exciter avec le fouet étincelant (II 218b).

At last, in an addition to the MS of La Fugitive, we learn that Bloch's style 'était devenu moins précieux' (III 589-91a, p. 590): even this information may not, of course, apply specifically to the Homeric imagery.

Marcel Gutwirth, in a most perceptive article, has brought out Bloch's rôle in the novel as another unsuccessful double of Marcel's,[1] and this interpretation is supported by the expansions made to his language, which, quite apart from their comic effect, give him, like Brichot, one of the most self-

---

1 M. Gutwirth, 'Le Narrateur et son double', Revue d'Histoire Littéraire de la France, 71e année, nos. 5-6 (1971), pp. 921-35 (pp. 926-35). R. Fernandez also makes this point in A la gloire de Proust, pp. 57-58.

conscious, almost self-parodying, modes of speech in the novel. Indeed, the mutual linguistic influence Bloch and Marcel exert on each other, and the narrator's implicit victory, is brought out by the addition to Le Temps retrouvé of that particular evolution which has led to Bloch's now borrowing Marcel's manner of speaking just as Marcel once borrowed his (III 953-56a, p. 954).[1]

Bloch's desire to distinguish himself, and the undue haste with which he adopts a mistaken pronunciation, appear in grosser form in the Balbec lift-boy, whose new linguistic abuses make up a mixed bag of grammatical errors, pretentious appellations, malapropisms and empty affirmations. The MS of Sodome et Gomorrhe already describes his use, inspired by 'orgueil démocratique', of 'collègue' and 'tunique' (II 790-91),[2] his idiosyncratic treatment of 'ne ... pas' (II 793),[3]

---

1 The passage in which Bloch starts to spell in Greek style, à la Leconte de Lisle, was also an inserted one (II 836a). For his Hellenisms, see too: I 740-48a, pp. 745-47; I 767-79a, pp. 770, 775, 777-78; II 201b; II 219b; II 234c,d; II 1101b; II 1102-4a; II 1103a.
This imagery was supposedly inspired not only by Proust's own former enthusiasm for Leconte de Lisle's translations, but also by Pierre Quillard, a classical scholar in Proust's and Mallarmé's circle. (See Painter, vol. I, pp. 46, 54, 224 n.1.) There is a trace of Bloch's classical style in the Jean Santeuil character Rustinlor (Jean Santeuil, Bibliothèque de la Pléiade ([Paris], 1971), p. 237); he on the whole, however, uses the non-classical style of the early Bloch (e.g. pp. 237-40, 480-83).

2 See also II 1025-26.

3 See also II 805.

his over-dependence on 'vous le savez' (II 794), and his firm belief that it is the marquise de Camembert who is acquainted with Marcel (II 805, 825, 857).[1] But his other curious verbal tics do not appear at all at this early stage. There were none, for example, in the 1914 galleys of A l'ombre: where the text now reads: '"Il y a plus autant de monde comme il y a un mois', the galleys gave simply ' - Cela commence à devenir vide' (I 799b); nor did they have the rapidly following revelation that for the lift-boy '"rentrer" était la forme usuelle du verbe "entrer"', and the further manifestations of 'democratic' vocabulary (I 799-800a). And Proust evidently felt that what was already in the MS of Sodome et Gomorrhe needed elaboration, for one addition makes the 'democratic' vocabulary extend wider still (II 790-91a), and others, explicitly stating that the lift-boy's language 'était défectueux', support the judgement by citing his supposedly amusing misapplied terms ('pédaler' for 'marcher vite'), his vigorous and frequent repetition of '"Vous pensez!"' or '"Pensez!"', and his exaggerated affirmation '"Oui, oui, oui, oui, je comprends très bien"' (II 791b, II 791-93a, II 792-93a). The 'rentrer/entrer' confusion inserted into A

---

1 This itself might be late; the MS paper on which it appears is, on the whole, very clean (n.a.fr. 16711:87, 113; 16712:10).

l'ombre is amplified with the further substitution of 'envoyer' for 'renvoyer' in Sodome et Gomorrhe (II 794a), and his old favourite reappears during the war in an addition to Le Temps retrouvé: he wishes to 'rentrer dans l'aviation' (III 746-47a).[1]

The lift-boy is, however, certainly capped in these mishandlings by his employer the hotel-manager, whose transformation into the French Malaprop is entirely post-1914. Initiating the series of mistakes is an insertion in A l'ombre: the 1914 galleys had simply informed the reader that the manager was cosmopolitan, but Proust subsequently adds:

> (en réalité naturalisé Monégasque, bien qu'il fût - comme il disait, parce qu'il employait toujours des expressions qu'il croyait distinguées, sans s'apercevoir qu'elles étaient vicieuses - "d'originalité roumaine") (I 666a).[2]

Thereafter, almost every time he appears, so too does an addition giving at best a double negative for a single one,[3] at worst some misplaced or mangled locution. In fact, he is

---

1 See also II 790b; II 793c,d,e; II 794c; II 825a,b,c; II 825-26a; II 826a; II 826-27a; II 1025-26a; II 1026a. R. Kempf, in an observant and entertaining discussion of the lift-boy, remarks that 'Tout se passe comme si, pour Marcel désenchanté, le mythe du lift se dissolvait dans les vices de son langage': 'Sur quelques véhicules', L'Arc, no. 47 (1971?), pp. 47-57 (p. 49).

2 (The tendency itself is commented on rather earlier: I 663a.)

3 See II 751-52a, p. 751.

occasionally introduced solely in order to provide the appropriate - or inappropriate - word: the MS of Sodome et Gomorrhe had read simply: 'Quand la nuit était tout à fait venue, si nous n'allions pas nous promener [...]', but Proust slipped into the margin, after 'tout à fait venue': 'et que, comme me disait le directeur de l'hôtel, le ciel était tout parcheminé d'étoiles' (II 1019e). The cluster of malapropisms around the beginning of the second visit to Balbec were all added either to the MS or to the typescript: no doubt the most exaggerated of all is that use of the word 'illustrées' which, Marcel concludes, may be a confusion with 'illettrées', itself, in that case, a confusion with 'lettrées' (II 775-76a). The manager's malapropisms are last seen in an insertion on the typescript of Sodome et Gomorrhe - 'le vent étant aujourd'hui assez craintif (à craindre)' (II 1125a) - but, in the same place as the lift-boy's 'rentrer', they briefly return during the war in additions to the MS of Le Temps retrouvé, with 'décrépir' and with 'défectuosités' for 'défections' (III 746-47a; III 747a,c,d,n.).[1]

---

1 See also I 682-83a, p. 682; I 696-97a; I 706-7a; I 866-68a, p. 866; I 951a; II 751a; II 751-52a; II 751c; II 752a; II 755a; II 763a,b,c; II 765a,b,c,d,e; II 772-75a, p. 773; II 778-79a; II 826-27a, p. 827; II 1035a.

The duc de Guermantes was already, in the 1914 galleys, saying of Rachel's influence on Saint-Loup that 'c'est probablement sa petite grue qui lui aura monté le bourrichon' (II 238), and telling Swann, in the MS, that 'c'est Boson, je ne sais plus quel numéro de Guermantes. Mais ça, je m'en fous' (II 580).[1] However, he is now given a host of new expressions, more than any of the characters so far discussed; furthermore, besides adding to the bizarrely comic sides of his character, some of these additions receive more direct commentary from Proust than is seen elsewhere, except in the case of Saint-Loup.[2]

This later duc de Guermantes practises unabashed imitation: where he had merely remarked that he was taking note of the newly fashionable 'mentalité',[3] Proust subsequently added the parenthesis 'Ce n'était pas une figure, le duc avait un petit carnet rempli de "citations" et qu'il relisait avant les grands dîners' (II 237d). And two occasions on which he directs attention to phrases he is evidently proud to have assimilated are post-1914 ones: 'très suffisant pour ce qu'on appelle un vulgaire pedzouille comme moi' (II 487b); 'elle vous aurait certainement pris comme sigisbée, comme on disait dans ma jeunesse, une espèce de cavalier servant' (II 724c). He now believes that it is 'à la fois bon enfant et comique de parler

---

1 In n.a.fr. 16760:24iv and 16707:83 respectively.

2 See below, pp. 154-57.

3 This itself was added to the pre-1914 typescript of Le Côté de Guermantes (II 234-39a, p. 237).

le langage du peuple' (II 416c), and makes efforts to be 'ancien régime', considering it 'vieille France' to call the bishop of Mâcon 'Monsieur de Mascon' (II 478b).[1] And many of his slangily jocular turns of phrase or forced decorations, rather like those of Cottard or Bloch senior,[2] are late, such as 'il ne faut pas nous raconter de craques. Il y a une donzelle, une cascadeuse de la pire espèce, [...] qui est précisément compatriote du sieur Dreyfus' (II 236-37a).

Furthermore, M. de Guermantes is held up as a representative illustrator of two of the most interesting aspects of the over-used expression: its 'filler-in' quality, and the strange ubiquity it possesses, employed as it is by widely differing groups of people, yet germinating from an unknown source. The discussion of the duc's 'que voulez-vous que je vous dise?' was added only late, in the margin of the third Gallimard galleys: these words, Proust remarks,

> étaient là tout à fait inutiles. Mais il avait un besoin perpétuel de les dire, qui les lui faisait rejeter à la fin d'une période s'ils n'avaient pas trouvé de place ailleurs. C'était pour lui, entre autres choses, comme une question de métrique (II 530e).[3]

---

1 See also II 418a,b,c; II 487a; II 724d. However, see II 418d, II 418-19a for the duc naturally slipping into the 'ancien régime' idiom in the sphere of manners (also in the MS on II 417).

2 See above, pp. 138-39 and p. 141 respectively.

3 See also II 534-35a, p. 535; II 535a.

And, as I have already mentioned, the generalisations following on from his 'quand on s'appelle' were not in the 1914 galleys,[1] and appear only in a layer glued to them:

> une autre loi du langage est que de temps en temps [...] il naît on ne sait trop comment [...] des modes d'expressions qu'on entend dans la même décade dites par des gens qui ne se sont pas concertés pour cela [...] je devais entendre souvent le "quand on s'appelle" (II 235-36a).[2]

Perhaps the most significant addition about the duc's language is, however, the one showing how indissolubly welded are the words 'bel et bien' to his thoughts on the Dreyfus Affair, and more especially to those on his own failure in the Jockey Club elections. This, we already knew from M. Suzuki,[3] was not inserted until the third typescript of La Prisonnière:

> [...] depuis l'élection du Jockey, dès qu'on parlait de l'affaire Dreyfus, "bel et bien" surgissait [...] Cinq ans pouvaient se passer sans qu'on entendît "bel et bien", si pendant ce temps on ne parlait pas de l'affaire Dreyfus, mais si, les cinq ans passés, le nom de Dreyfus revenait, aussitôt "bel et bien" arrivait automatiquement
> (III 40b; see also III 40c and III 42a).

This mechanical quality, and the close linking of the hackneyed expression with a disagreeable experience which its victim is internally trying to smother, no doubt characterises and explains a number of the easy phrases the other characters too may

---

1 See above, Ch. 1, pp. 31, 64.

2 See also here II 929a.

3 See 'Le comique chez Marcel Proust', BSAMP, no.11 (1961), pp. 377-91 (p. 390).

use.[1]

As the reader has seen, Françoise's picturesque expressions and even her mistakes, for a different reason, are directly vindicated by Proust.[2] But he equally gave her some less lovable linguistic traits, occasionally, indeed, pointing out the speed with which her originally pleasing language is deteriorating.[3]

He now makes her imitate current rhetoric and stereotyped sayings, adding to Le Temps retrouvé her energetic stress of the word 'boche' (III 844-45a), and, a few pages later, her comment on Saint-Loup's death: '"Toutes ses richesses ne l'ont pas empêché de mourir comme un autre, et elles ne lui servent plus à rien"' - for, says Proust, there are 'des clichés dans les offices aussi bien que dans les cénacles' (III 849d). Post-1914

---

1 The news of Amanien's illness calls forth a number of slack banalities from the duc, some added after the main 'story' (II 578b; II 588-89b; II 588b; see also II 725b); on Swann's death, see II 597e. For further additions to the duc's speech, see: II 227b; II 235d,e; II 237e; II 238a,c,d; II 238a,c,d; II 239a,b; II 338-39a; II 338a; II 429b; II 490-91a, p.490; II 490b; II 499a; II 505-6a; II 505a,b; II 524-26a, p.524; II 530d; II 532b; II 546-47a, p. 547; II 576a,b; II 580b,c; II 597a; II 666-68a, p. 667; II 677-78a; II 720a; II 826b; III 38-42a, pp. 41-42; III 589a.

2 See above, pp. 130-32.

3 Bardèche interestingly affirms that the very first Françoise of all in fact consistently used, not a 'langage savoureux', but 'une langue vulgaire et basse' (vol. I, p. 342).

too are her ponderously vague phrases 'Le fait est', 'C'est quelque chose!', 'c'est possible', 'je ne sais pas', as well as the commentaries to which they give rise (I 691-94a, pp. 693-94; II 301a); and her weak expressions of sorrow during the grandmother's last illness were added only on the first Gallimard galleys:

> Françoise, quand elle avait un grand chagrin, éprouvait le besoin si inutile, mais ne possédait pas l'art si simple, de l'exprimer [...] c'était ses impressions à elle, Françoise, qu'elle tenait à nous faire connaître. Et elle ne savait que répéter: "Cela me fait quelque chose" [...] (II 340-41a).[1]

However, it is Françoise's borrowings from her daughter that incur Marcel's greatest displeasure. It is not true, as M. Bardèche says, that this daughter was invented simply for the sake of all the slang Proust wished to attribute to her; she is in fact mentioned in _Du Côté de chez Swann_ and in the MS of _Le Côté de Guermantes_.[2] But her actual appearances from _Le Côté de Guermantes_ on are all post-1914, as is the extreme annoyance provoked in Marcel by her speech. In additions made to different stages of the Gallimard galleys, she stretches words to a wider usage than they can meaningfully bear, insisting on 'radical' cures (II 331-32a) or giving 'intéressant' a sense that is said to be 'affreux et nouveau'

1 See also II 335a; II 777-78a, p. 778; III 748-50a, pp.748-49.

2 I 53, 54, 122; II 367. See Bardèche, vol. I, p. 342, _n_.1; Feuillerat also makes this mistake (p. 80).

(II 147-48a, p. 148);[1] equally late are her facetious formations ('pétrousse', 'cambrousse') (II 340-41a; II 147-48a, p. 148), her Parisian slang, and her arch puns ('Charles attend/ charlatan') (II 726-28a, p. 728). And her mother is now all too susceptible to this influence. When Proust came to revise a rather earlier addition crediting Françoise with the language of Saint-Simon,[2] he slipped in the qualifying 'quand elle ne voulait pas rivaliser avec les "jeunes"' (II 69b), and in the same place added a concrete example of the 'danger':

> Et comme le démon du pastiche, et de ne pas paraître vieux jeu, altère la forme la plus naturelle et la plus sûre de soi, Françoise, empruntant cette expression au vocabulaire de sa fille, disait que j'étais dingo (II 69a,n.).

Hereafter, all the passages in which Françoise the 'traditionaliste' none the less smiles indulgently at 'l'esprit d'innovation' incarnated in, for example, her daughter's use of 'pneu' (II 147-48a, p. 148),[3] or besprinkles her own conversation with such terms, are added ones. Proust inserted very late that La Prisonnière sequence in which, now that Marcel understands her patois, Françoise begins speaking with her daughter 'un français qui devint bien vite celui des plus basses époques', telling Marcel that 'Je vais me cavaler et presto': 'Ainsi perdent leur pureté toutes les langues par l'adjonction de termes nouveaux' comments the narrator sadly (III 154-55b).[4]

---

1 Mentioned above, Ch. 2, p. 81.

2 II 68-69a, inserted on the 1914 galleys. (See above, p.130.) The modifications were inserted on the first Gallimard galleys.

3 See also II 308a.

4 Inserted in separate pages in the third typescript.

And the imitation in Le Temps retrouvé not only of her daughter ('Et patatipatali et patatatipatala'), but also, with some slight modification, of the maître d'hôtel ('pissetières'),[1] was added to the MS, with the final seal set on the passing of her former vocabulary: 'elle ne parlait plus bien comme autrefois', having now adopted, from those she admires, 'leur vilain tour de langage' (III 748-50a).[2]

Although on one occasion in the pre-1914 Côté de Guermantes typescript Saint-Loup is said to be copying Bloch's intonation just as he borrows his ideas (II 255),[3] and although some comparatively early additions give him forced or lazy phrases,[4] Proust now, in the post-1914 years, makes him the principal model for linguistic imitation and for the adoption of pretentious and vague fashionable expressions. And, like that of M. de Guermantes and Françoise, this new phraseology is more

---

1 See here III 182-92a, p. 190.

2 See II 64-65a for a similar, but non-linguistic, deterioration. Proust gives the speech of Mme de Guermantes too a few 'negative' additions; these are largely vague generalisations about art or minor affectations: see II 203a; II 232b; II 249c,e,f; II 501c; II 517a; II 526a; III 38-42a, p.41; III 1003d; III 1027b,c.

3 n.a.fr. 16736:279, 284.

4 E.g. II 103a, II 161a - both additions to the CG typescript.

consistently commented on by Proust than is the language of most other characters.

The reshaping starts in A l'ombre: not in the 1914 galleys are Saint-Loup's questioning of Charlus about Racine and his horrified whisper to Marcel:

> Préférer Racine à Victor, c'est quand même quelque chose d'énorme! Il était sincèrement attristé des paroles de son oncle, mais le plaisir de dire "quand même" et surtout "énorme" le consolait (I 763c).

So the additions go on. Proust alters a 'Vous êtes épatant' to the still slangier 'Dites donc, ça vous en bouche un coin, mes enfants' on the 1914 galleys (II 107a), and returns to an already glued-on layer to write above the line and in the margin:

> Et comme il donnait lui-même dans le genre de prétention agaçante qu'il réprouvait: "A quoi ça te sert-il d'avoir fait du charme pour eux avec tant de persévérance si tu ne veux pas les revoir?" (II 859b).

His penchant for 'des phrases qu'il croyait grand siècle [...] par là il imitait les manières de Guermantes' was added to the MS of Le Temps retrouvé (III 703-4a, p. 704); and apart from these, ranging from the over-vivacious to conscious archaism, Saint-Loup now appropriates numbers of flatter, more meaningless phrases. His 'C'est quelqu'un de gentil, tu sais, c'est quelqu'un de bien' was added in the margin of the first Gallimard galleys: 'C'étaient des expressions nouvellement - d'autant plus ardemment - adoptées par Robert' (II 147-48a,

p. 147); and, as in the case of M. de Guermantes,[1] Proust now discusses the dissemination of phrases - if Saint-Loup uses 'Ça "fait" [assez "vieille demeure historique"]' at every turn, it is because

> la langue parlée, comme la langue écrite, éprouve de temps en temps le besoin de ces altérations du sens des mots, de ces raffinements d'expression [...] le vocabulaire, la diction même de Saint-Loup étaient faits de l'imitation de trois esthètes différents dont il ne connaissait aucun, mais dont ces modes de langage lui avaient été indirectement inculqués (II 71-72a).

A more direct influence, however, that of Rachel, is also introduced. Thus, added to the 1914 galleys is the information that Saint-Loup 'était imbu d'un certain langage qu'on parlait autour de cette femme dans des milieux littéraires' (II 125a); where an insertion on the Sodome et Gomorrhe MS showed Mme de Cambremer-Legrandin borrowing 'le dialecte de Robert' (II 819-20a), Proust added to this, on the typescript, 'qu'elle ne savait pas emprunté à Rachel' (II 820a); and Marcel's astonishment at the couple's use of each other's expressions 'comme si c'eût été un langage nécessaire et sans se rendre compte du néant d'une originalité qui est à tous' appears only in the margin of the 1914 galleys (II 167b).[2] Finally, both Mme de Guermantes's mockery of Saint-Loup's 'sublime' (II 509c)[3] and its disappearance, which exemplifies the five-yearly changes

---

1 See above, p. 150.

2 Rachel herself had always used 'le jargon des cénacles et des ateliers' (II 167), but now 'elle l'étendait [...] à tout'. See II 167a. Also II 167-68a; II 168b; II 169c; II 170e; II 172b; III 1003c.

3 See also here II 549-51a, p. 551; II 551a.

in his speech, are new:

> "[...] Elle ne te dira pas des choses définitives (les choses "définitives" avaient été substituées aux choses "sublimes" par Robert qui modifiait, tous les cinq ou six ans, quelques-unes de ses expressions favorites tout en conservant les principales)
> (II 753c,d);

and Proust added even later here not only Robert's 'elle n'est pas toujours <u>à la page</u>' (II 753f), but also such illuminating definitions as 'c'est une nature, elle a une personnalité' (II 753e).[1]

Of all these characters, none, however, is paid so much attention as Norpois. As Feuillerat says, Proust, in the revision, 'appuya sur les ridicules de l'aristocratique ambassadeur' with 'un visible plaisir'[2] - although again, it was less a question of 'les ridicules' in general than of particularly linguistic ones, on which Feuillerat himself draws almost exclusively in order to make his point.[3] The

---

1 The MS shows Saint-Loup reverting, during the war, to his more critical self, and agreeing that phrases like 'passeront pas' are regrettable (III 752); but nevertheless, Proust adds his subsequent remarks that in these circumstances 'les mots ne font plus rien', and that '"poilu"' is 'déjà prêt pour de grands poètes' (III 753a). (See, however, III 760-62a, the relatively favourable addition about his word-play.) For further additions to or about Saint-Loup's speech itself, see: I 733-34a; I 750c; I 755a,c; II 100a; II 106a,<u>n</u>.; II 108-117a, pp. 108, 109; II 110a; II 112c; II 117b; II 125b; II 157a; II 279c; II 399a,b; II 412b; II 502-3a; II 691b & Pl. <u>n</u>.2; II 693a; II 1058a; III 61a; III 513a. For his imitation of others' <u>ideas</u>, see II 79a; II 119a,b,d.

2 p. 23.

3 See his pp. 23-26.

representative diplomat of the novel, Norpois is, by virtue of the additions, made its master cliché-monger. The other characters' affectations may be found against a background of less pretentious language, but Norpois is now singled out to make speeches composed of nothing but stereotypes. The typescript version of the _A l'ombre_ dinner had already given him such phrases as 'écrit d'une plume alerte' (cp. I 453)[1] or 'c'est tout simplement un coup de maître' (I 460),[2] and by the time Proust drew up the near-definitive MS of _Le Temps retrouvé_, he was incorporating Norpois's ready-made phrases into the main body of his text, where they are commented on by Charlus (III 781ff.);[3] but until he reached this point, we can see from the earlier material how much extra care was to be devoted to the skilful manoeuvres of Norpois as he contrives to make his point, or to give away as little as he can, with as much emphasis as he can summon up.

The expressions Proust put into Norpois's mouth at the _A l'ombre_ dinner are almost all, in their hybrid fusion of ponderousness and attempted levity, what Fowler would call 'battered ornaments'.[4] Such classical or foreign scraps as _mutatis mutandis_ (I 453a) and 'un véritable oukase' (I 459b) were added

---

1 n.a.fr. 16732:71, 16735:74.

2 n.a.fr. 16732:74, 16735:77.

3 Even here, he still added one or two: III 782a,b,c; III 784a.

4 H.W. Fowler, _A Dictionary of Modern English Usage_ (London, 1968), pp. 51-52.

after 1914; so were emphatic 'fillers-in' like 'disons, pour être exacts' and 'tranchons le mot' (I 475c, d), fancifully facetious circumlocutions like 'loin d'être un maître sot' (I 467b), and such quaintly old-fashioned words and phrases as 'de bon aloi' (I 457b), 'maître en l'art de dire' (I 463b), 'Une personne digne de toute créance' (I 463e), 'certaine personne qui n'est pas femme à en faire fi' (I 464d), and 'auquel cas' (I 466b).

However, the largest category of additions, both in _A l'ombre_ and elsewhere, shows Norpois relying on, even extending with a certain fluent inventiveness, those over-blown or blurred turns of phrase that range from the speech-maker's stock-in-trade to the pronouncements of the politician and the leader-writer seeking to confer a solemnity and a value on their subject which it does not possess, or simply trying to escape from an awkward question. These new passages may be short asides, like the concluding comment on that successful young man whom Marcel is urged to imitate:

> En somme, sans pouvoir dire encore qu'il soit au pinacle, il a conquis de haute lutte une fort jolie position et le succès qui ne va pas toujours qu'aux agités et aux brouillons, aux faiseurs d'embarras qui sont presque toujours des faiseurs, le succès a récompensé son effort (I 453i);

or, covering a page and more, they may be burlesquely drawn-out exercises. These longer speeches will be well-known to readers of Proust.[1] Norpois's substantial description of Vaugoubert's ordeal, in the course of which he not only impresses his listeners with an Arab proverb but goes so far as to pause and look around to see its effect, is post-1914: this addition includes the narrator's remarks on the fashionable use of threadbare political personification and of imported or supposedly historical sayings, culminating, of course, with the revelation that Norpois, owing to his more original reworkings of such expressions, has been thought by some to be a not unsuitable candidate for the Académie française (I 461-63a). Proust came back, too, to Bloch's interrogation of Norpois in _Le Côté de Guermantes_ and embellished the diplomat's already equivocal replies with large numbers of those 'accessoires de rhétorique' which, as Charlus observes in a later addition, are so dear to him (III 796d). Thus, part of a reply which, in the typescript, read merely:

> "Il est certain répondit Monsieur de Norpois que sa déposition à la première audience a produit une impression singulièrement heureuse[2]

---

1 Norpois understandably attracts much critical comment. P. Kolb's observations on him are useful: 'Proust's Portrait of Jaurès in _Jean Santeuil_', _French Studies_, XV (1961), pp. 338-49 (p. 338) (see also P. Kolb, 'Le Marquis de Norpois: Encore les "clefs" de Proust', _Mercure de France_, 1 mai 1951, pp. 178-81); and both J. Mouton (_Le Style de Marcel Proust_, p. 192) and M. Bardèche (vol. I, p.338) make, in different ways, the observation that Norpois, as a character-creation, is nothing _but_ language (this applies to other characters too, of course).

2 n.a.fr. 16736:257.

is now, after margin additions and corrections in both the 1914 Grasset galleys and the first Gallimard ones, four times as long, replacing 'Il est certain' with 'Il est hors de conteste', and swollen with unintentionally comic mixed metaphors:

> On ne sort pas d'une pareille impasse par une simple pirouette, ou alors on risque de tomber dans un bourbier (see II 240a, b, c, d).

Fullest of all are those two pages of Norpois's address to Bloch which are entirely compounded of journalese, overstretched circumlocutions, tautology or synonyms used for the sake of emphasis, and empty exhortation doubtless proffered partially in the hope of making the listener forget the actual subject of discussion. This speech, the one beginning 'Je sais que le parti socialiste réclame sa tête à cor et à cri' and ending 'S'il est avéré qu'il y ait eu erreur judiciaire, [le gouvernement] sera assuré d'une majorité écrasante qui lui permettrait de se donner du champ', was manipulated and reworked by Proust in unusual detail; he elaborated the original addition, made in a margin and on a layer in the 1914 galleys, with no less than sixteen further separate insertions (II 245-46a, with all indented additions, and II 246i).[1]

Finally, in a commentary on the forgetfulness of society people, added to the first typescript of La Prisonnière, Proust

---

1 The speech is cited by Feuillerat (p. 101) as a new and excellent example of 'la facilité inépuisable avec laquelle Norpois pouvait assembler des expressions toutes faites'. For other additions to this Côté de Guermantes section, see particularly II 240f,g; II 242a; II 242-43a.

had written simply that Norpois, for example, at some mention of his former prognostications, would say without intention to deceive, '"Vous devez vous tromper, je ne me rappelle pas du tout' (III 38-42a, p. 38). But when Proust returned to this, now typed out in the third typescript, he worked in not only the subject of these prognostications ('une alliance avec l'Allemagne qui n'avait même pas abouti', III 38c), but also, exploiting a still rich source, the string of over-clever or facile phrases now in the text:

> [...] je n'aurais jamais prédit le succès d'un de ces coups d'éclat qui ne sont souvent que des coups de tête et dégénèrent habituellement en coups de force [...] je n'en ai jamais parlé, parce que la poire n'est pas mûre encore, et, si vous voulez mon avis, en demandant à nos anciens ennemis de convoler avec nous en justes noces, je crois que nous irions au-devant d'un gros échec et ne recevrions que de mauvais coups
> (see III 38d, e, f, and III 38-39a).[1]

---

1 M. Suzuki mentions this expansion (again referring to the first TS as the second: see above, p. 136 n.1) in 'Le comique chez Marcel Proust', BSAMP, no. 11 (1961), pp. 377-91 (pp. 390-91).
See too, for Norpois, both versions of his dinner in Venice: III 630-39a, *passim*, and III 630 n.1: III 1052-53a. Also: I 431-34a, p. 431; I 437a; I 453c,e,f,g; I 456c,e; I 457c; I 458d; I 458-59a; I 460b; I 461a; I 463a,c,d; I 463-64a; I 464a; I 466d; I 467a,c; I 472a; I 473b,c; I 474a,b,f,g; I 475e,f; I 476a,b; II 222-23a; II 222a; II 225-26a (this and other additions to these 2 pages are prepared by II 150-51a); II 225a-f; II 226a,b; II 243c; II 259a,b; II 259-61a; III 774n.2: III 1127a.

An account of all the other abuses of language that Proust added to his drafts would make this chapter nearly twice as long as it is already. The rest of the aristocracy and 'gens du monde', in proportion to their more infrequent appearances, are given nearly as much thought as those already cited, especially Mme de Cambremer-Legrandin[1] and her husband.[2] The dowager Mme de Cambremer does not escape,[3] nor does the Cambremers' friend, the lawyer.[4] A few vague or pretentious expressions are added for Mme de Villeparisis,[5] for the Guermantes as a family,[6] for Mme de Marsantes,[7] the princesse d'Épinay,[8] the Courvoisiers,[9] the prince Von,[10] and other habitués of high society.[11] And

---

1 II 203d; II 811d; II 811-12a; II 814a,c; II 817a; II 819-20a; II 820a,b,d; II 922-23a; II 923c; II 928b; II 929a; II 944-45a,b; II 978a; II 1095a,b,c.

2 II 914b; II 918-19a; II 922-23a; II 923a,b; II 925a; II 965a, II 965-66a; II 976c; II 1094-95a; II 1094b; II 1109d; II 1124-25a, p. 1125; III 88c.

3 II 807a; II 817-18a; II 822a; II 946b.

4 II 806a; II 812a; II 821-22a.

5 I 721a; II 193-94a; II 217-18a.

6 II 461-62a; II 534 n.2: II 1169a,b; II 818d; II 819a,b.

7 II 251-52a; II 283a.

8 II 466-67a. (See, however, II 488, where this expression is in the MS.)

9 II 449b; II 467a.

10 II 262b; II 509a,b; II 510a; II 528c,e. See II 527 for some mispronunciations in the MS.

11 I 513-15a, p. 513; I 780b; II 477-78b; II 478a; II 649a; II 699-702a, p. 702; III 35-36a; III 38-42a, p. 41.

similar jarring usages come late in the speech of Vaugoubert, Froberville and M. de Crécy,[1] as well as in that of Marcel's middle-class friends and acquaintances - Gisèle,[2] Gilberte,[3] and Professor E... .[4]

Proust inserts, too, generally-used hackneyed expressions without attributing them to any one individual, such as phrases from the newspapers;[5] and the word 'intelligent' comes to be used more and more as a cliché during this period.[6] As for miscellaneous figures, the Paris maître d'hôtel is given more slang and jargon during the war than most other minor characters;[7] Proust bestows some idiosyncratic expressions on Aimé[8] and attributes to him one mistake _à la_ Françoise and a spelling error;[9] and in Françoise's footman, Joseph Périgot,

---

1 II 642-47a, p. 644 and III 45-47a, p. 46; II 676a; II 1110a, respectively.

2 III 177-80a, p. 178. See here I 869-951a, pp. 928-29.

3 I 507b; III 984-85a; III 985a.

4 II 313-14a; II 640-42a.

5 I 477-78a; I 480c; III 144c; III 199-201a; III 522b; III 630-39a, pp. 637-39 (written by Norpois); III 775-76a; III 784-93a; III 842-43a.

6 See I 604-5a; II 106a,_n._; II 117b; II 167-68a; II 293a; II 546-47a, p. 546; II 712a, II 712-13a; II 747-48a; II 940-41a; III 38-42a, p. 42; III 301e.

7 III 748a; III 748-50a; III 842e; III 842-43a; III 844a.

8 I 767f; II 772-75a, p. 772; II 1083-84a.

9 III 515a,_n._, and III 516a respectively.

who in passages all added writes the letters that are a hotch-potch of quotations he believes to be in common parlance, Proust gives one of his most indulgent renderings of the kind of wholesale borrowings he spreads throughout the novel.[1]

This post-1914 expansion, so comprehensively illustrated, is marked off from the others not only by its scale but by its diversity. To class the additions into the traditional and local, the forcedly original, the stereotyped and vague, or the distorted, is inadequate, glossing over the finer subdivisions: there is a difference, for example, between the incorrectness of Françoise's 'Nev-York',[2] that of the lift-boy's

---

1 II 321-22a, p. 322; II 322a,b; II 550a; II 566-67a; see also II 17c; II 25f,g; II 27a. Other additions illustrate the use of a private 'language' or patois, sometimes bringing out the feeling of superiority it creates in its speakers: see I 581-92a, p. 583; I 767-79a, p. 774, 774n.; II 818d, II 819a,b; II 850-51a; III 154-55a; III 325-26a.
For further miscellaneous, or general, new linguistic idiosyncrasies and clichés, see especially II 406a,b,c; and also: I 435a; I 459c; I 492c; I 560c; I 576-77a; I 675b,c,d; I 687b; I 703-4a, p. 703; I 732c; I 740-48a, p. 742; I 818a; I 869-951a, pp. 878,879,929,936; II 62-63a; II 93b; II 94b,c; II 105a; II 139a; II 161b; II 163a; II 182a; II 237b; II 257a; II 337b; II 401c; II 474a,d; II 481b; II 508a; II 537a; II 544a; II 610a,b; II 633-34a, p. 634; II 690b; II 749a; II 771a; II 771-72a; II 824b; II 934c; II 1078a; III 147-48a; III 147b; III 227d; III 243b; III 244a; III 288-89a,n.; III 596b; III 614a; III 723d; III 727a; III 729-30a; III 732-33a; III 754a; III 798a; III 814-15a; III 821a,b,c; III 822-23a; III 825-26a; III 852a; III 864a; III 886a; III 892-94a.
For the Norwegian philosopher's difficulties with language, see II 930-31a; II 931a; II 935a.

2 See above, p. 131.

'rentrer',[1] and that of the manager's 'défectuosités'.[2] But the additions do share obvious characteristics.

As I said in the preceding chapter, on a first level they are comic:[3] set in the right context, bombast, or simply the surprise of mistakes when the usual form is expected, can be immediately amusing.[4] Whereas the _Sodome et Gomorrhe_ draft discussing the problem in the abstract is flat, humourless, and almost solemn,[5] the specific examples, by contrast, lend the novel tautness and wit.

The additions clearly modify, too, the personalities of some figures in _A la recherche_: Norpois and Bloch now become performing monologuists; and in others, there is a down-grading, not quite in the directly personal sense in which Feuillerat understood it, but more in the sense that these insertions can contribute to a general atmosphere of decline, as in the case of the spoiling of Françoise's language, or Saint-Loup's use of rather cheaply fashionable expressions.

---

1 Above, pp. 145-46.

2 Above, p. 147.

3 See above, p. 81.

4 L. Pierre-Quint stresses the _mechanically_ comic side of the characters' tics of language, which follow them like _leitmotive_ throughout the novel (_Après Le Temps retrouvé: Le Comique et le mystère chez Proust_ (Paris, 1928), pp. 26, 36-37).

5 See above, Ch. 1, pp. 40-41.

More generally, the discussions of speech amplify other post-1914 developments - also oral ones. The easy spread of cliché, which rises from an unknown source, then to be passed on inside groups and move out from them with the occasional concomitant alteration of the original matter, resembles the dissemination of rumours, a theme much expanded in this period too.[1] The milder abuses of language shown in this chapter link with the post-1914 elaboration of lies; both Albertine's fabrications and the manager's malaproprisms, for example, are distorted material which needs to be interpreted.[2]

However, as I implied at the beginning of the chapter,[3] the most serious implications of this expansion lie in the contrast it sets up, in a subdued manner in most of the novel and overtly in Le Temps retrouvé,[4] between the cliché, either fashionable or private, and the language of the writer. This clearly should not be automatic, like the duc de Guermantes's, nor imitative like Saint-Loup's; the writer must not, like Bloch, copy a master (Leconte de Lisle), or strive to give himself false distinction: like La Berma, whose delivery is so much in harmony with its subject that no 'originality' of the flamboyant kind is noticeable, the successful writer has to search for the best means of conveying an impression, and not

---

1 See below, Ch. 6, pp. 255-64.

2 See below, Ch. 6, pp. 264-72.

3 pp. 124-25.

4 See, e.g., III 890, III 890-91a.

subordinate that impression to a wish to parade his own intelligence. Most of the phrases cited here flow forth with an ease which eventually lends new depth to the emphasis in _Le Temps retrouvé_ on the labour that has to go towards the final apt expression in literature.[1]

The younger Marcel, as his reactions to Françoise, her daughter, and others, show, is perhaps rather too conscious of faulty, imitated, or pretentious language, and lets it irritate or baffle him.[2] The older narrator can, however, stand back and view it more understandingly as an almost inevitable distortion, as the propelling force in the growth of any language, but a force whose negative aspects can be surpassed; he sees that it is a force transformed by the best writers - those who can, with as much self-awareness as is possible, both use the traditional resources of the language, and shape it so that it does go beyond those schemata which are normally so difficult to abandon.[3]

---

1 See, e.g., III 896.

2 See above, pp. 131-32, 152; e.g. II 147-48a, p. 147.

3 Additions to _TR_ about style, or discussing banalities or stereotypes, are III 881a; III 881-82a; III 895-96a; III 896c; III 898c; III 900a. (See also I 551a.) III 720a,_n._, mentions Elstir's former 'irritantes façons de parler', now discarded by 'l'homme de génie'.

4 Morel

The last chapter 'extracted' a chosen aspect from each separate character and brought these aspects together according to one classification; this is the procedure followed in most of the remaining discussion. However, there is one figure above all who, whilst exemplifying in some ways changes made elsewhere, received such particular reworking in the post-1914 expansion, and became the subject of so many entirely new episodes or generalisations, that he deserves a closer, more individual study than do any of the other characters. This figure, who, as it clearly emerged from Chapter 1,[1] was only sketched out in the drafts but who is now, by virtue of the additions, in a position of prominence that makes him comparable to Albertine herself, is Morel.

As the Pléiade edition had already told us, Morel is designated in the main MS, and in a number of the additions themselves, by the name Bobby Santois.[2] The name Charles Morel is used in the insertion introducing him into Le Côté de

---

1 See pp. 31, 44, 45, 57-58, 64.

2 I xxxiv.

Guermantes (II 264-67a), and since this addition was made to the first Gallimard galleys, the second name dates back at least to 1919-20.[1] Proust's reasons for the change are a matter for discussion. The name Charles held a special attraction for him - witness Charles Swann, M. de Charlus; Saint-Loup's first name, too, was Charles at one stage.[2] Claude Vallée ingeniously points out that 'Charlie' is almost an anagram of 'Rachel', and sounds like a feminisation of 'Charles' or 'Charlus'.[3] Whatever further interpretations can be put upon it, the new first name at any rate links the violinist with both of the other failed artists in the novel, the baron and Swann.

It would be useful if the exact date of the change could be established; but meanwhile, the two names show which are the later, which rather earlier, additions.[4] Some of these later developments must have been inserted in haste, since often the first name, Bobby or Santois, is left uncorrected in the MS page

---

1 See above, Ch. 1, pp. 18-19, for dating of the BN material.

2 See Bardèche, vol. II, pp. 372 n.1, 393, 407, and below, Part II, p. 55.
Gilbert le Mauvais had also been Charles le Mauvais: see J. Milly, 'Sur quelques noms proustiens', Littérature, no. 14 (1974), pp. 65-82 (pp. 74-75).

3 La Féerie de Marcel Proust (Paris, 1958), pp. 354-55.
S. Gaubert takes this approach even further in his 'Proust et le jeu de l'alphabet', Europe, 49e année, nos. 502-503 (1971), pp. 68-83.

4 (The Pléiade edition, from La Prisonnière on, notes all uses of the early name.)

where a passage in the same margin gives 'Morel'.[1] More interesting still, it is not quite true, as the Pléiade editors imply (I xxxiv), that the second name never appears in the main MS; 'Charlie', not 'Bobby', occurs, at infrequent intervals, actually on the page, in what must be late sections incorporated bodily from some other Cahier.[2]

Anthony Pugh's unpublished thesis devotes some space to the expansions made to Morel, giving details of the structural shift of an important episode, mentioning, of one or two passages, that they are late,[3] and considering, in a more general chapter, the changes in aesthetic perspective indicated by the new treatment of the musician. Here, Pugh remarks that Morel interested Proust increasingly, but had nevertheless 'always caused [him] trouble'; he brings out Proust's difficulties in placing the violinist's adventures satisfactorily in the framework already constructed, and notes the resultant troubles with narrative voice, troubles which forced Proust to assume omniscience or to introduce some such phrase, occasionally clumsy, as 'I later learned'.[4] These comments are thought-provoking; but they stress the injurious nature of the changes

---

1 See, e.g., III 311 paragraph 1, and III 311-12a (n.a.fr. 16718:24).

2 The most spectacular example of this occurs in the MS of La Fugitive, where the name 'Bobby' appears on n.a.fr. 16722:60 (III 682 n.2), and 'Charlie' on the very next page, which is in different writing (n.a.fr. 16722:61; III 685). 'Charlie' also appears in the MS on, e.g., II 1064-65, 1068-69, 1071; III 211, 212, 219, 221, 222, 242, 686, 1030.

3 Pugh, pp. 352, 408-10, 442-43, 482.

4 pp. 516-19.

rather heavily, and most readers probably do not find the narrative devices just mentioned as jolting as Pugh implies, if indeed they notice them.[1] However, rather than their structural effects, it is the actual substance of the expansions that I shall examine in this chapter, starting, for the sake of clarity, with a picture of the virtuoso as he is in the unexpanded MSS.[2]

Santois's first main entry came, it seems, in that sequence given by the Pléiade notes for <u>A l'ombre</u> (I 777<u>n</u>.1): Marcel, at a concert in the Balbec casino, recognised in the main player Santois, the son of his uncle's former 'valet de chambre', who had already paid him a short visit; and after the piece, during which the young instrumentalist was careful to let a lock of hair fall over his forehead, the two met briefly. Unfortunately there was no trace either of this encounter, or of the preliminary visit, in the material I was working on, but the passage evidently belongs to an early version of Morel, who was, here, credited with a 'gentil visage français' - although showing at the same time a certain 'hardiesse du paysan', and adopting a cavalier tone with Marcel: but, 'fils d'une race qui a fait la Révolution', he was said to be just as French as Françoise

---

1 Of course such devices are anything but a late invention in Proust, being wholly operative for 'Un Amour de Swann' - see, e.g., I 186.

2 Feuillerat makes brief and, in a passable majority of examples, fairly accurate conjectures (as far as my material is concerned) on the changed rôle of the young musician (pp. 107, 180-83; see also pp. 177-78).

(I 981).[1]

The earliest MS appearance of Santois which I myself found was at the moment of his meeting Charlus at the station.[2] This was in the same position in the MS of Sodome et Gomorrhe as it now is in the text (II 861); but there were interesting variations. Santois was carrying a bugle, not a violin,[3] and Marcel, although recognising him, was not sent by Charlus to fetch him: rather, this recognition was the cue for a somewhat digressive discussion of the type of set phrase described in the last chapter:

> Quand j'avais vu Santois[4] au concert de Balbec, si j'avais parlé le langage de la plupart des gens, je lui aurais certainement dit: "Que diable faites-vous ici", [C'est la][5] phrase consacrée, particulière à la vie en voyage et de bains de mer [...]
> (n.a.fr. 16712:16).[6]

---

1 Although the Pléiade edition notes tell us that this sequence was found in one of the MS passages glued by Proust to the 1920 edition of A l'ombre (I 978-79), this seems not really to be its place. Painter (vol. II, pp. 244-45) deduces that the concert was at one point planned to take place during the second out of the then three visits to Balbec; this is probably confirmed by a few lines in the MS of SG coming after the description of Santois on the station platform: 'Quand j'avais vu Santois au concert de Balbec [...]' (n.a.fr. 16712:16: see just below, this page).

2 (Compare this with the earlier meeting still, described by Bardèche, vol. II, p.155.)

3 n.a.fr. 16712:16, 18; it became a violin only in additions to 16712:18, 19.

4 Corrected from 'Quand je l'avais vu'.

5 Words in brackets crossed out.

6 And further expressions like this are given in the margin, n.a.fr. 16712:16, and (crossed out) in 16712:17.

There was thus no occasion for Santois to be 'sec' or 'hautain' to Marcel in the MS, as there is now (II 861). Charlus, who had come up to Santois, apologised for his abruptness and, talking 'beaucoup plus haut qu'il n'aurait voulu', asked if he played the bugle (n.a.fr. 16712:18). At this, Santois,

> qui n'avait pas répondu jusqu'ici et avait gardé l'air avenant et [fier] "hardi" d'un jeune français qui n'a pas froid aux yeux,[1]

interrupted Charlus with the information that he had the first violin-prize[2] of the Conservatoire; Charlus cunningly enquired if anyone of Santois's acquaintance would play a Bach sonata that night for 100 francs, to which the young man replied that, although otherwise comparatively unengaged, he was not, this once, free. Here the railway-employee announced: 'Le train est signalé, Monsieur' (n.a.fr. 16712:19; II 863), and events unfolded roughly as in the present text, Santois's display of firmness with the flower-seller delighting Charlus (II 863-64).[3]

From this point onwards, Proust added to, rather than reworked, Santois's history (with one substantial exception);

---

1 Crossed out, n.a.fr. 16712:18. Brackets signify a still earlier crossing-out; underlining, an above-line addition.

2 *Sic*; see above, p. 173 *n*.3.

3 This section may not have reached its final form until quite late in 1921, since in a letter to Gaston Gallimard of October 1921 Proust says of 'la première rencontre de M. de Charlus avec Morel' that it is 'entièrement changée ces jours-ci': *Lettres à la NRF* (Paris, 1932), p. 155. (Date derived from P. Kolb, *La Correspondance de Marcel Proust* (Urbana, 1949), p. 223.)

so that to describe the violinist's rôle in the early versions will now be much less an account of variants and excised passages than a summary of those sections at present in the novel that had also always been in the MS.

Santois, a 'discovery' of the Patronne's, normally came regularly to the Verdurins', and, as the principal event of the Wednesdays, Mme Verdurin was, as she is at present, careful to manage his feelings with tact. Two days previously he had 'lâché', owing, he said, to a migraine, but was coming that night with an old friend of his father's whom he had met at Doncières; this friend proved on arrival to be Charlus, of course (II 884, 893, 901-2, 904, 906).

The main MS does not now mention Santois at all until Mme de Cambremer-Legrandin's enquiries about him (II 923, 927). However, shortly before this, one MS page is torn,[1] and there occurs at this juncture in the proofs, although not in the MS or the typescript, the long passage already referred to as the object of an important structural displacement and as the source of noteworthy variants.[2] This is the early version of the revelation by Morel that Odette is the 'dame en rose'. The proofs mention a visit Santois had already paid to Marcel,[3]

---

1 At the equivalent of II 911, and just above a marginal mention of Elstir: see below, p. 176 n.3 (n.a.fr. 16712:68).

2 See above, p. 171, and p. 174, last paragraph.

3 Cp. I 982.

during which he had given him, amongst others, the photograph of Elstir's portrait of Odette, Miss Sacripant (cp. II 266). It now occurred to Marcel that he wanted to ask Santois two questions, but could recall only one: had Santois remembered to ask how his uncle was in possession of the photograph of Mme Swann?[1]

> [...] - Parfaitement j'y ai pensé me dit-il, car il avait à côté de terribles défauts que je ne connus que plus tard quelque chose de poli, d'exact, d'adroit, qui était extrêmement agréable; il n'oubliait rien de ce qu'on lui demandait".

He then told Marcel that the lady at his uncle's so many years ago was Odette, and ended: 'J'ai entendu causer que mon père (sic) était fou de celle-là. Elle lui a emprunté deux mille francs qu'il n'a jamais revus".' Here followed a discussion, not of the surprising fact that Odette now has to be identified with the 'dame en rose' (cp. II 267),[2] but of Elstir's vision:

> je compris combien ce qu'Elstir avait connu, avait aimé en elle était différent de ce que nous voyions tous, était une torsion des traits [...]. De tels portraits quand ils représentent, - pour le peintre seul - une femme aimée, expliquent tout un amour, toute une vie vouée à un être que nos regards déforment perpétuellement [...] (n.a.fr. 16766:242-43).[3]

Proust later thoroughly fragmented this sequence, shortening the

---

1 (n.a.fr. 16766:241.) The other question is no doubt about the paralytic at the concert (see I 982), who evidently has some connection with Vinteuil (see III 252 n.2), whether or not he is, as Painter concludes, Vinteuil himself (Painter, vol. II, p. 245).

2 The proofs simply read: 'Mme Swann était la même personne que la dame en rose que j'avais vue chez mon oncle' (n.a. fr. 16766:242).

3 This part appears also in an MS margin, n.a.fr. 16712:68, with only one minor variation: 'vu' for 'connu'.

consideration of Elstir's art, or possibly rewriting it to swell the description of Miss Sacripant already, perhaps, inserted into A l'ombre (I 847-50, I 860-63),[1] but omitting, there at least, any specific indication that Elstir might have been Odette's lover; instead, this suggestion, and a little of the discussion, were transferred to La Fugitive.[2] As for the information that Odette was the 'dame en rose', Proust placed this 650 pages earlier, in a large layer addition to Le Côté de Guermantes which amalgamates the discovery with both the visit from Morel and the gift of the photographs, and gives the revelation, now, the emphasis it deserves (II 264-67a).[3]

The MS of Sodome et Gomorrhe resumes, then, with Mme de Cambremer-Legrandin's questions. Hereafter, further mention of Santois himself at the dinner occurred only in the context of Charlus's manoeuvres to impress or to be near him, and in the card-game with Cottard. Mme Verdurin assured the baron that he must come often with Santois; this latter, although not knowing what the Gotha was, none the less was 'ébahi' by Charlus's references to the nobility of his family. The baron, hearing Mme Verdurin invite Santois for two days hence and hoping to be included, complimented her, whereupon she remarked to the

---

1 This is post-1914; see below, Ch. 8, pp. 353-54.

2 Here they appear on an unlined page in the MS, with some reworking (n.a.fr. 16719:35; see III 439-40, III 440a). Odette as Miss Sacripant appears briefly in the MS of La P too (III 299).

3 See also II 273a.

violinist on his friend's agreeable qualities (II 932, 948, 951, 953). Santois, 'comme il avait oublié son violon',[1] now asked to play cards. He sat down with Cottard; Charlus, who would have liked the game to be whist so that he could join in, stood nearby, and the conversation between the two players was punctuated by Charlus's fulsome praise of Santois and his insistence that the young man had to be back by midnight 'comme un enfant [...] bien sage', a comparison that gave him a 'sadique volupté' (II 953, 955, 958, 963-65). Mme Verdurin bemoaned Santois's unwillingness to play for them (II 967); Cottard, the winner of the card-game, promised Santois a chance for revenge (II 974-75); and that was the last we saw of the violinist until the general descriptions of the 'fidèles' in the train.

There once again the MS focused on Charlus's reactions to him; the baron, it explained, would arrange joint invitations for himself and Santois, and would publicly state that he found him handsome, in the belief that such activities or observations would be understood in all innocence, and unaware that his love for Santois was common knowledge (II 1042-43, 1049-50). When, however, the violinist boarded the train at Doncières, Charlus 'surveillait soigneusement sa conversation', as a father would with a daughter; his use of such phrases as 'un petit très honnête' made it evident that he considered inversion as dangerous for young men as prostitution for women (II 1053-54).

---

1 n.a.fr. 16712:113.

The relations of the couple with others were sketched out too: Charlus, afraid lest on their return to Paris the young man's family might intervene, consoled himself nevertheless by finding something '"très balzacien"' in his situation; and Santois, realising that Marcel was 'animé d'intentions bienveillantes' towards him,[1] sincerely attached, besides, to Charlus, ended by talking to his protector of Marcel in the same way that Rachel had to Saint-Loup, and even asked Charlus to invite him to dinner (II 1058, 1060). However, the first signs of deterioration were creeping in, with 'orages' in the relationship; belying Charlus's praise of Santois's behaviour with him, the violinist often, even in front of the 'fidèles', took on an irritated rather than a happy and submissive air, occasionally going so far as to give Charlus, 'sur un ton dur, une réplique insolente' (II 1060-61).

The incident of the pretended duel, provoked by Santois's departure with the words 'j'ai à faire', was in the MS, which described, as now, the letter sent through Marcel, Santois's first movements of gaiety, succeeded by sudden gloom at the mention of Charlus, his outbursts ('Alors je suis un esclave!'), - couched in crude terms and qualifying Charlus as 'ce vieux dégoûtant' -, and the final submission, which entailed Santois's rolling his eyes coquettishly at Charlus and asking tenderly if he might stay, to the delight of the baron, thus able to keep

---

1 n.a.fr. 16713:73.

him 'tant qu'il voudrait'[1] (II 1063-69, 1071). The MS drew this sub-plot of Sodome et Gomorrhe to its temporary conclusion with the story of the Cambremers' discomfiture: they were foolish enough to invite only Santois and Cottard to dinner, but Santois, having taken quite literally Charlus's 'esquisse hautaine et sommaire' of high society, and longing to act upon it, did not reply to the invitation and excused himself at the last moment by telegram, 'ravi comme s'il venait d'agir en prince du sang'. The Cambremers, furious, invited Charlus, now, without Santois, and then, worried, asked the violinist after all; the latter arrived alone and informed his hosts, to their horror, that the baron was unable to come, being 'un peu indisposé, du moins je crois que c'est pour cela' (II 1088-93); and the last reference to him appeared in Marcel's reflection that the name Doncières had come to represent to him only the station at which Santois boarded the train (II 1110).

The reader of the base MS from La Prisonnière onwards again has the impression that although in some ways Santois himself was more in the foreground, playing in the Septet, delivering the final blow to Charlus, and writing scurrilous articles, Proust was still primarily concerned to illustrate, through him, aspects of the baron. The MS of La Prisonnière, for example, showed Charlus 'living' only in the little clan because of Santois, talking about him in rather too revealing a manner, telling both Brichot and Marcel that he had invited guests who

1 n.a.fr. 16713:82 (cp. II 1071a).

might be useful in as much as they would make Santois's name known in 'le monde', and imparting the novel information that Santois wrote 'comme un ange', even that he would like Bergotte to help him. However, there was, perhaps, a foreshadowing of the changes Proust was later to make in the fact that it was through Santois that Charlus had learned of the proposed arrival of Mlle Vinteuil and her friend that night (III 211-14, 219-22).

Apart from a few further general statements on the development of the relationship - on Santois's increasing respectfulness and civility, on the hint of incest in Charlus's affection for him, and on the worry of some acquaintances that the baron might even adopt him (III 242) - the MS now moved into the plan for Charlus's 'execution' and remained in the dramatic action. Santois's refusal of an invitation from friends of Mme Verdurin because Charlus could not go kindled the Patronne's fury, and her desire to 'enlighten' Santois; and once Charlus, who enjoyed publicly showing his intimacy with the young man, had taken him to one side, she explained to Brichot the need for a serious warning: but 'cette exécution' was better left until after the concert, for fear of upsetting Santois (III 228, 230, 243-45).

Santois performed (a lock of hair falling, as now, at a well-timed moment), and reminded Marcel of Balbec, of the 'deux côtés' of Combray, and of the parallels between Santois's relationship with Charlus and Mlle Vinteuil's with her friend;

subsequently, the violinist was engaged by some of the guests (III 248, 251, 264-65, 273). Charlus waxed enthusiastic over the playing, ignorant of the fact that, in Mme Verdurin's words to Brichot, M. Verdurin was on the point of drawing his 'Dulcinée' aside; Brichot, who was both friendly with the baron and amiable to Santois, discussed with Marcel Charlus's feelings, and the coming execution, in sympathetic tones; and Charlus came up to enthuse once more over the playing and to comment ecstatically on the falling of the lock, Brichot all this time worrying that he might try to get back to Santois (III 275, 279-80, 282-83, 287-88, 290, 294-95).

The successive revelations then took place, both M. Verdurin's and, more clumsily, his wife's; and Santois, with tears in his eyes, was forced to feign surprise and hide his shame, though redder, and sweating more, than if he had played all Beethoven's sonatas in a row, 'et dans ses yeux montaient des pleurs que le maître de Bonn ne lui aurait certainement pas arrachés' (III 309-10). Mme Verdurin alleged that not only was he 'la fable du Conservatoire', but that he had also been called 'mon protégé', even 'mon domestique', by Charlus; and when the baron returned, Santois shouted: 'Laissez-moi, je vous défends de m'approcher', leaving him thunderstruck. Unfortunately for Santois, the Queen of Naples, whom he had wished to meet, here returned and made her second exit with Charlus, allowing no such introduction to take place (III 311-14, 316-17, 319-22).

This, apart from a brief mention (III 332), was all one saw or heard of Santois in the MS until very late in La Fugitive, when he reappeared as the object, now, of Saint-Loup's love. The letters signed 'Bobette' proved to be from the 'violoniste-chroniqueur dont nous avons parlé', and although Jupien, indignant, believed the liaison had been initiated by Santois, Marcel remembered a comment Robert, for his part, had once made on the violinist's resemblance to Rachel, and speculated that it might not have been solely 'méchanceté' or rancour, but also self-interest, that made Santois turn to Saint-Loup, who gave him financial support (III 670, 682, 684-86). Whatever the case, and despite Santois's daily demands for more money, Saint-Loup would relate thinly-disguised details about the love this former was supposed to have for him; eventually, he repeated to Gilberte what Santois had told him about Charlus (III 701-2, 703, 705-6).

Santois next appeared in the war-chapter, in four main capacities. In the first, a subdued comparison, he was said to have been, once, the centre of attraction in Mme Verdurin's salon in the same way as talk of the war now was (III 730). In the second, he was held up as a representative of the French of Saint-André-des-Champs, who fell into two divisions - one the Santois branch, the other the Françoise branch - both of which met again at the frontier (III 739). Principally, he acted in the MS as the 'interprète inlassable' of Charlus's Germanism, having managed to keep that place in the newspapers and in society which Charlus had found for him, and wrote chronicles with such titles as '"Les mésaventures de la Baronne"' just before the war, and during it '"Frau Bosch"' (III 766-67). Fourth and last, Marcel observed that the man from the abattoirs and 'Maurice' both looked somewhat like Santois, and wondered whether his relations with Charlus might have been platonic, love having the power to make the lover give up his desire itself (III 817-18). Santois reappeared briefly, though not in person, during the aesthetic meditation and the 'bal costumé', first to illustrate the subjectivity of perception, in so far as he and a bus-driver were objects of love for Charlus (III 912),[1] and finally, as during the Vinteuil Septet, to be cited as a connection between disparate elements in Marcel's life (III 972, 1029-30).

The skeletal attributes of the violinist were therefore the same in the MS as they are at present, in that he had risen from a servant family attached to Marcel's uncle, he was not at pains to be respectful ('fils d'une race qui a fait la Révolution'),[2] he was a talented virtuoso, and he infatuated Charlus. But he emerged from the MS as the object of Charlus's love more than anything else; in as much as he had a character, he was empty-

---

1 See II 716 n.1.

2 See above, p. 172.

headed, temperamentally unartistic (playing cards, rather than music),[1] and coquettish: he was, in fact, a mediocre, even a simple, good-looking young man. The only point at which he came alive was in his outbursts to Marcel,[2] and perhaps in the articles written during the war, although even here there was a certain anonymity in Proust's treatment. Santois's worst trait was a childlike rudeness, discernible in his reactions to Charlus and blossoming fully in his high-handed manner with the Cambremers, understandable in the first case and, in the second, springing merely from a gullible belief in Charlus's summary social judgements.[3] It is true that the probably early 'dame en rose' sequence of the proofs mentioned his 'terribles défauts', but the reader was given no concrete examples of these, and, after thus skimming over them, the passage was full of praise.[4] All in all, the first Santois may have had his proletarian pride, but he was not insolent or base, and was a pleasant, though weak, character who was not clearly delineated: he may stand in the same relation to the present Morel as the prototype of Albertine (usually called Maria, according to M. Bardèche[5]) does to the much more complex and sometimes baffling

---

1 See above, p. 178.

2 II 1065-66; see above, p. 179.

3 See above, pp. 177, 179-80.

4 See above, p. 176.

5 See particularly Bardèche's vol. I, p. 299; vol. II, pp. 25, 27, 29 n.1, 31, 32, 34, 36, 37 n.1.

figure now in the novel.

Proust must have felt that, in himself, Santois needed more definite outlines, and must have seen in him, too, both the possibility of exploring certain phenomena increasingly interesting him and the scope to create a further series of links in the novel. He picks out this late dual rôle himself in his Baudelaire article, writing that he has confided to 'une brute, Charles Morel', the median ground between Sodom and Gomorrha[1] - although there is more to be seen in the changed Morel's character than this rather summary placing of Proust's implies. At any rate, during the war and until the end of his life, he paid a great deal of attention to this young parvenu - sometimes using almost the same words in different places to emphasise the new features -, making him still more the object of Charlus's fascination and attempted tyranny, and above all bringing out his bisexuality, giving him inclinations to volte-face, and divesting him of scruples.

First, Proust dwelt on a side of Morel already there, the likeable Saint-André-des-Champs side, asserting, in the margin of the MS of _Sodome et Gomorrhe_, that Morel's apparent charming simplicity or frankness has its source in 'le génie de l'homme

---

1 'A propos de Baudelaire', in _Contre Sainte-Beuve [...]_, Bibliothèque de la Pléiade, p. 633.

du peuple de France' (II 1061a). And the brief MS statement that the two Saint-André-des-Champs types, 'sous-embranchement Morel et sous-embranchement Françoise', met at the frontier[1] is now elaborated by Proust, albeit with contradictions, in additions about Morel's attitude to the actual fighting: at first he is a deserter (III 730a); then, 'son sang français bouillant dans ses veines comme le jus des raisins de Combray', he enlists, in spite of all Mme Verdurin can do to prevent him (III 768-69a); then, a deserter once more, he is sent back to the front, 's'y conduisit bravement', and is eventually decorated (III 852-53a).[2]

Second, Marcel's attitude to his old acquaintance is modified. As we have seen, the narrator was in the MS 'animé d'intentions bienveillantes pour lui':[3] Proust corrects this on the typescript to the less enthusiastic 'sans méchanceté pour lui' (II 1060b). And, shortly after the beginning of the Sodome et Gomorrhe Verdurin soirée, he inserts the passage stressing Marcel's tolerance of Morel - a tolerance said to be inherited from his grandmother - as if to imply that this is now rather more necessary! (II 909-11a, p. 911).[4] Indeed, the baseness and ingratitude referred to in this same addition do

---

1 See above, p. 183.

2 See also II 1062-63a, p. 1062.

3 See above, p. 179.

4 Marcel comments on this tolerance and freedom from rancour in himself à propos of Bloch too: I 740-48a, p. 746.

eventually personally affect Marcel when, overhearing Morel's abuse of his fiancée, he is thrown into a state of agitation, even saying that his heart is beating violently and that the violinist's words 'm'avaient bouleversé' (added in a layer to the La Prisonnière MS: III 162-64a, pp. 163-64). In spite of this, riding the vicissitudes of Morel's new amatory career and the unsavoury impulses the additions bestow upon him, a certain sympathy almost always shows in Marcel's comments.[1]

More directly involved with Morel, Charlus's feelings are also developed in the revision. The MS depiction of his love for Santois did not, except in the pretended duel episode, convey a sense of turbulence: certainly he wished for physical proximity to Santois (for example during the card-game), was downcast, even wept, when the young man was short with him, and felt a 'sadique volupté' in talking of him as he would of a well-behaved child.[2] But it seemed to be rather the paternal nature of this love that Proust wanted to stress,[3] more than any urgent anxiety or anguish. Now, however, in three additions he brings into doubt whether the relations between the two were platonic or not (II 987-93a, p. 993; II 1011a; II 1032b);[4] and the baron's other emotions are exacerbated. Charlus, demonstrably not understanding how to deal with Morel (II 1061-

1 See also II 861b.

2 See above, pp. 178-79.

3 See above, pp. 178, 181.

4 See also III 817-18a. Cp. the brief MS discussion (III 817-18), noted above, p. 184.

63a, II 1062a, II 1062-63a), is said to have been much humiliated by 'certaines scènes' (II 1068-69a, p. 1068); he play-acts with him when they go out for meals (II 1006a); he showers curious gifts on Morel, whose unappreciative, even violent, responses 'plongeaient M. de Charlus - jadis si fier, maintenant tout timide - dans des accès de vrai désespoir' (II 1011a); and he builds him a 'pigeonnier', flattered to do so in spite of Morel's humble extraction, but also because he is 'surexcité' by his protégé, who recounts to him the many propositions he receives (II 1059-60a, II 1059a). This provoking, deliberate or accidental, of Charlus's jealousies recurs in _Le Temps retrouvé_ with the addition of those passages in which the baron threatens to revenge himself (III 779-80a) and later discovers to his sorrow that he has a rival in M. d'Argencourt (III 852-53a). Finally, it is Charlus's love for Morel that is held at least partly responsible for his social decline (III 1018-19a).

The numerous sequences in which Morel's life emerges as shadowy and impenetrable also bear directly, of course, on the new frustrations in Charlus's love for him; I shall discuss these a little later.[1] Meanwhile, Proust adds an unexpected dimension to the young man's feelings for Charlus. What was mere irritation in the first Morel may largely remain so, but it is, on occasions, now combined with actual fear of his protector. The secret Morel confides to the narrator in _Le_

1 Below, p. 199.

Temps retrouvé, that he is too frightened to visit Charlus, and Marcel's later discovery of the baron's indeed murderous intentions, are late (III 803-6a). And Proust added to the Sodome et Gomorrhe typescript the long Maineville episode which shows Charlus 'fou de jalousie' - his feelings are like a sculpted mountain-range 'où se tordaient [...] la Fureur, la Jalousie' - and which ends with the portrayal of Morel as so terrified that he looks like one dead, and the next day rushes away in a panic at the sight of a photograph of Charlus (II 1075-81a, pp. 1080-81; II 1078b; II 1081-82a).[1]

The revision also brings Morel's artistry to the fore. The MS told us only that he had the first prize of the Conservatoire and that, according to Charlus, he played like a god;[2] we knew too that he wrote, but the only illustrations of this were his scurrilous and heavy-handed attacks on Charlus.[3] Now, however, we actually see more of Morel's playing: where at the La Raspelière soirée he had simply settled down to a card-game, he does, in the final version, play to the 'fidèles', although

---

1 Both the sculpture and the death imagery are noted above, Ch. 2, pp. 121 n.1, 114 respectively. For other additions bringing out Charlus's feelings for Morel, see II 901d; II 901-2a; II 914-15a; II 915a; II 964a; II 1037a; II 1039b; II 1043-44a; II 1047-48a,b; II 1047b,c; II 1060-61a; II 1066b; II 1067-68a; II 1073-74a; II 1074-75a; II 1075a; III 44a; III 45-47a; III 51b; III 208a; III 210-11a; III 213-14a; III 241-42a; III 330b; III 525-26a,n.; III 597-98a; III 819-20a.

2 See above, p. 174, and III 287.

3 See above, pp. 180-81, 183-84.

with some trickery (II 953-54a, II 954-55a). And both here and elsewhere Marcel discusses the limitations of his talent, saying that his art

> n'était guère qu'une virtuosité admirable, mais me faisait (sans qu'il fût, au sens intellectuel du mot, un vrai musicien) réentendre ou connaître tant de belle musique (II 909-11a, p. 911),

and concluding that Charlus will give Morel, 'merveilleusement doué pour le son et la virtuosité, précisément ce qui lui manquait, la culture et le style' (II 953-54a, p. 953). Indeed, this side of Morel is used to extend the implications of an important problem as yet unresolved by the narrator. Marcel has just, in an MS addition to La Prisonnière, been pondering the rôle of technical ability in the composition of music, reflecting that, if this is what lies at the bottom of its apparent originality, then art is no more real than life (III 161-62a): in the next addition, made on the same MS, his thoughts move to Morel's virtuosity, and, perhaps implying connections, he gives an example (enacted that very afternoon) of the violinist's lack of self-control (III 162-64a). And Saniette's interesting, if timidly ventured, suggestion that Morel's virtuosity runs counter to the spirit of the work he is playing was also inserted on the MS (III 265-66a,n.).[1] Morel's 'literary' capacities too are extended from the invective against Charlus to calumny of the comtesse Molé (III 220-21a), and he acquires

---

1 For further discussions of this virtuosity, and for musical advice which Charlus gives Morel, see II 1006-7a; II 1009-11a; II 1029-34a, pp. 1032-33.

an entirely new gift, that for mimicry and pastiche. The information (reproduced only in the Pléiade edition notes) that 'Santois imitait Bergotte à ravir' is late (III 700n.6: III 1120a), and so is the explanation for, and ultimate condemnation of, his written style, which derives from Bergotte's speech:

> Cette fécondation orale est si rare que j'ai voulu la citer ici. Elle ne produit, d'ailleurs, que des fleurs stériles (III 767-68a,n.).[1]

Santois's social position was unambiguously defined in the MS. He was of a servant family, had a certain class-pride, and eventually, thanks to Charlus, achieved and maintained a position in higher society.[2] But there was no indication of the energetic, and sometimes heated, feelings that Morel has about his own status: Santois's rudeness to the Cambremers was inspired by credulity rather than by the specific desire to advance or to prove his position. What Proust now overlays on this character is a much sharper awareness of his prestige, of his advantages, and of actions which may threaten these; at the same time, discrepancies appear in his generally disrespectful attitudes.

Thus, although Santois assumed a cavalier tone with the narrator in the early draft of the concert (I 981), Proust now,

---

1 For Morel's writing, see too III 767a,b,c; III 768-69a, p. 768; III 775-76a. In two of the late passages, Proust stresses Morel's lack of taste: II 264-67a, pp. 264, 266; III 131-36a, p. 134.

2 See above, pp. 183-84.

in the Côté de Guermantes addition describing his visit (II 264-67a), emphasises his pleasure in using the second, not the third, person to Marcel, writes that he 'tint [...] à couper le câble avec la domesticité d'où il sortait', being 'très "arriviste"', tells us of his first attempts to penetrate 'le monde "aristo"', and, more immediately, reveals his shame about his origins in the request to Marcel not only for discretion in front of Jupien's niece, but also for some such form of address as 'cher grand artiste'. This is not the only unabashed demand the aspiring parvenu now makes of Marcel, since the passage in which he is also asked to imply that Morel's father was 'l'intendant de domaines si vastes, que cela le faisait presque l'égal de vos parents' seems to have been an added one (II 909-11a, p. 909); and, although Mme Verdurin did tell Morel in the MS of La Prisonnière that Charlus had referred to him as 'mon domestique' (III 314), the final incitement was added in the margin and on a layer:

> il nous raconte, en se tordant, que si vous désirez la croix, c'est pour votre oncle[1] et que votre oncle était larbin (III 314-16a, p. 315).[2]

Morel's jealousy over the position he holds with Charlus, and his fear that this may be usurped by others, are late too (II 1068-69a; II 1069a,b; II 1107a); but by far the most

---

1 This should no doubt be 'père' (Proust's slip).

2 See also II 861e; III 279a; III 283g; III 301e; III 309b; III 311-12a, p. 311; III 312b; III 314-16a; III 316c; III 320a,b.

important new sources of social conceit or worry are his Conservatoire prize and the violin class. This prize, as I have said, was mentioned in the MS, and Santois did interrupt Charlus on the subject; but in the present text it is with 'un sourire satisfait' that he lets Marcel know of it, rather than imparting the information more or less neutrally, as he originally had[1] (II 264-67a, p. 264); and Proust added all those passages in which Morel betrays anxiety about the opinion of the violin class, or is said to value this, and his artistic reputation, more highly than even money and the aristocracy (II 1009-11a, p. 1010; II 1011a; II 1029-34a, pp. 1033-34;[2] III 49b; III 193-97a, p. 196). Whereas in the MS it was Santois's fear of the consequences of the duel on his life in the <u>regiment</u> that made him so willingly accede to Charlus's demands (II 1067), in an addition it is the class, by its links with the regiment, that becomes once again the main cause of apprehension (II 1069-71a, pp. 1070-71). And Proust gave him too the pride in his Conservatoire reputation that makes him refuse to take another name, for his own is inseparably associated with his prize and therefore impossible to modify (II 1011a; II 1062a; II 1062-63a).[3]

The new Morel's ambition, then, is to become, 'avec une respectabilité intacte, maître du jury de violon aux concours

---

1 See above, p. 174.

2 (Here the flute or counterpoint classes, not the violin class.)

3 See also III 310b.

de ce prestigieux Conservatoire' (II 1029-34a, p. 1034), and Proust added to Le Temps retrouvé the fulfilment of this desire for impeccable respectability (III 956b,n.; III 991b,n.). However, he attributed to the violinist another characteristic which rounds out this later picture of unmitigated, if sometimes naïve, self-seeking: he bestowed on Santois/Morel an unshakeable admiration for Oncle Adolphe and for everything that surrounds him:

> Le jeune Morel avait beau chercher à s'évader de ses origines, on sentait que l'ombre de mon oncle Adolphe, vénérable et démesurée aux yeux du vieux valet de chambre, n'avait pas cessé de planer, presque sacrée, sur l'enfance et la jeunesse du fils
> (II 264-67a, p. 265).

And Morel's enthusiastic assurances that 'dans tout Paris il n'existe rien qui vaille le 40 bis' (a house of Adolphe's) were added only on the typescript of Sodome et Gomorrhe (II 1057-58a).[1]

The self-satisfaction accompanying not only Morel's use of the second person to Marcel, but also the information about the violin-prize, shows that Proust has made him more snobbishly

---

1 See also II 1056b,c; II 1056-57a.
J.-F. Revel, in his discussion of snobbery in A la recherche, says that all the characters must have one object of snobbery, and that 'Morel lui-même, si veule, si peu affecté par le mépris d'autrui, á pourtant, lui aussi, son secret talon d'Achille: la sacro-sainte classe de violon du Conservatoire' (Sur Proust, p. 79): one could certainly add to this the equally strong veneration for Oncle Adolphe. J. Rousset, incidentally, most perceptively remarks that Morel resembles Odette not merely in that they are both virtuosos (she for clothes, he for the violin), but also in that both 'prennent leur source' in Adolphe's flat ('Proust. A la recherche du temps perdu', in Forme et Signification (Paris, 1962), p. 148; see also p. 149).

complacent; what else happened to his personality? He is now haughty towards the narrator, although able to display, when convenient, the greatest deference (II 861e; II 909-11a; II 909c; II 1031-32a, p. 1032); and the addition to Le Côté de Guermantes shows, both in the attempts to break into high society and the more successful scheme to impress Jupien's niece favourably, a haste to profit by Marcel from which Santois was free (II 264-67a, pp. 265-66). Proust brought out this tendency to use others in an earthier manner, mentioning Morel's mercenary qualities in many of the later passages, and making specific additions to illustrate them. Once the young man has met Charlus, an insertion tells the reader that 'l'offre des 500 francs avait dû remplacer pour Morel l'absence de relations antérieures' (II 862a). Other additions show him wishing to supplant Jupien in the belief that Charlus gives him money (II 1006-9a, p. 1008), demanding twenty-five thousand francs at a time from the baron (II 1074-75a), and enjoying the prospect of the night at Maineville with the prince de Guermantes, which offers him the chance both to earn money and to be surrounded by partially undressed women (II 1075-81a, p. 1078). He borrows 5,000 francs from Nissim Bernard (III 51-54a, pp. 53-54) and regrets the rupture with Jupien's niece in as much as it may entail the loss of his income from Charlus (III 195-96a). And the affirmation that Morel would do anything for money, - would plunge into misery, even into mourning, whole families were it in his interest to do so - forms part of a long handwritten insertion into the typescript (II 1029-34a, p. 1033).[1]

This provides some introduction to the other changes. Santois was simply coquettish; but Proust now builds up a picture of overt sensuality, eventually sadism, telling us in the important 'dame en rose' insertion that Morel 'semblait avoir, à côté de l'ambition, un vif penchant vers des réalités plus concrètes' (II 264-67a, p. 266) and adding to the typescript of Sodome et Gomorrhe his wish, outlined to Charlus, to seduce a 'jeune fille bien pure' and then leave her (II 1006-9a, p. 1008).[2] Almost immediately following, Proust wrote into the same typescript the discussion from which it emerges that one of Morel's not dissimilar enjoyments is to 'aller chercher des petites filles' (II 1011a).[3] And all the descriptions of him as base and primitive, odd, 'neurasthénique', mad, even violent, are late ones. The very first Sodome et Gomorrhe addition of any substance about the violinist warns of his 'étranges retours à sa sauvagerie primitive et aveugle'

1 (This passage was mentioned briefly above, p. 194.) For other additions in which Morel tries to acquire money, or Charlus gives it to him, see: II 1006-9a, p. 1006 (see here also II 1027-28a); II 1059-60a; II 1063b; II 1075-81a, p. 1077; III 162-64a, p. 163.

2 See also III 51-54a, p. 51.

3 See also III 599-600a.

(II 909-11a, p. 911); his nature is now 'folle dans son genre, mais ingrate et mesquine', and Charlus's generosity provokes in him only 'une sécheresse ou une violence toujours croissantes' (II 1011a). The neurasthenia itself is introduced in shortly following insertions on the typescript:

> Parallèlement à cette bassesse de nature, il y avait une neurasthénie compliquée de mauvaise éducation (II 1063a,b);

it combines with the 'méchanceté à la fois violente et sournoise' to bring about the scenes in which Marcel overhears him abusing his fiancée and is led to comment baldly on the animality of his behaviour (III 162-64a; III 193-97a, pp. 193-94, 196-97; III 197a). It is at this point that occurs the image of Morel as the perpetrator of unspeakable misdeeds:

> cette méchanceté [...] que Morel avait à la fois, disait-on, laissé éclater et dissimulée dans les milieux successifs, les différentes villes par où il avait passé, et où on ne parlait de lui qu'avec un frisson, en baissant la voix, et sans oser rien raconter (III 162-64a, p. 163).

This image, here rather comically gangster-like, is always more hinted at than elaborated in the novel.[1] Perhaps Proust meant to remind us of it, and the other unpleasant traits, at the very end of <u>A la recherche</u>, since he came back to the addition in <u>Le Temps retrouvé</u> about Morel's eventual respectability[2] and inserted further, after the reference to his morally valuable and universally esteemed evidence in a celebrated trial: 'et

1 See below, pp. 202-3, and Chapter 6, pp. 282-83.

2 Already cited, above, p. 195.

qui avait entraîné la condamnation de deux personnes' (III 956c,n.).[1]

However, some of these features are modified by Proust himself, either in the same or in further additions which show that he wanted to reveal in Morel what is to be so important in Albertine: varying angles of vision from others, and contradictions. These either surround Morel's activities, or seem to be embodied in his very character. Charlus's picture of the young man's life is now uneven and cloudy:

> Morel ne pouvait ainsi s'empêcher de présenter une image de sa vie, mais volontairement, et involontairement aussi, tellement enténébrée, que certaines parties seules se laissaient distinguer
> (II 1075-81a, p. 1077);[2]

the only trace of this in the MS was Santois's brusque 'j'ai à faire', hardly nebulous.[3] Linked with this new opacity is the imperfect or fragmentary knowledge attributed to Morel himself (II 1029-34a, p. 1033; II 1033a; III 162-64a, p. 164); but the central paradoxes, or strange gaps, are those in his personality. These are adumbrated in the first main addition to Sodome et Gomorrhe, which describes Morel's fluctuations between disdain and charm in his treatment of the narrator (II 909-11a, p. 911).

---

1 See also II 1032b; II 1029-34a, p. 1033. Morel maintains that algebra is good for his neurasthenia in II 1075-81a, pp. 1077-78, and III 162-64a, p. 163. Bardèche, with shades of melodrama, brings alive the 'névropathe' side of Morel (vol. II, pp. 245-46).

2 See also III 162-64a, pp. 162-63.

3 See above, p. 179.

The long tale of Howsler's contrived dismissal, inserted into the Sodome et Gomorrhe typescript, breaks off to insist that 'je ne veux cependant pas laisser le lecteur sous l'impression d'une méchanceté absolue qu'aurait eue Morel. Il était plutôt plein de contradictions, capable à certains jours d'une véritable gentillesse' (II 1029-34a, p. 1031), and concludes:

> Il ressemblait à un vieux livre du Moyen Age, plein d'erreurs, de traditions absurdes, d'obscénités, il était extraordinairement composite. [...] Mais c'est peut-être encore trop de logique dans la cervelle de Morel que d'y faire sortir les unes des autres les contradictions. En réalité, sa nature était vraiment comme un papier sur lequel on a fait tant de plis dans tous les sens qu'il est impossible de s'y retrouver [...] (II 1029-34a, pp. 1032, 1034).[1]

And a number of the other additions underline similar polarities, showing Morel veering between sullen aggression and open affection, even on one occasion feeling shame for a display of 'brute' anger (III 193-97a, pp. 193-94).[2]

As a final ambiguity - that which Proust himself brought out in the Baudelaire article - the violinist is now made bisexual. The MS gave no clear idea of his sexual orientation, but he could be assumed to be an invert, and certainly there

---

1 A long layer attached to the TS page after this addition (n.a.fr. 16741:37) continues to describe Morel's volatility and sensuality, saying that his attention is distracted too easily for him really to carry through any evil projects: 'Il avait été me dit plus tard son père soigné dans son enfance comme un peu idiot et je le crois volontiers' (words underlined above-line).

2 And III 197a. See also II 1061-63a, p. 1062; II 1063a,b; III 51c.

was no mention of any feeling for women. Now, however, not only is he attracted to Jupien's niece, an innovation I discuss a little later, but Proust also specifically comments on his bisexuality, at once exploiting, for example, the double entendre in Mme Verdurin's remark that social origins are unimportant 'Pourvu qu'on soit d'art, pourvu en un mot qu'on soit de la confrérie':

> La façon dont Morel en était - autant que j'ai pu l'apprendre - était qu'il aimait assez les femmes et les hommes pour faire plaisir à chaque sexe à l'aide de ce qu'il avait expérimenté sur l'autre
> (II 909-11a, p. 910; II 910a).

The later Morel points out lesbians to Charlus, maintaining that he possesses special insights in this respect: 'Et qui eût regardé en ce moment Morel, avec son air de fille au milieu de sa mâle beauté, eût compris l'obscure divination qui ne le désignait pas moins à certaines femmes qu'elles à lui' (II 1006-9a, pp. 1007-8). The direct discussion of this bisexuality in La Prisonnière was added at two stages: in the first expansion (earlier, since the name Santois is used), Proust tells us that Charlus is not jealous of Morel's relations with women (III 216-19a; III 217a); but in the later one (where 'Morel' is used), Charlus, reading a letter to the young man from Léa, finds the phenomenon more disturbing (III 214-16a; III 215a). And it is in an addition to the MS of Le Temps retrouvé that Morel eventually returns to heterosexuality and to fidelity

(III 780-81a; III 781a).[1]

Finally, Proust not only elaborated Saint-Loup's relationship with Morel, dropping a hint some 800 pages before its actual discovery (II 973a), telling the reader that Morel is 'reçu comme l'enfant de la maison' (III 700a), and speculating that Morel's dark colouring may play some part in Saint-Loup's attraction to him (III 705a),[2] he also gave the violinist five important new liaisons or partnerships. The first, as is clear by now, is that with the prince de Guermantes - if the abortive skirmishes of the Maineville episode can be characterised as a liaison (II 1075-81a, pp. 1078, 1081; II 1081-82a). The second, less clearly defined, is with Léa (III 214-16a). Third, Morel now bands with the chauffeur, helping him cheat Charlus of money (II 1006-9a, p. 1006), going out with him to find little girls for shady purposes (II 1011a), and laying the complicated plot to have Howsler dismissed and the chauffeur established in his place (II 1029-34a, pp. 1029-31, 1033-34; II 1030a; II 1031a, b; II 1031-32a).[3] (This is the chauffeur who will later

---

1 An interesting aside is reproduced in the Pléiade notes: 'Mais il [Charlus] sentait que cet enfant était déjà un homme; et il ne se trompait pas, car, comme il y a des exceptions à toutes les règles, c'était la première fois peut-être que dans ses amours il allait donner le nom d'homme non plus à un hermaphrodite, mais à un mâle' (II 863 n.2: II 1198a). Proust had added this to the MS just after the pair had met at the station; but he subsequently crossed it out on the typescript (n.a.fr. 16740:6). As can be seen, it casts doubts even on Morel's *bi*sexuality, implying complete heterosexuality.

2 See also III 683-84a; III 757-58a; III 841b,*n*.; III 956b,*n*.

3 Howsler has been introduced in II 895c, II 977c. For other additions about Morel and the chauffeur, see III 17a; III 64-67a, p. 66; III 131-36a, p. 134.

reappear to connive with Albertine.[1]) More noteworthy still, Morel now has an 'understanding' with Albertine herself. Two premonitory remarks appear in additions to Sodome et Gomorrhe - the narrator's complaint that, although Morel had made a bad impression on him, 'hélas! je ne sus pas assez tôt en tenir compte' (II 909b); and the undisguised statement of his later discovery that Albertine knew Morel very well (accompanied, however, by a caution about Andrée's veracity) (II 1031-32a; II 1032a). And the full revelation comes in La Fugitive, almost immediately after Morel's and Charlus's added visit to Marcel (which may even have been inserted there to remind the reader of the violinist: III 597-98a): we learn that Albertine and Morel would between them seduce young girls, for 'Tout de suite ils s'étaient compris' (III 599-600a).

However, Morel's most substantial new relationship is the one with Jupien's niece. All phases of this, from the initial attraction (II 264-67a, pp. 266-67)[2] to the engagement (III 44b, III 44-45a, III 47a, b), from the girl's imitation of 'l'être adoré' (III 47-49a) to her recognition of the 'profondeurs de méchanceté et de perfidie' in his nature (III 64-67a, pp. 66-67; III 67a), finally Morel's abuse of her (III 162-64a) and the rupture (III 193-97a; III 208a), were added, some perhaps very

1 See below, Ch. 6, pp. 282-83.

2 See also II 862a,c; II 1006-9a, p. 1009.

late.[1] This affair provides a suitably direct commentary on some of the traits, from the comically thick-skinned to the sadistic, now given to Morel, since it sets him in contrast to a fine sensibility other than Charlus's, concisely demonstrating the nature of his personality with, for example, the plans to persuade his fiancée to enter into schemes of debauchery so that he need not work for a living (III 51-54a, pp. 51, 52, 54), his blank unawareness of her good points (III 44-45a, p. 45), and his return to her to joke about his abandonment of her (III 311-12a).[2]

The principal changes made to Santois/Morel, many of which stand out well in a comparison of the early 'dame en rose' passage[3] with the final one (II 264-67a), are, then, an elaboration of his Saint-André-des-Champs side, together with some modification of Marcel's attitude towards him, and an intensification of Charlus's feelings for him; the limitations of his virtuosity are discussed, new depths added to his social fears and ambitions, and his character on the one hand becomes more distinctively unattractive, on the other hand, so contradictory is he, can betray real charm; he turns to bisexuality, and he

---

1 III 64-67a, for example, was added to the first TS of <u>La P</u>.

2 See also, for Jupien's niece, II 20b,c; II 602d; III 48a; III 49a,b; III 49 <u>n</u>.2-51a.
For other additions about Morel, see II 901c; II 953a; II 957a; II 964c; II 974b; II 1089a; III 42-44a, p. 44; III 212-13a; III 278-79a.

3 See above, pp. 175-76.

conducts liaisons and relationships which were never attributed to Santois, notably that with Jupien's niece.

The reasons for the development are now more evident than they were immediately after the outline of Santois's rôle in the MS.[1] Proust is, as I said, giving this important but unrealised figure an at last satisfactory delineation, and, with the added liaisons, joining threads in the novel; but he is doing more than this. In the person of the virtuoso instrumentalist, he is creating yet another counterbalance to the end of the novel: the new opposition of Morel's technical gifts to Charlus's understanding of music, and the former's talent for pastiche rather than original writing, throw into relief, in a different way from the inserted linguistic abuses, the narrator's final more thorough commitment to his art. Morel's later personality also helps to tighten the structure of the growing novel in two ways. It provides a paradigm for some of the most striking changes to take place in the other characters (which I shall describe in the next two chapters), in its new inclinations to pride, callousness and violence,[2] and its display of a bi-sexuality that is reflected, in the post-1914 additions, in many others;[3] and he stands out, by virtue of the additions, as the single most important object of attraction to those of equivocal sexuality, like the prince de Guermantes and Léa. But, most

---

1 See above, pp. 184-86.

2 See below, Ch. 5.

3 See below, Ch. 6, pp. 283-94.

important of all, his relationship with Charlus now fully complements Albertine's with Marcel, and from this point of view alone, the novel would have been both structurally and psychologically much the poorer had Santois remained the pale figure he was. To attach to Morel contradictory behaviour, and actions or character-traits which have to be interpreted, to a point where he bears comparison with a document full of errors and absurd traditions[1] is to make several crucial associations: these paradoxes not only resemble other such post-1914 'distorted material' as the etymologies or the linguistic manglings of Françoise;[2] they join, above all, the chaotic information Marcel painfully gleans about Albertine's private life. Morel may be a cruder double of Albertine (in that Proust openly attributes sinister deeds or motives to him whilst preferring to keep their presence in Albertine an enigmatic possibility), but certainly the two often parallel each other exactly. Morel's sudden 'grand pied de grue', for example, is close both in content and consequence to Albertine's 'me faire casser le pot', both of which, on the same day, so startle Marcel.[3] And, even if Albertine does not work on Marcel's feelings deliberately, she no doubt seems the same to him, in the provoking of his jealousy, as Morel does to Charlus.

---

1 See above, p. 200.

2 See above, Ch. 2, pp. 91-95; Ch. 3, pp. 131-32.

3 For Albertine, see below, Ch. 6, pp. 281-82.

The expansion of the Morel-Charlus relationship in Sodome et Gomorrhe now, therefore, sets the stage for the events, at the end of the volume and in La Prisonnière, of the Albertine affair, which will also follow a course of attempted possession, interrogation, spying, jealousy, and suspicions about secret meetings. Albertine herself was, as will be seen, elaborated in similar ways to Morel; but her contradictory or bisexual behaviour was already in the MS, whereas at that stage it was entirely absent in Santois.[1]

I shall now sketch out changes in the other characters, some of them, as I have said, surprisingly like those that took place in Morel.

---

1 For Albertine, see below, Ch. 6, pp. 267-83.
Since the post-1914 expansions to the Gilberte affair have been described so lucidly and thoroughly by Feuillerat (although with occasionally questionable general conclusions) (pp. 36-41, 118-22), I have not thought it necessary to explore them in this study.
(I have, however, given explicit page-references for the late passages - above, Ch. 1, p. 24 n.1 - and should like to add to Feuillerat's discoveries the fact that a number of other additions to Sodome et Gomorrhe, clustered for the most part around Albertine's late-night visit, remind the reader of Gilberte further than the MS did, thus inviting comparisons: II 713-14a; II 729-30a; II 737-38a; II 738b,c; II 739a; II 742a; II 746a. See also, for Gilberte, III 505a; III 561a; III 644b; and some of the discussion below, Ch. 5, p. 243, and Ch. 7, pp. 308-9.)
Nevertheless, this would certainly be one place to consider the changes to Gilberte, to Albertine and to Morel all together, and to define tentatively the development in Proust's depiction of love. A careful comparison of the trend of these late passages with the Swann/Odette relationship in 'Un Amour de Swann', complete in 1913, would probably yield a good deal, and serve as a useful corrective to exaggerated claims of radical innovation in Proust's descriptions of love.

5 Some Moral Aspects

In the description of the MSS in Chapter 1, I mentioned at a few points that some individual character-portraits in the early versions do not yet have certain small but important touches now familiar to readers of the final text.[1] This chapter is an attempt to group these new details, where suitable, as moral traits; it is inevitably somewhat fragmented, since, given the number of characters in A la recherche, any full account of what each was like before and after the revision, on the scale of the preceding pages on Morel, would be impossibly long.

The narrative tone of these additions, which can be light-hearted or sardonic as often as it is serious, is more varied than the actual attitudes described, which may be reduced to three preoccupations of Proust's. He was increasingly concerned to describe scenes of investigation and control; acts of cruelty and ill-treatment; and above all, manifestations of extreme pride (it is these expansions that are most often comic). He made too a number of additions about nationalistic prejudice

---

1 See, e.g., pp. 42-43, 46-47.

or anti-semitism, and a brief account is also given here of these.

Attempts to control others' lives, or lack of response towards death and illness, were evident in Du Côté de chez Swann;[1] but, as in the case of the caricatural descriptions,[2] it can be said that some of Proust's most arresting examples of characters' efforts to impose their will on others, or their most extended displays of indifference towards, even glee about, pain, do belong to the post-1914 period.

INVESTIGATION AND CONTROL

Proust's renewed interest in investigation is noticeable, for example, in the addition of a number of relatively mild passages about spying and close scrutiny. The fright the narrator's mother takes on seeing, in the salon of a distant cousin, 'le meilleur ami du plus susceptible de mes oncles auquel il allait rapporter que nous n'avions pas commencé notre tournée par lui' was not in the 1914 A l'ombre (I 486a). Proust came back to Saniette's unwelcome visit, already added to the MS of

---

1 See, e.g., Tante Léonie's treatment of Françoise (I 117-18); or the discussion of sadism after the Montjouvain scene (I 163-65).

2 See above, Ch. 2, pp. 86-87.

Sodome et Gomorrhe (II 1022-24a), and worked in still further, on the typescript and later, his uncontrollable and fascinated scrutiny of a 'lettre quelconque' of Marcel's (II 1024a,b).[1] And, as has been mentioned in the context both of Proust's later imagery and of Charlus's new feelings for Morel, the important scene in which Morel, aware that he is being spied on, looks like one dead, forms part of a long addition to the Sodome et Gomorrhe typescript (II 1075-81a, pp. 1080-81).[2] As for Marcel himself, some of those occasions of his detailed scrutiny of Albertine or others are late ones, as when, yearning to be accepted by the other Balbec holiday-makers, 'je les regardais avec une curiosité passionnée [...] je suivais tous leurs mouvements' (I 674-75a), or when much later, in La Fugitive, 'Tout mon espoir était qu'Albertine fût partie en Touraine, chez sa tante où en somme elle était assez surveillée' (III 431b). One addition to the first typescript of La Prisonnière which ran:

> Sans me sentir le moins du monde amoureux[3] d'Albertine [...] j'étais resté jaloux d'elle

was later corrected by Proust to end: 'j'étais resté préoccupé de l'emploi de son temps' (III 21c); and Marcel's arrangement to have his last captive girl watched by a friend, and the episode of the little girl which culminates with Marcel himself being

---

1 See here III 73-74a for Marcel's curiosity about Albertine's letters.

2 Referred to above, Ch. 2, p. 114, and Ch. 4, p. 190.

3 First version: 'Sans être amoureux le moins du monde'.

watched by the police, were both added to the MS of La Fugitive (III 677a,n.; III 432c,n.; III 442-45a, pp. 443-44; III 443a; III 446-47a).[1]

These additions show the onlooker, feared or actual, at least keeping his distance; but several of the more concerted attempts in the novel to explore the doings of some elusive subject were also late. Swann's mechanical persistence in investigating Odette's life long after his love and jealousy have died down was, for example, added to A l'ombre after 1914 (I 523-24a). And Marcel now indulges in more questioning, either of others or of Albertine. Proust added to La Prisonnière the sudden pinning-down of Albertine about Gilberte

---

1 The concierge's spying plays a considerable part in the late story of the valet Poullein, an expansion discussed below, pp. 228-30.
A certain number of insertions refer to political spying, especially additions to the war-chapter: thus Marcel's initial belief that Jupien's hotel is a 'lieu de rendez-vous à des espions' was added (III 810-11a; III 811a; III 812b), and the large hotels are now said to be peopled with spies who note the news telephoned by Bontemps (III 733-34a, p. 734). See also II 582-83a, p. 582; III 830-31a. For other additions in which spying or detailed scrutiny are apparent, see: I 489-90a; II 215a; II 558-59a, p. 559; II 610-13a, p. 613; III 434-35a,n.; III 630-39a, p. 633; III 748-50a, pp. 748-49; III 834-36a, p. 836.
Possibly connected, numerous references to the police were added: see II 752d; II 862-63a, p. 863; II 1057-58a; II 1075-81a, pp. 1078, 1081; III 24a; III 162-64a, p. 163; III 216-19a, pp. 216-17; III 280-82a, pp. 280-81; III 830-31a, p. 831; III 833-34a; III 837c,n.

(III 23c), and, even later, both the characterisation of this brief dialogue as 'ce genre de causeries investigatrices' (III 23d) and its introductory phrase 'Je l'interrogeais à brûle-pourpoint' (III 23d, b). The lines taken by one critic as a comic comment on Marcel's behaviour are new ones:

> Il est déjà difficile de dire "pourquoi avez-vous regardé" telle passante, mais bien plus "pourquoi ne l'avez-vous pas regardée?"
>
> (III 89b);[1]

inserted too is the well-known conclusion about 'les résultats négatifs de mes incomplètes enquêtes': 'aucun être ne veut livrer son âme' (III 150-51a). The difficulty the jealous lover has in obtaining information, and the alleviation of suffering it is hoped investigations will bring, are now stressed (III 288a; III 430a); finally, Proust inserted into <u>La Fugitive</u> the passage describing the survival of Marcel's 'désir de connaître sa vie' even after his love for Albertine has faded away, and his realisation that it would now be possible to question Saint-Loup as well as Gilberte, were it not for the fact that he has lost virtually all curiosity about Albertine (III 599a; III 679a, III 679-80a).[2] (This is not to mention, of course, the long added interrogations themselves, which are

---

1 M. Suzuki, in 'Le comique chez Marcel Proust (II)', <u>BSAMP</u> no. 12 (1962), p. 575.

2 Marcel now also assures Swann he does not know what jealous curiosity is (II 702-3a); see too, for more questioning, I 759-60a, p. 760; II 363b; III 59-61a; III 60c,d; III 62a; III 169a; III 612-14a, pp. 613-14. Norpois on two occasions becomes, comically, inscrutable and frustrating in conversation (with Marcel and his father): I 452-53a, I 455-56a (see also II 244c).

discussed later in connection with Marcel's suspicions about, and apparent proofs of, Albertine's lesbianism. The two outstanding new ones are those mentioned in Chapter 1: the questioning and evasion scene in Sodome et Gomorrhe (II 798-802a) and the quarrel in La Prisonnière (III 333-39a).[1])

An even closer form of interference, however, was developed in the revision of the drafts. Three important references to meddling in others' relationships, with a view to breaking these up, were added to La Prisonnière; perhaps the position of these additions is significant, since, although Marcel is the interfering agent in none of them, this is nevertheless the point of the novel at which his concern to disrupt Albertine's possible unions with others is greatest. Charlus's inclination to 'mettre [...] la zizanie' between Morel and his fiancée (III 47a, III 47-49a, p. 49), and even, 'les soirs où il s'ennuierait, de mettre la guerre entre les époux' (III 49 n.2-51a, p. 51) occurs only in relatively late Morel additions. Mme Verdurin's interfering capacities, firmly established in Du Côté de chez Swann and in the MS of other volumes,[2] now move into new territories. Marcel's fear that she may start some work of intervention between Albertine and himself, and the growing urgency of her need to prevent private friendships in the clan, even at the risk of the 'fidèles' breaking with *her*, were added to the MS in a

---

1 See Ch. 1, pp. 43, 48; and see below, Ch. 6, pp. 270-72.

2 See, e.g., I 190; II 1091-92 without the additions.

margin and on a layer (III 280-82a, pp. 281-82; also III 281 a, b, c); and the reverse side of the possessiveness displayed by both herself and her husband is fully explained only in separately-typed pages in the third typescript:

> L'assiduité aux mercredis faisait naître chez les Verdurin une disposition opposée. C'était le désir de brouiller, d'éloigner. Il avait été fortifié, rendu presque furieux par les mois passés à la Raspelière, où l'on se voyait du matin au soir [...]
> (III 228-30a, pp. 229-30).

In the Verdurins and in Charlus, this desire to interfere is put down to boredom, a cause also implied in Mme de Guermantes's victimisation of her valet.[1]

Such behaviour leads easily to the authoritarian. Again this was, in the early versions, an indispensable character-trait of, for, example, Mme Verdurin's;[2] but Proust now slips in comments - some only brief or humorous, but growing in numbers - on domination, control, or resistance to these. The two speculations that M. Verdurin may be shaking off his wife's 'tutelage' were added to the MS of Sodome et Gomorrhe (II 900a; II 902a). The narrator himself, in four additions, remarks, sometimes incredulously, on Albertine's docility towards him

---

1 See below, p. 230.
For similar attempts to provoke discord, see III 154-55a, p. 154; III 277b. See also III 314-16a; III 315a; III 316a, for Mme Verdurin, and II 997-1006a, pp. 1002-4, for her imposition of her company on Marcel and Albertine; Bloch behaves similarly in I 866-68a; I 869-951a, p. 880.

2 Her domineering traits too were, however, explained or further illustrated in a few additions: II 969-71a; II 971-72a; III 244b,c; III 277-78a; III 278a; III 278-79a; III 984a,n.

(II 1124c; III 157b; III 158b; III 351a),[1] and Proust added to the MS of La Prisonnière two direct references to Marcel's mastery or 'reign'. One is both comic and dramatically ironic: Marcel, at the very end of La Prisonnière, congratulates himself on the '"sévère loi"' which (unfortunately for him, at this point)

> faisait que [...] aucun "timide mortel", fût-ce Françoise, fût-ce Albertine, ne s'aviserait de venir me troubler "au fond de ce palais" où
> une majesté terrible
> Affecte à mes sujets de me rendre invisible
> (III 412b);

and the other arises from his glimpse of the sleeping Albertine:

> je sentis ce demi-cercle immobile et vivant [...] je sentis qu'il était là, en ma possession dominatrice
> (III 365-66a,n.).[2]

More extremely, Proust adds three passages in which Marcel expresses a wish to threaten Albertine or make her fear him, including the aside to the effect that 'La jalousie n'est souvent qu'un inquiet besoin de tyrannie appliqué aux choses de l'amour' (III 91c);[3] and, after Albertine's departure, Marcel now asks himself whether her complete liberty would really have been so very painful to him, assuming a moment later, however, that 'Une fois épousée, son indépendance, elle n'y tiendra pas' (III 422a, b). But perhaps the most transparent indication of Proust's wish to

---

1 For this docility (mentioned in the MS on III 408), see also III 351a; III 370-71a; III 402a (and III 424a); III 405a.

2 Discussed in Ch. 2, p. 114.

3 The other two are II 1097a; III 474-75a, p. 475.

emphasise this element of tyranny in his narrator's feelings may be seen in the fact that on five separate occasions he corrects the MS so that where, in the first version, Marcel was saying that he was frightened Albertine might leave him, he is now saying that he does not want her to have too much liberty. To give only one example: where a layer glued to the MS read simply 'j'avais peur qu'elle me quittât', Proust corrected and expanded this, with an above-line addition, to:

> j'avais peur qu'elle voulût une liberté (je n'aurais pas trop su dire quelle était cette liberté qui me faisait trembler, mais enfin, une liberté telle qu'elle eût pu me tromper, ou du moins que je n'aurais plus pu être certain qu'elle ne me trompât pas) (III 346-47a).[1]

Such corrections as these and the one cited earlier, in which 'jaloux' was changed to 'préoccupé de l'emploi de son temps',[2] show interestingly the meeting-point between moral insights and precise expression.[3]

---

1 The others are: III 344b; III 345a; III 345 n.2: III 1090a; III 361d. See also III 361-62a, p. 362.

2 See above, p. 210.

3 See too III 432a for Albertine's wish for freedom (this, her liberty, etc., are however mentioned in the MS on III 360, 472). She is compared to an untamable wild animal in III 610c. For Marcel, see also II 68-69a; II 804c; II 845-50a, p. 847; II 848d; III 78b; III 333a; III 530a. Mastery or tyranny, or attempts to escape from them, are brought into play too in: I 691-94a, pp. 691-92; II 64-65a; II 285c; II 671b; II 825-26a; II 855c; II 960-62a; III 24b.

CRUELTY AND ILL-TREATMENT

Perhaps as a complement to other newly cruel instincts, Proust added to his novel a few curious passages about pity, some discussing weeping (some, too, not without a measure of irony);[1] but for the most part during the post-1914 period, he staged in his novel, rather than compassion, overtly violent incidents or reactions to them, illustrating callousness towards death or illness, specially inserting smaller references to aggression or to physical violence, and considering in a number of late sequences the rôle of the victim and the relationship between him and his persecutor.

Swann's announcement of his imminent death, and the sweeping aside or weak acceptance of the news by M. and Mme de Guermantes, was, as I have said, always in the MS;[2] but this, and the Verdurins' lack of response to the deaths of Dechambre and the princesse Sherbatoff, were the only memorable examples in the novel, after

---

1 See II 769b; II 777-78a; II 794b; II 953-54a, p. 954; II 1128c; II 1129c; III 480-81a; III 849a,c,d; III 902c,d. References to the Queen of Naples, and implicitly or explicitly to her kindheartedness, increase: II 511b; III 246a; III 247a,b; III 274-75a; III 274a; III 275a; III 282b; III 301e; III 312b; III 313a; III 320a,b; III 321-22a,b.

2 See above, Ch. 1, p. 33.

Combray, of such indifference towards illness and death.[1] It now, however, reappears in numbers of additions. As already mentioned, M. de Cambremer's hilarity over Marcel's choking-fits, and his delighted comparison of these with his sister's, seem to be almost entirely new;[2] less comically, Proust invented an extra character, the marquise d'Amoncourt, solely for the purpose of letting her say, in the margin of the _Côté de Guermantes_ manuscript, that she regrets her father's dying at a moment of the year 'où on a à sa glace des centaines de cartes d'invitations' (II 477a); and he added to the _Sodome et Gomorrhe_ MS Cottard's refusal to dress the arm of an old cook who has cut herself, in such a hurry is he to get to one of the Verdurins' 'mercredis' (II 879-80a, p. 880).[3] Besides making the Verdurins themselves far more resistant to grief, or even sympathy, than they previously were, over both Dechambre and the 'fidèles' in general,[4] Proust added to _Le Temps retrouvé_ the

---

1 For Dechambre see II 899-900, 901, and for the princesse Sherbatoff, III 227-28, 238-39, without additions.

2 They appear in the MS on II 977; but this passage is on quite clean paper (n.a.fr. 16712:127), and refers to what is certainly late everywhere else: see II 926-27a; II 975-76a, p. 976; II 1096-97a; II 1109c,d; II 1124-25a; III 932-34a.

3 Professor E... and the dinner he is rushing to, also of course added, should be remembered here: see above, Ch. 2, pp. 83-84.

4 In II 895-97a, p. 896; II 897-99a, p. 899; II 900a; II 901a; II 928-29a, p. 929. The account of the Verdurins' reactions to the princesse Sherbatoff's death was also expanded slightly: III 228a comments on M. Verdurin's use of the same words as M. de Guermantes on the occasion of Amanien's death; and see too III 239a,b,c; III 240a.

long description of Mme Verdurin's expression of 'douce satisfaction' as she resumes her breakfast croissants whilst reading about the sinking of the Lusitania (III 772-73a);[1] he inserted too, into La Prisonnière, both her light-hearted dismissal of Cottard's death, and M. Verdurin's instructions when Saniette, after a stroke, falls to the ground: '"Faites-le ramener chez lui, ce ne sera rien"', for 'la soirée n'était pas finie' (III 240-41a, p. 241; III 265-66a,n.; III 266a,n.). But, of course, the outstanding new example of this attitude is that of the duc's reaction to the illness and death of Amanien d'Osmond. This tale, written into the novel in additions made to the first and third Gallimard galleys and on documents later than the MS of Sodome et Gomorrhe, must have been composed after 1918.[2] M. de Guermantes mentions his own stomach in one of these Amanien d'Osmond passages (II 588-89b, p. 589); and Proust adds two more references to it on the very last page of the volume (II 597a, b), thus highlighting the duc's preference for his appetites to thoughts about the death of relatives or friends (here, Swann), and foreshadowing Mme Verdurin's love for her croissants, as well as all those dinners for the sake of

---

1 See also III 769a for similar tendencies of Mme Verdurin's during the war.

2 See II 574-76a; II 575b; II 578b,c,d; II 586-88a; II 588-89b; II 588b; II 662a; II 725b.

which others will be pushed to one side.[1]

If certain of the characters are thus more reluctant than before to consider the unsavoury, they also now feel and occasionally practise violent or cruel impulses. In the 1913 Du Côté de chez Swann there was, of course, play on Françoise's killing of the chicken (I 121-22); but the drafts show that when Proust was revising his later text, he amplified the theme of violence further than he had originally planned to, sometimes providing unpleasantly sharp details.

It is an addition to the 1914 galleys of Le Côté de Guermantes which tells us that M. de Guermantes 'avait dans son ménage l'habitude d'être brutal' with his wife (II 235a, b); and, some two hundred pages later, Proust added to the MS the

---

1 M. Raimond sees a 'lien structural constant' in CG, at any rate, not merely between others' deaths and general social pleasures, but, even more narrowly, between 'la mort et le dîner en ville' (his emphasis), in 'Note sur la structure du "Côté de Guermantes"', Revue d'Histoire Littéraire de la France, 71e année, nos. 5-6 (1971), pp. 854-74 (p. 871).
The duc's concern with his stomach was introduced in two earlier additions (II 423a, II 433b).
Proust may have meant Mme de Guermantes's brittle wit in sending the gigantic envelope to Mme Molé to contrast with her lack of feeling for Swann; if so, it is relevant here that all the passages narrating the story of this riposte were worked into the end of CG at a late stage (II 574b; II 585a,b; II 586a; II 588-89a; II 589b; II 590-92a; II 593-94a; II 594a).
For other additions about similar lack of feeling, see II 250-52a; II 335b; II 338-39a; II 340-41a; II 511a; II 1115a; III 951-52a; III 995-99a.

corroborative passage '[...] le duc était si mauvais mari, si brutal même, disait-on, qu'on lui savait gré, comme on sait gré de leur douceur aux méchants, de ces mots "Mme de Guermantes" [...]' (II 416-17a).[1] Moreover, five other characters develop 'haines violentes'. These, springing out suddenly and pointing to 'intermittences' in the personality, are, in their way, volte-faces similar to those described in Chapter 2;[2] but the basic phrase, a new entry into the vocabulary of the novel that is repeated with only minor variations, deserves consideration here. One of these five characters makes only a single appearance - he is the young Peruvian of La Prisonnière with his 'haine atroce', already mentioned (III 266-72a, p. 271);[3] the others are, however, familiar enough. Andrée's 'haines courtes et folles' and Françoise's 'colères haineuses' come in additions to La Prisonnière (III 59-61a, p. 60; III 96-99a, p. 99). An insertion on the MS of Le Temps retrouvé tells us that the war is for Charlus 'une culture extraordinairement féconde de ces haines qui chez lui naissaient en un instant, avaient une durée très courte, mais pendant laquelle il se fût livrée à toutes les violences' (III 775-76a); and that paragraph in which Bloch's nature takes an unusually disagreeable turn was written in only in the margin of the first Gallimard galleys of Le Côté de

1 See also II 437a: Proust, in the first version of a remark about the duc, had written that he was 'rempli de gentillesse et dénué de coeur'; the final version reads: 'attendrissant de gentillesse et révoltant de dureté'.

2 pp. 75-79.

3 Ch. 2, p. 72.

Guermantes: 'Il commençait à avoir des haines, et on sentait que pour les assouvir il ne reculerait devant rien', and indeed, he plans to drive one of his friends to despair (II 228a).[1]

These additions are on the whole confined to the psychological, but Proust made others describing, or referring to, the physically violent. On a comic level, the harking back to Françoise's cruelty at Combray, with her later killing of the rabbit and Marcel's anxious enquiries about the pain she has caused it, was not in the 1914 version of A l'ombre (I 484a); and Proust adds to his novel a number of butchers, for example the one who appears in the midst of the street-cries (III 138b, c), or the young butcher-boy 'timide et sanglant' to whom Françoise takes a liking during the war (III 750a; III 756-57a). Françoise's niece, who appears only in additions, is also 'une bouchère' (II 147-48a; II 148a; II 726-28a, p. 727). And, on the night of the fog, the restaurant-owner's advice to Saint-Loup and Marcel about their menu forms the sole subject of a new parenthesis that does not appear until the third Gallimard galleys:

> (il insista beaucoup pour que nous prissions de la "viande de boucherie", les volailles n'étant sans doute pas fameuses) (II 409a);

Proust must have inserted this aside to provide, underneath the stock phrase 'viande de boucherie', a link with the other new references to butchers. Such additions by suggestion conjure up images of bloodshed and killing: it is interesting that some are

---

1 II 275-76b gives an explanation of Bloch's hatreds.

again associated with Françoise, even if only indirectly.[1] Mme de Guermantes is now shown to have been a crueller little girl than she at first was: in an addition to the MS of Le Côté de Guermantes, she merely drowned cats in her childhood (II 502-3a, p. 503), but Proust corrected this on the third Gallimard galleys to: 'cassait les reins aux chats, arrachait l'oeil aux lapins' (II 503a). And, reworking the MS of Le Temps retrouvé, he made the deaths of both Saint-Loup and, earlier, his comrades, more grotesque than they were before (III 849b and III 753b respectively). Finally, Charlus is given murderous tendencies: not only does he now want to kill Morel,[2] but Marcel's conclusion during the interview scene that

> cet homme était capable d'assassiner et de prouver à force de logique et de beau langage qu'il avait eu raison de le faire

does not appear until the third Gallimard galleys (II 555b).[3]

As often as callousness or direct violence, spectacles of

---

1 These additions can be 'derived' à la Painter from probable events in Proust's own life: see Painter, vol. II, pp. 265-70.

2 See above, Ch. 4, pp. 189-90.

3 Another addition refers to Charlus's 'violences' and 'brutalité postiche' (II 603-4a); see below, pp.234, 248-49, for his new sadistic feelings towards Jews; and this side of his character is amplified too in II 558a,b,c; II 567-68a; II 602b; II 1070a; III 220-21a. For other late references to physical or psychological violence, see: II 181a; II 182-83a; II 279-80a; II 533-34a; II 607-9a, p. 609; II 735-36a; II 736-37a, p. 737; II 917c; III 138d; III 262b; III 346a; III 379-80a; III 815b; III 816-17a; III 842a,b,c,d; III 842-43a; III 843a.
Two brief additions bring out curiosity about (psychological) pain: III 310-11a; III 319a.

persecution find their way into the novel during the post-1914 period. As I mentioned in Chapter 1,[1] the laughing off stage of the timid actress in Le Côté de Guermantes is late, added to the 1914 galleys (II 173-74a; II 174a). The narrator's comments on the pain this episode causes him are therefore also new ones ('l'idée de la méchanceté ayant pour moi quelque chose de trop douloureux'), and another important elucidation of his feelings for the victim was added, in a margin and on a layer, to the MS of La Prisonnière: discussing Charlus's imminent execution, he observes that

> le sentiment de la justice, jusqu'à une complète absence de sens moral, m'était inconnu. J'étais au fond de mon coeur tout acquis à celui qui était le plus faible et qui était malheureux (III 290-91a).[2]

Certainly an increasing number of incidents are of a nature to stir up this soft-heartedness. Proust, in insertions, makes two victims of the duc de Guermantes's insolence go so far as to tremble: the first unfortunate is the Bavarian musician M. d'Herweck, whose only appearance in the novel is this one (II 682-84a, pp. 682-83); and the second is the historian at Mme de Villeparisis's matinée, who merely, in the typescript, 'rougissant encore davantage répondit que non en balbutiant',[3] but now, instead,

---

1 See above, p. 30.

2 For elaborations on Charlus's 'execution', see also III 316-17a; III 317-18a.

3 In a layer glued to the TS (n.a.fr. 16736:257).

> flairant une insolence et ne la comprenant pas, se mit à trembler de tous ses membres (II 237f).

And Proust introduced after 1914 two characters who, humble themselves in one sphere, ill-treat their social inferiors as soon as they find themselves more powerful. In the novel for the first time in the third Gallimard galleys, and invented specially for the purposes of this description, is

> la vicomtesse d'Égremont, que Mme de Guermantes ne pouvait souffrir mais qui, ne bougeant pas de chez la princesse d'Épinay où elle s'abaissait volontairement à un rôle de soubrette (quitte à battre la sienne en rentrant) restait, confuse, éplorée, mais restait quand le couple ducal était là [...]
> (II 163a, see also b);

and the sister of the squinting hotel-boy, who was added only to the typescript of Sodome et Gomorrhe, excretes in hotel-rooms or carriages in order to incommode those of her own former class, telling her brother that there will always have to be 'de[s] malheureux [...] pour que, maintenant que je suis riche, je puisse un peu les emmerder' (II 773a; II 979-80a).[1]

Proust also brought out more clearly than before the rôle of the victim himself, to show him, in the additions, provoking attack by his very blandness, or displaying such irritating qualities that sympathy with the persecutor is not inconceivable:

---

1 Feuillerat remarks (p. 85) that Rachel becomes crueller, and some of the additions do show that Proust wished to make her, inconsistently it is true, an exemplar of similar behaviour: see not only the scene with the timid actress (above, p. 224), but also I 782c; II 169b; II 179d; III 1013-15a; III 1015a.

for example, one hypothesis to explain M. Bloch's constant insults to Nissim Bernard is that he may be 'excité par la bonhomie sans défense de son souffre-douleur' (I 767-79a, p. 774), and Proust added to the MS of Le Temps retrouvé the passage in which Saint-Loup admits that M. de Guermantes is 'un mari terrible', but remarks too that the duchesse 'est une sainte mais [...] le lui fait terriblement sentir' (III 738-39a, p. 738).

However, the unfortunate now more thoroughly and consistently victimised than any other is Saniette. He was always to be in the position of scapegoat, singled out by his timidity, his speech-defect, and his unsuccessful attempts to be witty,[1] and the MS of Sodome et Gomorrhe portrayed him as still shy and aware that he bored (II 871-72, 875, 882). Even before the expansion, he trembled at M. Verdurin's questions about La Chercheuse d'Esprit and was shouted at for his pronunciation, his pedantry, and his inability to play whist, - weakly joking that he knew how to play the piano instead (II 931, 933-34, 936, 957-58); Mme Verdurin referred publicly in the MS to his poverty (II 936), deplored the effect on M. Verdurin of his rages with Saniette (II 973-74), and treated him well so that he would return the next day (II 975-77); and his last two appearances in the MS of the novel were to tell M. Verdurin of the princesse Sherbatoff's death, receiving a 'brutal' reply (III 228), and

1 See I 203, 260, 261, 276-77, 300.

to protest when it was said that the princesse had a 'mauvaise réputation' (III 239).

Proust built considerably on this already solid base, inserting Saniette's unwelcome visits to Marcel (II 1022-24a; II 1023a; II 1024a, b)[1] and adding to the MS of Sodome et Gomorrhe at more than eight points elaborations of the part he plays in the clan. Three new passages explain or illustrate the tendency of his jokes to fall flat (II 872-73a; II 937b; II 938-39a, b, II 939a[2]). Two smaller insertions show M. Verdurin putting 'le malheureux' out of countenance yet again (II 931d; II 933f); and the apparent collusions against him by the Verdurins as a couple are late. Proust added to the MS their seeming kindness in smiling at him or requesting water for him, kindness belied by the parenthesis 'Les généraux qui font tuer le plus de soldats tiennent à ce qu'ils soient bien nourris' (II 930a); and Mme Verdurin now feigns intervention on his behalf, with unlucky results:

> "Voyons, ce n'est pas sa faute [...]. - Ce n'est pas la mienne non plus, on ne dîne pas en ville quand on ne peut plus articuler (II 934b).

The most important passage, that in which Proust attributes the Verdurins' treatment of Saniette to boredom, is also a late one:

---

1 See above, pp. 209-10.

2 II 938-39a may not be a very late passage; see the note to it in Part II. See also II 1022a.

> Mme Verdurin et son mari avaient contracté dans l'oisiveté des instincts cruels à qui les grandes circonstances, trop rares, ne suffisaient plus [...] grâce à sa sensibilité frémissante, à sa timidité craintive et vite affolée, Saniette leur offrait un souffre-douleur quotidien
> (II 900-901a).[1]

And all references to Saniette in La Prisonnière except the two mentioned above are additions, such as the descriptions of the recently acquired greyness of his face, his now constant breathlessness, M. Verdurin's attacks on him for his use of old forms of the language, and his death (III 225b; III 228b; III 265-66a,*n*.).[2]

Two more discoveries to be made in the post-1914 material for Le Côté de Guermantes firmly establish Proust's extended interest in the scapegoat or the victim. First, that curiously stylised tableau of the unhappy people living in Marcel's neighbourhood was added only in the margin of the third Gallimard galleys:

> Ce qui me faisait de la peine, c'était d'apprendre que presque toutes les maisons étaient habitées par des gens malheureux. [...] Toute une moitié de l'humanité pleurait. Et quand je la connus, je vis qu'elle était si exaspérante que je me demandai si ce n'était pas le mari ou la femme adultères (qui l'étaient seulement parce que le bonheur légitime leur avait été refusé [...]) qui avaient raison [...]
> (II 372a).

Second, the entire sorry tale of Mme de Guermantes's arbitrary interference in the meetings between her footman Poullein and

---

1 See also II 1092a for Mme Verdurin's boredom.

2 (He re-appears, alive but ruined, in III 324-27a.) For other additions about Saniette, see II 933e; II 934a,d; II 934-35a; II 957b; II 973-74a; II 974a; III 228c.

his fiancée was late too, added on or between the first and the third Gallimard galleys.[1] (Perhaps the name 'Poullein' was intended to remind the reader of Françoise's chicken, 'poulet'.) The elements holding this sub-plot together, elements to be found on a larger scale elsewhere in the novel, are Françoise's tender feelings for the afflicted footman - it is she who introduces his fellow-employees and himself as worthy of sympathy: 'les concierges sont jaloux, et ils montent la tête à la Duchesse' (II 23g; also II 147c; II 153c; II 307a); the revelation of the real rôle of the spying concierge, at first blamed by everyone, including Marcel, but later seen to be merely a pawn, used by the duchesse 'comme on joua longtemps du cléricalisme, de la franc-maçonnerie, du péril juif, etc.' (II 586-88a, p. 588; also II 62-63a; II 298a); the gullibility not only of the other servants, who quite absolve Mme de Guermantes, but also of Poullein, who 'célébra la bonté de Madame la duchesse' (II 422b) and, when the truth at last becomes inescapable, simply turns pale and seems even now not to understand (II 483-84a; also II 307a; II 586-88a); and the emotions of Mme de Guermantes

---

1 There is, however, an earlier addition, made to the 1914 galleys (margin, n.a.fr. 16760:2viii) and crossed out on the first Gallimard galleys (n.a.fr. 16762:2v), which, inserted after 'de leur maître d'hôtel' (II 28), runs: 'lequel n' était du reste pas destiné à rester longtemps d'après ce que Françoise apprit bientôt de la [...] durée éphémère de chaque équipe de serviteurs dans l'hotel (sic) Guermantes'. The final additions are II 23g; II 62-63a; II 147c; II 153c; II 298a; II 307a; II 372b; II 422b; II 483-84a; II 493a,b,d; II 586-88a; II 587a.

herself. When, having covertly deprived Poullein of his rendez-vous, she is complimented on her generosity to her servants, she makes the ambiguous reply 'Mais je ne fais qu'être avec eux comme je voudrais qu'on fût avec moi' (II 483-84a); she twice either criticises Poullein or ill-treats him following promptly on her own complaints of boredom (II 493b; II 586-88a); and, where Poullein was betraying a joy which she already 'remarqua et comprit' (II 586-88a, p. 587), Proust added still further the lines:

> Elle éprouva comme un serrement de coeur et une démangeaison de tous les membres à la vue de ce bonheur qu'on prenait à son insu, en se cachant d'elle, duquel elle était irritée et jalouse (II 587a).

This sequence epitomises many of the additions described so far in this chapter, in that it shows at work spying, domination, and interference in others' relationships; it hints at the passivity of the victim and demonstrates both the jealousy and the boredom that can lie behind arbitrary tyranny. Mme de Guermantes now resembles Mme Verdurin in her dislike of smoothly-running relationships that are outside her control; but above all, the story mirrors Marcel's relationship with Albertine, in that he hampers her 'outings', whether he is with her or not, and relies on her wanting to keep her 'place' to regulate or thwart her plans.[1]

NATIONALISM AND ANTI-SEMITISM

A note should be made at this point about one expansion only sporadically noted by Feuillerat: that of the subject of the Dreyfus Affair and, more generally, Jews.[2] Proust's aim in elaborating his treatment of the Dreyfus Affair seems to have been twofold: he was exploring, on the one hand, personal reactions to the Affair and anti-semitism, and on the other was revealing its rôle as a catalyst in society. This second broader aspect will be discussed later, together with other social changes,[3] but the place of the additions showing individuals' attitudes is in this chapter; not only do many of

---

1 Cp. Poullein, who 'avait failli aller gifler le concierge, mais s'était contenu, car il tenait à sa place': II 153c. (In fact, Proust added to the novel some passages about servants losing their posts: especially noteworthy are the engineering of Howsler's dismissal by Morel and the chauffeur (see above, Ch. 4, p. 202) and Saint-Loup's proposed tricks to have a servant removed (see above, Ch. 2, pp. 78-79), but see also I 596-97a, p. 597; II 826-27a, p. 826; II 917-18a, p. 918.)
For further additions about the victim or scapegoat, see II 699-702a, p. 701; II 892e; II 950a, II 950-51a; III 943-44a, p. 944.

2 See in Feuillerat, for example, pp. 47, 90, 106, 115, 137.

3 Below, Ch. 7, pp. 298-301.

these attitudes derive from forms of snobbery or national pride, they also, in a more subdued manner, evoke the theme of victimisation, in the person of Dreyfus, and even that of spying, around which the Affair revolved.[1]

These additions equally, of course, illustrate in yet another sphere that partisan appraisal of all types of phenomena which is fundamental in Proust:[2] indeed, two of the important Côté de Guermantes passages explaining that choice of sides in the Affair is based always on emotion, not reason, and describing the immutable and stereotyped nature of such choices, once made, were added to the first Gallimard galleys and to the MS (II 296-98a; II 406a, b, c). And not all the characters become anti-

---

1 Nationalism itself is discussed in the MS of the war-chapter in TR (see above, Ch. 1, p. 55; e.g. III 773, 778), but this discussion is extended with a few additions on chauvinism (and patriotism), including that which Feuillerat again takes to be purely denigratory (Feuillerat, p. 27), describing Bergotte as 'fort exclusivement de son pays' (I 556a). See also II 845-50a, p. 849; III 743a; III 837c,n.; III 841a; III 843b; III 883-89a, p. 888.
Charlus's defeatism or Germanism is somewhat elaborated: II 947a; II 1100b; III 760-62a, p. 761; III 784-93a, pp. 784-89; III 796b; III 797-98a; III 799a; III 800-801a; III 821-22a; III 825-26a; III 830-31a.

2 This view of the rôle of the Dreyfus Affair in the novel has been taken by, amongst others, G. Giorgi in 'L'Affaire Dreyfus dans la "Recherche"', BSAMP, no. 17 (1967), pp. 631-41; E. Carassus, 'L'affaire Dreyfus et l'espace romanesque: de "Jean Santeuil" à la "Recherche du Temps perdu"', Revue d'Histoire Littéraire de la France, 71e année, nos. 5-6 (1971), pp. 836-53 (particularly pp. 845-49). G. Brée interestingly brings out the relative detachment of the narrator of Jean Santeuil, as well as of the mature novel, to the Affair: see her 'Proust et l'Affaire Dreyfus, à la lumière de Jean Santeuil', in Marcel Proust: A Critical Panorama, edited by L.B. Price (Urbana, Chicago and London, 1973), pp. 1-23 (particularly p. 14).

Dreyfusards in the revision. Saniette and Mme Sazerat are now pro-Dreyfus (II 583a; II 151-52a; II 325b) (are there echoes, in the former's persuasion, of the fact that he himself is increasingly a victim?). The duc's change to Dreyfusism under the influence of three charming ladies was inserted into the typescript of Sodome et Gomorrhe (II 739-41a).[1] And Saint-Loup, now openly if temporarily Dreyfusist, seems, surprisingly, not to have been strongly so before the expansion: although Marcel mentioned his Dreyfusism in the MS for the last part of Le Côté de Guermantes (II 582), and the duc commented on it in an addition to the pre-1914 typescript (II 234-39a, pp. 234-36, 238), the 1914 galleys told us of his Doncières friend that 'seul d'eux tous il était partisan de la révision du procès Dreyfus'. Proust then, however, corrected this on the galleys to the present text, in which Saint-Loup is particularly friendly with the same comrade, 'car ils étaient dans ce milieu les deux seuls partisans de la révision du procès Dreyfus' (II 105a).[2]

However, it is anti-Dreyfusism or anti-semitism that is revealed in most of the additions on the topic. Brichot (II

---

1 See too III 782-83a, an exactly similar about-turn in the duc's war-time opinions: this is a very late addition, referring to 1919 as in the past.

2 Also II 105-6a. For this apparent change, see too II 108-117a, pp. 108-9; II 118b; II 147-48a, p. 147; II 164c; II 179a; II 583c. Feuillerat seems to overlook it (see his p. 78). Saint-Loup's change back again was in the SG MS (II 698). See II 164c for Rachel too; for Swann, II 582-83a; II 712a; II 712-13a; II 714a; for Marcel, II 607-9a, p.608.

583a), Mme de Marsantes (II 164c, II 236-37a, II 252-53a, II 582a) and Aimé (I 806-8a, pp. 806-7) now become anti-Dreyfusard; and a large number of insertions show anti-semitism at work, on complex levels of motivation.

The passage in which Bloch himself thunders against the Jews at Balbec is post-1914 (I 738a).[1] And Proust gave Charlus a new trait, adding all the sequences in which the baron shows interest in Bloch, allows free range to his sadistic fantasies about the young man's family, and expatiates at length on the 'curieux goût du sacrilège, particulier à cette race' (II 1101-8a, p. 1105). This last tirade is described by Proust as 'Ce discours antijuif ou prohébreu - selon qu'on s'attachera à l'extérieur des phrases ou aux intentions qu'elles recelaient' (II 1107a), and certainly Charlus's actions belie, and no doubt account for, the expression he gives to the most virulent anti-Jewish feelings in the novel.[2]

These two cases of ambivalent prejudice apart, Proust now brings out a more straightforward anti-semitism. If Mme Sazerat

---

1 Bloch's feelings about his Jewishness are also brought out in I 740-48a, pp. 746-47; II 247-48a; III 317a; III 952-53a, III 953a.

2 For Charlus's interest in Bloch, and Jews, see I 764c; II 190-91a; II 191a; II 287-90a; II 288-89a; II 379-80a; II 381-82a; II 1101-8a, pp. 1104-7; II 1102-4a, p. 1104; II 1104a; II 1105a; III 216-19a, pp. 216, 219. It is implied in II 505b that M. de Châtellerault, another invert, is also attracted to Bloch.
This 'anti-semitism' of Charlus's is a correlative to his religious pride, equally an entirely added feature. See below, pp. 248-50.

is a Dreyfusard, she is anti-semitic too (II 289-90a); and it is in an interpolation on the Côté de Guermantes MS that Mme Bontemps is said to have taught Albertine 'la haine des Juifs' as an integral part of her upbringing (II 356f).[1] As for the 'gens du monde', M. de Guermantes's remarks to the effect that all Jews are Dreyfusard appear only in additions to the typescripts of La Prisonnière (the conversion has apparently been forgotten here) (III 38-42a, pp. 41-42; III 42a); Proust inserted on the 1914 galleys the brief paragraph in which the prince Von is said by Mme de Marsantes to be 'l'antisémitisme en personne' (II 256b);[2] and he added to the Côté de Guermantes MS the duc's observation that his cousin the prince 'tombe en attaque quand il voit un juif à cent mètres' and that his normally amicable feeling for Swann 's'aggrave de l'affaire Dreyfus' (II 578a). The MS of Sodome et Gomorrhe does not yet describe the entire Guermantes milieu as so anti-semitic that the duchesse is afraid to greet Swann openly (II 672-73a). Finally, Proust added to Mme de Villeparisis's matinée all the references to the anti-semitism of her family and friends, her consequent unwillingness to introduce Bloch, the anti-Dreyfus activities of the archivist, and, in a slightly later series, Mme de Villeparisis's fear of this archivist 'dont les opinions nationalistes la tenaient pour ainsi dire à la chaîne' (II 190a, b; II 217a; II 219-20a, b; II 237a, c; II 248a;

---

1 See also, for Albertine, I 869-951a, p. 903.

2 Cp., however, II 677-80a, p. 678.

II 248-49a).[1]

PRETENCE AND PRIDE

Perhaps the character-trait most conspicuously drawn out in the post-1914 novel was, however, a more private kind of pride than chauvinism. Pretence, and the attempt not to 'lose face', were always at the very base of Marcel's relationship with Albertine, and as such had already motivated important exchanges in the MS of La Prisonnière, for example the feigned separation;[2] but Proust wishes now to bring them still more prominently into the novel, adding to the MS of La Prisonnière the long general consideration of the risks the lover takes in bluffing

---

1 For other additions about opinions on the Dreyfus Affair, and anti-semitism, see: II 252-53a; II 263-64a; II 505-6a; II 592a; II 668-69a; II 676a; II 677-80a; II 677-78a; II 965-66a; III 51-54a, pp. 53, 54; III 580-81a.
There are also a number of additions about Jews, not necessarily in the context of anti-semitism: thus the Bloch dinner is doubtless late (I 740-48a, pp. 747-48; I 767-79a; I 786a); Nissim Bernard is a new character (see Ch. 6, pp. 290-91); and the increased reference to Esther and Athalie, as well as to La Juive (sic) (II 845-50a, p. 845), reinforces this theme (see Ch. 2, pp. 84-86). It is an addition which compares Marcel, sobbing after the letter from Mme de Stermaria, to Jews 'qui se couvraient la tête de cendres dans le deuil' (II 393c) - a comparison again most interestingly discussed in M. Gutwirth's article 'Le Narrateur et son double', Revue d'Histoire Littéraire de la France, 71e année, nos. 5-6 (1971), pp. 921-35 (pp. 923, 926). See too I 738-40a; II 190e; II 190-91a; II 191-92a; II 400a; II 408-9a; II 408b; II 1039a; II 1039-40a; II 1040a; III 702a.

2 See above, Ch. 1, p.47, and, e.g., III 341-43 without the additions.

(III 353-54a),[1] and giving Marcel a pride which often makes him revert to pretence. I give details of this a little later:[2] meanwhile the dissimulations of the lesser characters echo those in the prominent relationships of the novel. M. de Guermantes's pretence that he does not mind his Jockey Club defeat, in spite of the fact that 'En réalité, il ne décolérait pas' (III 38-42a, p. 40, III 40a) is late; so is the pride in Françoise's character which, we learn, leads her to pretend that she already knows news in fact just revealed to her (I 694-96a, p. 695).[3] Where Proust had written: 'la Patronne, si au retour elle trouvait les cartes de quelque mondain "de passage sur la côte", était désolée d'avoir manqué sa visite', he later corrected the text to 'feignait d'être ravie mais était désolée' (II 1000a).[4] This, it could be objected, simply reinforces Mme Verdurin's characteristic supposed disdain for the 'ennuyeux', but, on the other hand, Proust adds on the very same typescript page a few lines making the 'mondain' in question pretend himself: he at first brought his hosts to La Raspelière 'pour eux leur donnant ce divertissement [...]', but now 'feignait d'offrir comme une sorte de politesse de leur faire connaître ce divertissement

---

1 For Marcel pretending with Albertine, see too III 341c,d; III 395b; and with his mother, III 567a.

2 Below, pp. 242-44.

3 Marcel similarly pretends to Albertine that he knows facts about her life. For Françoise, see also II 19b.

4 See also III 282b for Mme Verdurin.

[...]' (II 1000c). Finally, the Cambremers had in the MS reacted merely with despair to the impolite behaviour of Charlus and Morel, but Proust now tells the reader that

> Les Cambremer feignirent que l'absence du baron était un agrément de plus à la réunion [...] Mais ils étaient furieux (II 1093c).[1]

However, the new exhibitions of pride or self-satisfaction in A la recherche du temps perdu are far more noticeable. Sometimes Proust worked in only a few lines, sometimes a whole page, but the movement towards a more vigorous depiction of this trait is unmistakable. The actual words 'orgueil' or 'fierté' now constantly recur, and the characters will blatantly and unashamedly refer to their own exceptional qualities.

The aristocracy develop, with the insertion of the well-known information that, notwithstanding her respect for things of the mind alone, Mme de Guermantes had never thought of asking her valet to call her simply 'Madame' and always refers to her husband as 'Monsieur le duc' (II 440a). The latter's 'Si c'est à voir, je l'ai vu!', attributed to his possessing less learning than pride, was added to the MS of Le Côté de Guermantes (II 523-24a); and three exposures of the princesse de Parme's seeming humility are late: she is now said to be 'dénuée de snobisme comme la plupart des véritables altesses et, en revanche, dévorée par l'orgueil' (II 55a).[2]

---

1 For a few other additions showing pretence at work, see: I 594-95b; I 605-6a, p. 605; I 706a; I 869-951a, pp. 913-14; II 810a; II 1022-24a, p. 1023; II 1104c; III 320a; III 422c.

2 The other two are II 426-27a, p.427; II 428a. See also II 788-89a; II 788c.

Marcel's bourgeois acquaintances are not exempt. Proust added to La Fugitive the discussion of the envy and pride on one level, at least, of Andrée's nature: she is ready to love

> toutes les créatures, mais à condition [...] de les humilier préalablement. Elle ne comprenait pas qu'il fallait aimer même les orgueilleux et vaincre leur orgueil par l'amour et non par un plus puissant orgueil [...] (III 604a).

Mme Verdurin's criticisms of Elstir were written into the margin of the Sodome et Gomorrhe MS:

> [...] Comme si la fréquentation d'une femme comme moi pouvait ne pas être salutaire à un artiste!" s'écria-t-elle dans un mouvement d'orgueil (II 943b).[1]

It is in an addition to the first Gallimard galleys that the narrator's charitable remarks to Bloch provoke the self-eulogy ending 'Rare est le mortel à qui le Père Zeus accorde tant de félicités', for amiability such as Marcel's 'persuade aisément de leur bonne chance ceux qui ont beaucoup d'amour-propre' (II 201a, b).[2] And, moving on to the domestic staff, Proust describes in the long 'jeunes filles' passage Françoise's habit of drawing herself up 'fièrement et rageusement [...] pour peu qu'on la trouvât en faute' and of assuming 'une ironique expression d'orgueil' when Marcel ventures to complain (I 869-951a, p. 896); even if this is not late, the deep offence she takes on being offered help *is*, appearing only in additions to

---

1 See II 971b,c, for a similar remark about Swann.

2 See also the passage about Bloch's 'haines', in which he posits 'en principe qu'il avait une haute valeur morale' (II 228a); and III 680-81a; III 943-44a, p. 944.

both sets of Gallimard galleys: 'Se voir prêter un concours lui semblait recevoir une avanie [...]. Elle ne voulait pas, elle la titulaire, se laisser chiper son rôle dans ces jours de gala' (II 321a; II 321-22a).

However, of all those so far cited, it is Mme de Cambremer-Legrandin whose pride is illustrated in the most detail. The base documents did show her longing to meet the Guermantes, her disdain for her mother-in-law's artistic notions and her scorn for the Verdurins.[1] But Proust paid particular attention to this semi-cultured snob, adding her oscillations between the sickly-sweet and the rock-hard according to the company she finds herself in (II 811b, c, II 914-15a), and specifying one of the factors contributing to the mother-in-law's prestige as 'l'impolitesse de sa belle-fille née Legrandin qui, par son arrogance, relevait la bonhomie un peu fade de la belle-mère' (II 765-68a, p. 767). She now interrupts her mother-in-law to assure Marcel that the Arrachepel family is indeed illustrious (II 809-10a); she is ashamed to speak of Combray (II 810b). Her arrogance towards the 'fidèles', especially towards Brichot, is new, 'la rage ou l'orgueil l'emportant sur l'ostentation du savoir-vivre' (II 914-15a). And Proust worked into the MS additional proprietorial comments about La Raspelière, proffered by her with 'un air familièrement aristocratique'; the information that her congenital and morbid snobbery has enabled

1 See II 55, 809, 811, 813-15, 817-20, 823, 914-15, 923, 964, 978 without additions.

her to overcome even penchants towards avarice and adultery; and her 'dédaigneuse' explanation of the Cambremers' proposed invitation to Mme Verdurin: 'à la campagne on voit n'importe qui, ça ne tire pas à conséquence' (II 914d, 922-23a, II 923c; II 923-24a; II 1088a).[1]

Proust perhaps wanted to make the reader pause before entering the period of the narrator's life during which he too, more than at any other point, will display an incurable susceptibility to the idea that he is unwanted or excluded: the passage ninety pages before the end of _Sodome et Gomorrhe_ which, discussing the sources of pride in general terms, comes as a climax to all the descriptions of snobbery given throughout the last two volumes, was added only at the typescript stage. It is that relating how Marcel has inadvertently offended the princesse Sherbatoff, and concluding:

> Il faut [...] savoir de quels dépits amoureux, de quels échecs de snobisme étaient faits l'apparente hauteur, l'anti-snobisme universellement admis de la princesse

---

1 The other main additions about her are: I 526-36a, p. 534; I 646-47a; I 682a; II 232c; II 435b; II 753a-f; II 807b; II 811-12a; II 812-13a; II 815a; II 817a; II 820b,c,d,e; II 822b; II 914c,d; II 915c; II 923c; II 925-26a, p. 925; II 928a,b; II 928-29a; II 929a; II 944-45a,b; II 944a; II 954-55a; II 978a; II 978-79a; II 1092-93a; III 662-64a, p. 663; III 664b.
See III 586a for similar shame about her origins in Gilberte.
M. de Cambremer too is attributed some vulgar snobbery: II 916a,b; II 925a,b; II 925-26a; II 926a; II 926-27a; II 958-59a; II 963-64b.

> Sherbatoff, pour comprendre que dans l'humanité la règle - qui comporte des exceptions naturellement - est que les durs sont des faibles dont on n'a pas voulu, et que les forts, se souciant peu qu'on veuille ou non d'eux, ont seuls cette douceur que le vulgaire prend pour de la faiblesse (II 1045-46a).[1]

Whatever the reasons for the position of this unusual statement, two central figures, Marcel and Charlus, do now act, in very different ways, with growing pride. In the revision of La Prisonnière and La Fugitive Proust weighted his narrator's anxieties increasingly towards the fear of appearing humiliated, adding his outbursts of anger over the discovery that Albertine knows of Saint-Loup's visit to Mme Bontemps (III 451b; III 472a),[2] and his relief on hearing that Mme Bontemps does not believe he intended marriage with Albertine: 'Ceci me rassurait un peu en me montrant que j'étais moins humilié, donc plus capable d'être encore aimé' (III 473b). Other than the offer of a yacht as well as a car, the only element added to Marcel's letter to Albertine in La Fugitive were the words: 'Ainsi je ne suis pas bien à plaindre' (III 454a).[3] The discussion of the coldness which the lover must simulate 'pour peu que celui-ci ait un peu de fierté, et dût-il mourir d'une séparation' forms part of a long passage not to be found until the third typescript of La Prisonnière (III 182-92a, p. 192); and Marcel's

---

1 See II 1046-47a, which illustrates the point.

2 See also III 429a.

3 For the yacht, see III 455a-h; III 456a.

pretence 'par orgueil, par habileté' of wishes opposite to his real ones (III 344-48a, p. 347),[1] or his lies to Albertine 'pour ne pas, par fierté, avouer que j'aimais' (III 458a), are cited, respectively, in the course of a more substantial addition, and in a special insertion on the MS.

More important even than these, one series of additions introduces a quite new element into La Prisonnière and La Fugitive. All Marcel's comparisons of the pride he displays in the Albertine affair to that on which he had relied so heavily in the separation from Gilberte appear only at a late stage. A reminder is introduced in the shape of the unexpected news that Gilberte had loved another young man at the time that she was receiving Marcel's visits too: 'je supposai que ma triste impression était due, en partie du moins, à mon amour-propre blessé' (III 134-35a; also III 135a). And, having thus jogged the reader's memory and implied certain links between 'amour' and 'amour-propre' (III 134-35a, p. 135), Proust now, in three separate additions, writes, with slight variations, that

> sans renoncer à elle, ce qui me restait de ce que j'avais éprouvé pour Gilberte, c'était la fierté de ne pas vouloir être à Albertine un jouet dégoûtant en lui faisant demander de revenir, je voulais qu'elle revînt sans que j'eusse l'air d'y tenir
> (III 429b; the others are III 451c and III 456-57a).

Finally, as I mentioned in Chapter 1,[2] Proust was yet to compose the paragraph in which Marcel abandons his pride and asks

---

1 See also p. 344.

2 p. 50.

Albertine to return, receiving, as soon as his telegram has left, another from Mme Bontemps (about Albertine's death); when Proust did insert this in the MS margin, he did not even correct the main MS properly to make room for it:

> Je laissai toute fierté vis-à-vis d'Albertine, je lui envoyai un télégramme désespéré lui demandant de revenir à n'importe quelles conditions, qu'elle ferait tout ce qu'elle voudrait, que je demandais seulement à l'embrasser une minute trois fois par semaine. Et elle eût dit: une fois seulement, que j'eusse accepté une fois [...] (III 476a,b).

The fact that there was previously no trace at all of this last plea from Marcel, at such a highly-charged moment of the novel, is enough to point to the significance Proust evidently now wishes to give to manifestations of pride and humiliation.[1]

If Charlus is one double of the narrator's,[2] then perhaps the expansions making him, too, prouder were meant partly as a humorous balance to the almost unrelievedly serious additions about Marcel. At any rate, it was the baron primarily whom the revision endowed with extremes of condescending insolence: his refusal to admit supposed attacks on his superiority becomes still more absolute than that implied in his already almost

---

1 The odd little paragraph in <u>TR</u> in which Marcel seems, in front of Charlus, to be ashamed of Combray, is late too: III 794-95a, p. 794. Possibly it arises from the passage quoted in I 754<u>n</u>.1, pp. 977-78.

2 Bersani's analysis of their similarities is valuable (<u>Marcel Proust: The Fictions of Life and of Art</u> (New York, 1965), pp. 160-61).

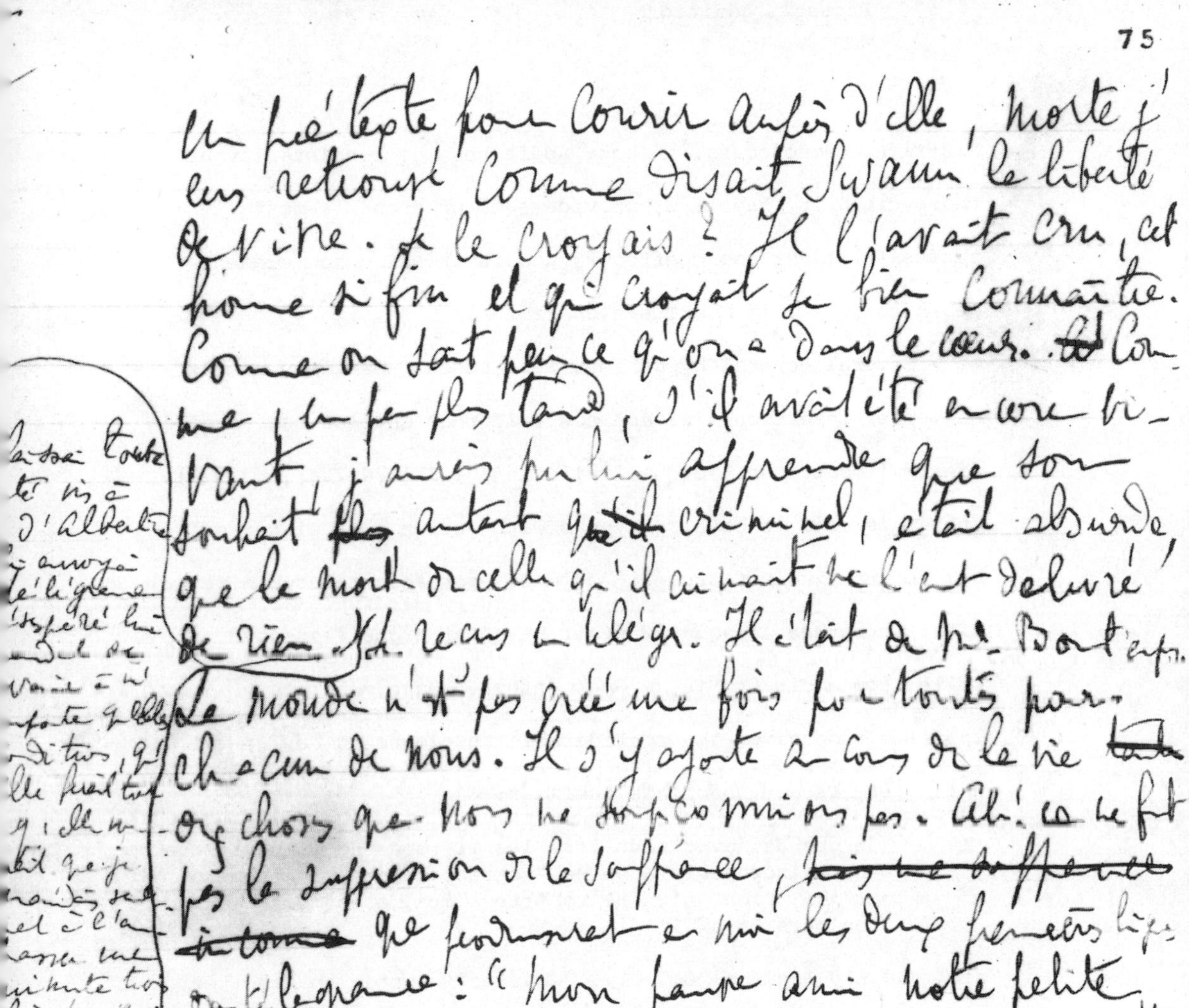

un prétexte pour courir auprès d'elle, morte j'eus retrouvé comme disait Swann la liberté de vivre. Je le croyais? Il l'avait cru, cet homme si fin et qui croyait se bien connaître. Comme on sait peu ce qu'on a dans le cœur. ~~Et~~ Comme, un peu plus tard, s'il avait été encore vivant, j'aurais pu lui apprendre que son souhait ~~plus~~ autant que ~~il~~ criminel, était absurde, que la mort de celle qu'il aimait ne l'eût délivré de rien. Je reçus un télégr. Il était de Mme Bontemps. Le monde n'est pas créé une fois pour toutes pour chacun de nous. Il s'y ajoute au cours de la vie ~~tant~~ de choses que nous ne soupçonnions pas. Ah! ce ne fut pas la suppression de la souffrance, ~~mais une souffrance inconnue~~ que produisirent en moi les deux premières lignes du télégramme: « Mon pauvre ami notre petite Albertine n'est plus, pardonnez-moi de vous dire cette chose affreuse, vous qui l'aimiez tant. Elle a été jetée par son cheval contre un arbre pendant une promenade. Tous nos efforts n'ont pu la ranimer. Que ne suis-je morte à sa place! » Non, pas la suppression de la souffrance, mais une souffrance ~~nouvelle~~ inconnue, celle d'apprendre qu'elle ne reviendrait pas. ~~Mais ne m'étais je dit je~~ ~~cela~~ c'était-ce donc inconnu? ~~Ne~~ Mais ne m'étais-je pas dit ~~pl~~ plusieurs fois qu'elle ne

[Marginal note, left: Laissai toute la vie d'Albertine, j'envoyai le télégramme [illegible] … Elle ne revenait … je reçus un … Il était de Mme Bontemps.]

Photo. Bibl. nat. Paris.

Plate 1 A page from the MS of La Fugitive (n.a.fr. 16719:75).
See III 476 a,b.

histrionic monologues.[1] These additions, as consistently as those cited in Chapter 2, provide some of Proust's most successful later comic effects; and interesting new elements begin to appear in Charlus's character.

Several general hypotheses were added, sometimes as part of longer insertions: we are now told that Charlus has 'enté la fierté féodale sur l'orgueil allemand' (II 1074-75a, p. 1075), and it is said to be his shyness with Jupien that either drives him to 'un excessif orgueil' or else, perhaps, makes him reveal his true nature, 'laquelle était en effet orgueilleuse et un peu folle, comme disait Mme de Guermantes'. More concretely, this last addition gives the considerable monologue to Jupien with which readers are doubtless familiar:

> je prends, avec peut-être les microbes de la peste, la chose incroyable appelée "correspondance", un numéro, et qui, bien qu'on le remette à <u>moi</u>, n'est pas toujours le n° 1!

etc. (II 610-13a, pp. 610-11). Charlus's letter to Aimé, strewn with hyperbolic impertinences, appears for the first time in the typescript of <u>Sodome et Gomorrhe</u> (II 987-93a, pp. 991-93; II 991b; II 992a); Proust added to the same typescript the lines in which, talking to Morel, the baron gives way to a 'délire de fierté et de joie', and 'dans un mouvement d'orgueil presque

---

1 Feuillerat remarks that in the additions (to the first half of <u>CG</u>) 'L'orgueil de Charlus prend des proportions incroyables' (p. 99).

fou, [...] s'écria en levant les bras: "Tantus ab uno splendor! [...]' (II 1069c, d); and Marcel's conclusion, near the end of the interview scene, that at last Charlus's 'bon coeur l'emportait sur ce que je considérais comme un état presque délirant de susceptibilité et d'orgueil' was also late (II 563a).[1]

Additions of this kind amplify the grandiose self-exaggeration already in the novel;[2] but Proust now extends the baron's repertoire of insolent imagery to include the openly scatological. His 'Cambremerde' was in the MS (II 1090), but the gross remarks during the interview scene about Mme de Villeparisis, remarks ostensibly made to accuse Marcel of ineptitude, were added only in the margin of the first Gallimard galleys (II 555a); his comparison of the smell of Mme de Saint-Euverte's breath to that of a cesspool, and her garden-party to a walk through the sewers, is not in the MS of Sodome et Gomorrhe (II 699-702a, pp. 700-701); and Proust inserted at two points on the typescript of this volume his likening of actors or nobles to excrement at moments when he wishes to exalt himself at their expense (II 1070b; II 1090a).[3]

---

1 For this scene, see also II 553-54a; II 554a,b,c; II 555a,b; II 555-56a; II 555c; II 556a,b; II 557a; II 558d,e; II 558-59a; II 561-62a; II 561a; II 562a; II 563b.

2 See, e.g., II 556 without additions.

3 See also III 44b; III 44-45a; III 266-72a, p. 268. In a brief account of this trait of Charlus's, J. O'Brien points out that he shares it with Swann: 'An Aspect of Proust's Baron de Charlus', The Romanic Review, LV (1964), pp. 38-41.

However, Charlus's principal new character-trait is his religious pride. The implications of this should not be immediately narrowed to the egocentric. One of the additions in this group explains that Charlus is pious with the piety of the Middle Ages, believing in prophets and angels, and choosing the archangels Michael, Gabriel and Raphael to intercede for him (II 1040c): his faith is thus connected with the feeling for the past (the religious past at that) so evident elsewhere in the novel,[1] as well as with the wish for defined hierarchies that brings about as disparate reactions as Marcel's indulgently-portrayed need to classify actors in order of merit (I 74), and Charlus's own feelings of confusion about bisexuality.[2] Nevertheless, nearly all the other insertions show how inseparable are Charlus's religious beliefs from his sense of glory in being a pillar of traditional France, from his evident conviction that he has in some way been singled out by, or may associate himself with, the Deity, and, still less creditably, from the sadistic mixture of contempt and fascination inspired in him by the Jews, to whom he attributes deliciously heathen impulses. All these latter passages are interpolations, whose tone is usually as follows:

---

1 E.g. the etymologies, the references to cathedrals, etc.

2 See III 214-16a, III 215a; discussed below, Ch. 6, p. 286.

> pensez, en ce moment où tous ces malheureux Juifs tremblent devant la fureur stupide des chrétiens, quel honneur pour eux de voir un homme comme moi condescendre à s'amuser de leurs jeux! (II 287-90a, p. 289).[1]

As for the more direct religious pride, it is in an addition to the interview scene that Charlus tells Marcel:

> je ne me suis pas laissé décourager. Notre religion prêche la patience. Celle que j'ai eue envers vous me sera comptée, je l'espère (II 555-56a);

and the other passages putting these associations into Charlus's mouth, until they reach near-insanity in Le Temps retrouvé, are all added ones - some very late, such as that in which the baron expatiates on Saint Michael to the literal-minded Mme Verdurin, given in neither the MS nor the typescript of Sodome et Gomorrhe (II 956-57a). Charlus also now compares himself to Christ, denied by Peter in the form of Aimé (II 987-93a, p. 992), waits for the archangel Raphael to bring him Tobias (Morel) (III 323-24a), and, in that letter to Marcel which mingles sexual, genealogical and religious pride, thanks the archangel Michael for saving him from killing Morel (III 803-6a; III 805a; III 805-6a). And the speech in which Charlus assimilates himself not merely to Raphael, but implicitly to God, is a very late one too, again appearing in neither the MS, the typescript, nor the proofs of Sodome et Gomorrhe:

---

1 For the others, see above, p. 234.

> Grisé par son amour, ou par son amour-propre, [...] il me dit avec un orgueilleux sourire: "[...] il [Morel] a tout de suite compris que le Père auprès duquel il allait désormais vivre, n'était pas son père selon la chair, qui doit être un affreux valet de chambre à moustaches, mais son père spirituel, c'est-à-dire Moi. Quel orgueil pour lui! [...] Je n'ai même pas eu besoin, ajouta le baron, fort persuadé qu'il siégerait un jour devant le trône de Dieu, de lui dire que j'étais l'envoyé céleste, il l'a compris de lui-même et en était muet de bonheur!" Et M. de Charlus (à qui au contraire le bonheur n'enlevait pas la parole), peu soucieux des quelques passants qui se retournèrent, croyant avoir affaire à un fou, s'écria tout seul et de toute sa force, en levant les mains: "Alleluia!" (II 1073-74a).[1]

Proust is, then, reminding his reader of the ubiquity of pride more consciously than in Du Côté de chez Swann and the base versions of other volumes, and he is introducing important new elements to illustrate it; simultaneously, he makes Mme de Cambremer-Legrandin, for example, emerge from her subdued position to become a fitting sister for the originally more closely-portrayed Legrandin of Du Côté de chez Swann; and he gives the figure of Charlus some of its most outlandishly

---

1 See too II 610-13a, p. 612, for the religious pride. For other additions describing or mentioning Charlus's insolence, snobbery or pride, see II 267a; II 287b; II 287-90a, p. 290; II 292h; II 293b,c,d; II 293-95a; II 293-94a; II 294a,b,c; II 446a; II 914-15a; II 915a,b; II 967-68a; II 986-87a; II 1067-68a; II 1068-69a; II 1068a; II 1069-71a; II 1071e; III 230-38a, pp. 230-34; III 234a,b; III 247-48a; III 266-72a; III 276-77a; III 277b; III 279b; III 290-91a, p. 290; III 301c; III 317a; III 318-19a; III 784-93a, pp. 786-87.

comic facets.[1]

In a few other additions Proust seems to be 'replying' to his own expansion of egocentric behaviour by setting out

---

1 As F.-C. Green says, Charlus's real 'comic vice' is not his homosexuality, but his 'morgue de grand seigneur': 'Le rire dans l'oeuvre de Proust', Cahiers de l'Association Internationale des Études Françaises, no. 12 (1960), pp. 243-57 (pp. 253-54).
The lawyer-friend of the Cambremers is now given his own source of pride (II 806a); so is Ski (II 873-74a, p. 874). Octave, in matters of fashion, displays 'une infaillibilité orgueilleuse' (I 869-951a, p. 878). Could the additions to A l'ombre bringing Swann's vainglory in Odette's social relations to the very beginning of the volume, and elaborating it still further, be connected with these other expansions? (I 431-34a; I 465-66a). Perhaps, too, it is relevant that Saint-Loup's anxious 'showing-off' of Marcel to his Doncières friends and to Rachel is late: this possibly foreshadows his inversion, but it also arises from a more obscure form of pride than those discussed so far (II 103-4a; II 104a; II 106-7a; II 106a,n.; II 107a; II 172a). (The duc acts similarly with his wife in II 239-40a; II 463-65a; II 485a; II 486c.)
For other additions showing pride, snobbery or humiliation in the characters, see: I 557-58a; I 694-95a, p. 695; I 767-79a, pp. 770-71; II 24-25a; II 251-52a; II 402-6a, pp. 402-3; II 439a; II 475-76a; II 577b; II 791a,b; II 791-93a; II 1086-87a; III 239b,c; III 240a; III 485-86a, p. 485; III 576-77a; III 606a.
The theme of professional self-importance was also expanded in this period. The great majority of these additions are about Cottard, and describe the bombastic self-assurance he has gained. The first addition to A l'ombre tells us, referring to Cottard, that 'les honneurs, les titres officiels viennent avec les années' (I 431-34a, p. 433); and almost all following references to his new status, and to its effect on him, are additions. One of them does, however, state that he has remained 'très simple malgré une couche superficielle d'orgueil' (II 932b). For the others, see: I 497-99a; I 515-16a; I 598e; II 869b; II 881d; II 893a; II 912a, b,c; II 919a; II 933d; II 960-62a; II 973a; II 1038a; II 1050-52a, pp. 1051-52; II 1052a; II 1071g; II 1072-73a.
Mme Cottard discusses her husband's professional commitments in II 964-65a; II 965a; II 1039a; and see Ch. 3 for his new linguistic confidence (above, pp. 138-39).

clearer alternatives to it than he had in the base versions of A la recherche. First, one of Elstir's new characteristics, as I shall show, is his lack of amour-propre.[1] Second, Proust made the unusual addition about Andrée directly advocating treatment of the proud not in kind but by 'l'amour': there is no equivocation or irony in this recommendation.[2] Third, elaborations of the aesthetic meditation and the 'bal costumé' take up, but aptly reverse, the concepts of pride, tyranny, or prejudice. Marcel's definition of the pleasure he felt during the involuntary memories as 'non plus égoïste, ou du moins d'un égoïsme [...] utilisable pour autrui' is late:

> tous les altruismes féconds de la nature se développent selon un mode égoïste, l'altruisme humain qui n'est pas égoïste est stérile (III 1036b);

so is the long development just before in which the narrator, talking of the book he will write, uses for the last time the imagery of both scrutiny and domination, but now in the sense that the 'rules' and restrictions come from him and are willingly applied to himself:

> cet écrivain [...] devrait préparer son livre minutieusement [...], l'accepter comme une règle, [...] le suivre comme un régime (III 1032-35a, p. 1032).

Finally, Proust added here the two important discussions of the relationship between the author and his readers, affirming that these 'ne seraient pas, selon moi, mes lecteurs, mais les propres

---

1 See below, Ch. 8, pp. 351, 354, 358.

2 III 604a; see above, p. 239.

lecteurs d'eux-mêmes': the first is that in which Marcel uses again the word 'liberté' which was such a source of fear for him during the Albertine affair:[1]

> d'autres particularités (comme l'inversion) peuvent faire que le lecteur a besoin de lire d'une certaine façon pour bien lire; l'auteur n'a pas à s'en offenser, mais au contraire à laisser la plus grande liberté au lecteur en lui disant: "Regardez vous-même si vous voyez mieux avec ce verre-ci, avec celui-là, avec cet autre." (III 910-11a).

And the second, part of the long insertion just mentioned and comprising a still further elaboration on it, shows a certain modesty in Marcel, and the final deprecation of anxiety about pride or humiliation:

> [...] je pensais plus modestement à mon livre [...]. De sorte que je ne leur demanderais pas de me louer ou de me dénigrer, mais seulement de me dire si c'est bien cela, si les mots qu'ils lisent en eux-mêmes sont bien ceux que j'ai écrits [...]
> (III 1032-35a, p. 1033; III 1033b).[2]

---

1 See above, p. 216.

2 This lack of self-assertion might be contrasted with Marcel's 'sentiment presque orgueilleux, presque joyeux' (also an addition) after the other major revelation in the novel, that at the end of Sodome et Gomorrhe (II 1115-16a).
For new considerations of changes in the self, and its release from egoism, see too III 873b; III 986d,e; III 986-87a; III 1039-41a.
To what extent the end of the novel can be seen as Marcel's break with characteristics like those described in this chapter is still open to discussion. Germaine Brée implies, possibly, that it is (see her Du Temps perdu au temps retrouvé, pp. 80, 242-246 - where she opposes Proust's character-creation to the art meditations - and also her The World of Marcel Proust, pp. 161, 232, 246); but René Girard is the only critic who unequivocally equates Marcel's discovery of his vocation with a moral change (Mensonge romantique et vérité romanesque (Paris, 1961), pp. 234, 296-98). If Girard is right, then such a change was always implied by the climax of the novel, of course.

6 Lies and Uncertainty

The traits described in the last chapter contribute to a clear-cut, definite view of individual characters; Proust also evidently wished, in his expansion of A la recherche, to amplify characteristics or situations marked by ambiguity and uncertainty, ranging from mistaken identity to proliferation of rumour, or from Albertine's lies to manifestations of bisexuality. Again, the additions may be only a phrase or two in length, or else they can introduce quite new characters or sub-plots to fill out this area of the novel, one which was always essential, as Odette's lies and the family's stubbornly incorrect notions about Swann in Du Côté de chez Swann show,[1] but which is now made far more prominent by Proust, with the appearance and constant re-appearance of further subjects for speculation or attempted interpretation. He added numerous examples of rumour, scandal and second-hand reports; of lies and liars; of suspicions about Albertine's lesbianism or seeming 'proofs' of it; and of bi-sexuality and inversion.

---

1 See, e.g., I 280-81, I 360-66; I 17-21.

RUMOUR AND SCANDAL

A survey of the drafts shows that many of the smaller illustrations in the novel of inaccurate reporting, slanderous tales, far-fetched gossip, and entirely mistaken information are post-1914.

Norpois, for instance, had originally answered Marcel's question about Gilberte in these words:

> [...] Je vous dirai que je l'ai peu vue, elle est partie après le dîner [...],

but Proust later corrected the diplomat's reply to the more casually vague

> Je vous dirai que je l'ai peu vue, elle est allée se coucher de bonne heure. Ou elle allait chez des amies, je ne me rappelle pas bien (I 476c).

At the opposite extreme, Mme de Guermantes's positive affirmation in Le Temps retrouvé that Rachel is still Robert's mistress was added to the MS ('j'ai la certitude que ça n'a jamais cessé [...]') (III 1028a). As for libel or slander, both Bloch and Morel, the reader will remember, are now inclined to these, the former planning to 'déposer d'une façon mensongère et dont l'inculpé ne pourrait pas cependant prouver la fausseté' (II 228a) and the latter writing 'des petits entrefilets bassement calomniateurs' against Mme Molé (III 220-21a);[1] and Proust added to the Côté de Guermantes MS and to the third Gallimard galleys respectively Mme d'Épinay's claim that the

1 See above, Ch. 5, pp. 221-22, and Ch. 4, p. 191, respectively.

princesse de Parme is immoral, 'faisant allusion à certains débordements purement imaginaires de la princesse' (II 466-67a), and the duc's quite untruthful statement that the dame d'honneur is 'légèrement sous l'influence de Bacchus', made merely because he likes to 'placer ses locutions favorites' (II 499a). The accusation which the hotel-manager levels against Albertine and her friends, to the effect that they have either been spreading slander or have been slandered themselves, appears only in the margin of the Sodome et Gomorrhe MS (II 775-76a).[1] The comments of 'le monde' on news of two expulsions are late: Bloch's exit from Mme de Villeparisis's matinée is now, in a layer addition to the 1914 galleys, 'universellement admiré et commenté le soir même dans divers salons, mais d'après une version qui n'avait déjà plus aucun rapport avec la vérité' (II 248-49a, p. 249), and the rumour that 'M. de Charlus avait été mis à la porte de chez les Verdurin au moment où il cherchait à violer un jeune musicien' occurs towards the end of another layer glued to the La Prisonnière MS (III 318-19a). Proust inserted too, at the beginning of La Prisonnière, Bloch's wrong conclusions about Marcel's activities, citing him as an example of those who see 'dans le fait nouvellement découvert l'explication de choses qui n'ont précisément aucun rapport avec lui' (III 9-10a); he

1 Mentioned above in Ch.3, p. 147. See here the long 'jeunes filles' section in A l'ombre, which refers to Gisèle's 'potin' about Andrée, and to the middle-class mothers who, jealous of Albertine's social success, accuse her of gossip and breach of confidence (I 869-951a, pp. 888, 937).

added to the war-chapter the remarks on the inaccuracy of Bontemps's information, always belied by the event, and on the forgetfulness of those who had once put out false news, but are now 'prêts à en propager sincèrement d'autres qu'ils oublieraient aussi vite' (III 733-34a, III 777b);[1] and the interesting discussion given in the Sodome et Gomorrhe Pléiade notes, which brackets the intractable spirit of rumour with that of the verbal stereotype, was written in the margin of the MS:

> [...] Sans s'arrêter au démenti, si probant soit-il, le potin, dans certains cas la calomnie, recommencent à pied d'oeuvre, en vertu de la même tendance qui les avait d'abord fait naître, ou peut-être de l'esprit d'imitation qui fait que les gens connaissant la phrase: "Oui, on a démenti, mais il paraît que c'est bien vrai, que c'était tout de même lui (phrase inachevée)". A cela rien ne fait [...]
> (II 724n.1: II 1191a).

However, more important are those topics or figures worked into the novel probably solely in order to illustrate the tenacious yet ambiguous nature of rumour and scandal. Suzanne Delage and Robert Forestier, whose mothers, Albertine assures Marcel, know his, although this relationship exists nowhere but in 'l'imagination de Mme Bontemps', make their one appearance in margin and layer additions on the first and third Gallimard galleys (II 368-69a,b). All instances of the dame d'honneur's

---

1 This theme of forgetfulness helping in the casting-off of old rumours and the maintaining of new ones has already appeared in a substantial La P addition: see III 38a; III 38-42a, pp. 38-39; III 38b; III 38-39a; III 39a,b.

stubborn belief that Marcel is related to the admiral Jurien de la Gravière are additions: nothing will convince her of her mistake (II 498a, b; II 498-99a; II 546-47a; II 547b).[1] The ambassadress of Turkey is also a new character, introduced on a version between the first and third Gallimard galleys (II 534-35a), and given her scandal-mongering tendencies in slightly later additions: she is now dangerous to listen to, being always mistaken and in the habit of telling tales 'qui semblent sortir d'un livre, non à cause de leur sérieux, mais de leur invraisemblance' (II 534c); she not only reintroduces the slander about M. de Luxembourg but insists that the duc de Guermantes is an invert - 'l'erreur, la contre-vérité naïvement crue étaient pour l'ambassadrice comme un milieu vital hors duquel elle ne pouvait se mouvoir' (II 537-40a, pp. 537, 539-40); and she reappears in an addition to Le Temps retrouvé as a paradigm of all who are most prone to accept rumour, and most forgetful of what has once been affirmed (III 971-72a, p. 971).[2] The scandal just mentioned about M. de Luxembourg, and the young man himself, are, too, entirely new in the novel: the whole 'épidémie' of malicious stories about him (II 533-34a), and Marcel's protests, appear only as insertions on the third

1 She is herself an entirely added character: the other late passages in which she appears are II 499a; II 544-45a; III 1006-10a, p. 1009.

2 See also II 535b and II 659-61a for the ambassadress.

Gallimard galleys, and although the last of them assures us that

> J'étais intimement persuadé que toutes les histoires relatives à M. de Luxembourg étaient pareillement fausses [...]. La suite montrera que c'était moi qui avais raison (II 537-40a),

the reader never learns what this 'suite' is.[1]

The rumour about the separation of the duc and duchesse de Guermantes is also a late _leitmotif_, first introduced in additions to the MS of _Le Côté de Guermantes_ in which Mme de Villeparisis's departing guests talk about 'la grande nouvelle, la séparation qu'on disait déjà accomplie entre le duc et la duchesse de Guermantes' (II 371a), and in which mention is made of the rumoured estrangement at the moment of Marcel's arrival for dinner at the Guermantes's.[2] Proust returned to both these additions, reworking the second to a more plausible form (II 416a), and amplifying the first with the paragraph in which some of the guests, seeing Mme de Guermantes in conversation with Marcel, assume that it is the duc who wants the separation because of the younger man, and 'se hâtèrent de répandre cette nouvelle' (II 375b). Finally, Saint-Loup's sensible observations in _Le Temps retrouvé_ about these rumours of divorce (once more, apparently, springing up) were added to the MS (III 738-39a).[3]

---

1 The other additions about M. de Luxembourg are II 329-30a; II 410-11a.

2 See under II 416a. (The original MS, before any addition, had, more innocuously, portrayed Marcel as so astonished to be invited by Mme de Guermantes that he expected the duc to be surprised or angry: n.a.fr. 16705:85.)

3 See also III 1006-7a, p. 1006.

mes qui n'ayant pas d'attrait physique à leur base sont les seules qui soient tout à fait mystérieuses. Tel de nature énigmatique m'était apparu à Balbec ce sentiment que Saint-Loup ressentait peur moi, qui ne se confondait pas avec l'intérêt de nos conversations, détaché de tout lien matériel, invisible, intangible et dont pourtant il éprouvait la présence en lui-même comme une sorte de phlogistique, de gaz, dont il parlait en souriant Et peut-être y avait-il quelque chose de plus surprenant encore dans cette sympathie née ici en une seule soirée, comme une fleur qui se serait ouverte en quelques minutes dans la chaleur de cette petite pièce. Saint-Loup m'avait parlé de sa jeune bonne ; je savais que seul d'eux tous il était partisan de la révision du procès Dreyfus.

— Il n'est pas de bonne foi me dit Saint-Loup ; au début il disait : il n'y a qu'à attendre, il y a là un homme que je connais bien, plein de finesse, de bonté, le général de Boisdeffre ; on pourra sans hésiter accepter son avis. Mais quand il a su que Boisdeffre proclamait la culpabilité de Dreyfus, Boisdeffre ne valait plus rien ; le cléricalisme, les préjugés de l'état-major l'empêchaient de juger sincèrement (quoique personne ne soit, ou du moins n'était, aussi clérical, avant son Dreyfus, que mon ami, ajoutait Saint-Loup). Alors il nous a dit qu'en tous cas on saurait la vérité car l'affaire allait être entre les mains de Saussier, et que celui-là soldat républicain, (mon ami était d'une famille ultra-monarchiste) était un homme de bronze une conscience inflexible Mais quand Saussier a proclamé l'innocence d'Esterhazy, il a trouvé à ce verdict des explications nouvelles, défavorables non à Dreyfus, mais au général Saussier.

C'était l'esprit militariste qui aveuglait Saussier (et remarque que lui est aussi militariste que clérical, ou du moins qu'il l'était, car je ne sais plus que penser

Photo. Bibl. nat. Paris.

Plate 2 A page from the 1914 Grasset galleys of Le Côté de Guermantes (n.a.fr. 16760:11viii).
See II 104c; II 104-5a; II 105a (and Part II, p. 10, n.1).

However, the most persistent new rumour in the novel is that of Saint-Loup's marriage, first to Mlle d'Ambresac, then to the niece of the princesse de Guermantes.[1] Two late passages cite Mlle d'Ambresac as a potential bride for members of the prince de Foix's group (II 403-5a) and reveal that this prince 'aimait à répandre tous les bruits pouvant faire manquer un mariage à Robert' (II 509a); but the marriage with Saint-Loup himself is implied to be imminent in the other added rumours, from Albertine's uncharitable comments in A l'ombre (I 869-951a, pp. 884, 886) to Françoise's reports (II 35b). After the two contradictions of the story, inserted into both Le Côté de Guermantes (II 104-5a) and Sodome et Gomorrhe (II 698b), the additions move on to the second young woman. each of Mme de Cambremer-Legrandin's declarations that Saint-Loup is engaged to the niece of the princesse de Guermantes was added to the MS of Sodome et Gomorrhe (II 928a;[2] II 1094-95a); and Marcel's memory of this in La Fugitive (III 442a),[3] followed three hundred pages later by Saint-Loup's final confirmation of its untruth, are, of course, late too:

---

1 Since all the other references to Mlle d'Ambresac are added ones, those in the 'jeunes filles' section are probably late too (I 869-951a, pp. 884-86, 893).

2 See also II 928c, d.

3 (She is the daughter of the prince de Guermantes here.)

> Il sursauta et m'assura [...] que ce n'était qu'un de ces bruits du monde qui naissent de temps à autre on ne sait pourquoi, s'évanouissent de même et dont la fausseté ne rend pas ceux qui ont cru en eux plus prudents [...] (III 738-39a).[1]

---

1 This is the addition that also mentions the divorce of the duc and duchesse (see above, p. 259); the MSS in fact provide evidence that Proust conceived these rumours together, and both in connection with the war. Thus, one margin addition in the MS of SG (at about the equivalent of II 714, before 'La passion qu'elle eut'), commenting on a rumour that the prince and princesse de Guermantes are going to separate, ends:

> [...] depuis le bruit de la séparation du duc et de la duchesse de Guermantes, et surtout avant du mariage de Robert avec Mlle d'Ambresac, je savais qu'il naît dans le monde, comme dans le peuple en temps de guerre, [...] des bruits qui ne reposent absolument sur rien [...] (margin, n.a.fr. 16710:18);

and the addition mentioned above (p. 257; III 777b) on the forgetfulness of those who propagate war-time rumours originally continued:

> comme ceux qui jadis annonçaient et oubliaient le mariage de St-Loup avec Mlle d'Ambresac et la ou la (sic) séparation du duc et de la Duchesse de Guermantes (margin, n.a.fr. 16725:1).

This was crossed out by Proust.
For further additions about rumour, indiscretion, or others' knowledge of facts about us, see: I 465a; I 478d; I 484-86a, p. 484; I 516-23a, p. 520; I 607-15a, p. 613; I 740-48a, p. 747; I 759b; II 27c; II 108-117a, p. 108; II 268-69a, II 269a; II 271-73a, II 272-73a; II 376b; II 816a; II 820c; II 873-74a, p. 874; II 902d; II 903a,c; II 917-18a, p. 918; II 1042-43a; II 1048-49a; II 1075-81a, p. 1081; II 1095c; III 589-91a, p. 590; III 740-41a; III 864b.

As usual, Proust exposes complex causes behind superficially similar effects, bringing out in his additions a variety of motives for the spreading of tales. The characters may simply wish to 'show off', like the duc de Guermantes;[1] they may be wounding deliberately, as do Bloch and Morel. They may have misunderstood some connection, then obstinately clung to the mistake, like the <u>dame d'honneur</u> - here the perpetuation of rumour joins that of mispronunciation, for example;[2] like Mme Bontemps and Bloch, they may be drawing false conclusions from apparently self-evident 'pointers'. One trait they share, however, is forgetfulness: Proust emphasises the uselessness of confronting rumour-mongers with their past errors.[3]

For whatever reason it sprang up, all this inaccurate reporting extends the elements in the novel conspiring to give the impression that the truth will never be known, elements that, in opposite ways, reinforce both the Albertine affair and the conclusion of the work. Proust may even have wanted to imply that it is a waste of time to speculate on the accuracy of the overt subject of the rumours, since the gossip about Saint-Loup's marriage is quite beside the point of what is, presumably, actually happening, that is, the gradual development of his

---

1 See also II 873-74a, in which Ski affects a 'fausse précision' for purposes of self-aggrandisement.

2 See above, Ch. 3, p.167. Proust shows another persistent mistaken belief in II 726-28a, p. 727.

3 In, e.g., II 104-5a; III 777b.

inversion.[1] Meanwhile, it is suggestive that two of the principal rumours - this, and the one about the divorce of the duc and duchesse - are about marriage and separation, reflecting the uncertainties of Marcel's relationship with Albertine.

LIES

If the characters are now more inclined to pass on rumours, they also increasingly resort to lying. This particular expansion is one of the most striking in the post-1914 drafts. As in the case of the characters' language, it is perhaps those additions of simply a few lines which most arrest the attention: when, for example, in three-and-a-half pages of text, the only addition made is one introducing a consideration of lying not previously there, the sign of a powerful new intention is unmistakable. (The addition in question was worked into *A l'ombre* just after the vague statements of the 'bâtonnier' that the Cambremers had wished to introduce him to M. de Stermaria: Proust now inserts, after 'dit le bâtonnier':

> qui comme beaucoup de menteurs s'imaginent (*sic*) qu'on ne cherchera pas à élucider un détail insignifiant qui suffit pourtant (si le hasard vous met en possession de l'humble réalité qui est en contradiction avec lui) pour dénoncer un caractère et inspirer à jamais la méfiance (I 688c).)

---

1 Interestingly, the addition to *Le Côté de Guermantes* mentioning Mlle d'Ambresac as a bride not for Saint-Loup but for others does actually set beside this, included in the same insertion, rumours about his inversion, which Marcel maintains he was able to 'démentir de la façon la plus formelle' (II 403-5a).

And, apart from these shorter examples, there are much longer added passages, indeed episodes, developing the _leitmotif_ of liars and lying.

Let us look first at what happens to those characters outside the main drama of the Albertine affair. Mme Verdurin's allegations about the war-time activities of acquaintances, uttered 'sans scrupule de mentir', and Mme de Cambremer's deformation of names, a 'procédé semblable à celui des menteurs', were inserted in the MSS of, respectively, _Le Temps retrouvé_ and _Sodome et Gomorrhe_ (III 768-69a; II 916c).[1] The prince de Borodino's hairdresser, who appears only in additions, has 'une faculté de mensonge extraordinaire' (II 127b);[2] Mme de Guermantes's claim that she was never at the Saint-Euverte soirée ('La duchesse avait toujours été un peu menteuse et l'était devenue davantage') is part of a long addition to _Le Temps retrouvé_ (III 1023-26a, p. 1024); and one of the late passages in _A l'ombre_ about Bloch and his family describes Bloch's habit of consolidating some falsehood with the words '"Je te le jure", plus encore pour la volupté hystérique de mentir que dans l'intérêt de faire croire qu'il disait la vérité' (I 740-48a, pp. 745-46). Similarly, one characteristic of Nissim Bernard's is 'l'habitude du mensonge perpétuel', a

1 See II 973a for a lie of Mme Verdurin's which may be true.

2 His other appearance is in II 217-18a.

trait which greatly embarrasses his family but interests Saint-Loup, said to be 'très curieux de la psychologie des menteurs' (I 767-79a, p. 775) - although Proust also added in the margin of the 1914 galleys of Le Côté de Guermantes the exoneration, this once, of Nissim Bernard ('"Dire que pour une fois il n'avait pas menti, c'est incroyable", eût pensé Bloch') (II 276-77a). As for the 'jeunes filles', Proust inserted into La Fugitive Andrée's assertion that Gisèle 'mentait avec une telle perfidie' (III 549-50a);[1] and the passage in which she herself tells everyone that Octave's father has committed a theft was not only itself an addition (III 59-61a),[2] but was further reworked to make Andrée a definite liar rather than simply a spreader of malicious tales, since what originally read

> Or, j'appris qu'on n'était nullement certain que le père [...] eut (sic) rien fait d'indélicat, qu'Andrée n'en avait pas plus de preuves que personne

now runs:

> Or, j'appris que le père n'avait rien commis d'indélicat, qu'Andrée le savait aussi bien que quiconque (III 60b).

No doubt, too, her lie in the long 'jeunes filles' section is of late inspiration ('Bien que ce mensonge fût, Andrée me connaissant si peu, fort insignifiant, je n'aurais pas dû continuer à fréquenter une personne qui en était capable') (I 869-951a, p. 886).[3]

---

1 Gisèle is also a scandal-monger: see above, p. 256 n.1.

2 It is however mentioned in the MS of La F, III 603-4.

3 See also, for Andrée, III 603a,b.

However, it is the lying in Marcel's relationship with Albertine which is the most thoroughly expanded. As I said in Chapter 1,[1] and as can be gathered from Proust's November 1915 résumé for Mme Scheikevitch,[2] the jealousy now rife in the Albertine affair was apparently much less prominent in the earlier plan;[3] and in the finished text, much of this jealousy is provoked by the new impenetrability of Albertine's evidence. Marcel himself is given a few further lies or dissimulations in La Prisonnière ('Moi aussi, depuis que j'étais rentré et déclarais vouloir rompre, je mentais aussi'),[4] but these are well outweighed by the lies, suspected or proven, freshly attributed to Albertine in Sodome et Gomorrhe, La Prisonnière, and even later.[5]

On the widest level, Proust added general remarks about her capacities for lying. The direct focus on her lies as one of the fundamental enigmas of her being is late: the narrator feels

---

1 p. 63.

2 Correspondance Générale (6 vols., Paris, 1930-36), vol. V, pp. 234-41. Bardèche (vol. II, pp. 168-69, 210-13) and Feuillerat (pp. 209-11) discuss this letter.

3 Bardèche refers too to 'la jalousie, si étrangement absente' from early sketches of Marcel's love (vol. II, p.34).

4 III 349-51a, p. 351; see also III 120b; III 332a; III 339a, b,c; III 341a; III 352-53a. (He lied in the MS on III 106, 355.)

5 The next section (pp. 273-76) gives a summary of those suspicious activities of Albertine's which were already in the MS; as for her actual lies in the unexpanded MS, the only concrete one was that about the possible visit to the Verdurins (III 90-91, 106). One important passage gave examples of her habitual self-contradictions (III 407-8), and a few other pages made brief reference to her lying (III 384, 525, 609, 622-23), but this was virtually all.

he must bring a judgement on her as a whole, 'savoir si elle m'avait menti, si elle aimait les femmes' (III 514a); two descriptions in La Prisonnière of Marcel's fear of her lies were added to the typescript and to the manuscript (III 21-23a, III 22a; III 29-30a, p. 30); and the long discussion provoked by the 'terrible intonation dédaigneuse [...] qui se retrouve dans toutes les classes de la société quand une femme ment' appears only wholly in the first typescript, leading into the important affirmation that Albertine 'ne se contentait pas de mentir comme tout être qui se croit aimé, mais [...] par nature, elle était, en dehors de cela, menteuse' (III 96-99a, pp. 96, 98). The three passages in La Prisonnière in which Marcel puts down Albertine's lies to her recognition of his jealousy were all added to the MS (III 57-58a; III 58a; III 61a),[1] and that series of rhetorical questions in La Fugitive about the mutual dissimulations of the pair, in the course of which Marcel asks 'mais notre vie ne reposait-elle pas sur un perpétuel mensonge?', was equally late (III 466-67a). And, to return to the beginning of the process, Marcel's premonition in Sodome et Gomorrhe of 'de longues souffrances' is not in the MS:

> je sentais que je n'apprendrais jamais rien, qu'entre la multiplicité entremêlée des détails réels et des faits mensongers je n'arriverais jamais à me débrouiller [...] (II 733-34a).[2]

Specific illustrations of Albertine's duplicity were added

---

1 See also III 58b; and III 23a; III 530b.

2 See also, for a general discussion, III 177-80a, pp. 178-80.

in numbers too. Proust inserted into the MS of La Prisonnière both examples of her habitual type of lie in the life with Marcel: she will forget her own falsehoods, stage by stage revealing a close relationship with a 'personne "insoupçonnable"', or will manage to '[rendre] vaines mes cruelles attaques et [rétablir] la situation' by rapidly changing 'je' to 'elle' in the course of some anecdote (III 144-47a, pp. 145-46; III 152-53a). And Proust situated other lies more definitely than these ones in the imperfect tense, as it were. He added, first, incidents to show Marcel discovering or guessing at falsehoods without either direct avowal or obvious evasion on Albertine's part. Her supposed meeting with Bergotte, related so naturally that Marcel is quite deceived, for 'je n'appris que bien plus tard l'art charmant qu'elle avait de mentir avec simplicité', and her fabrications of other encounters with individuals of whom Marcel is jealous, which she has gone so far as to concoct simply because she 'trouvait que nier complètement était peu vraisemblable', come towards the end of a long section appearing for the first time in the third typescript (III 182-92a, pp. 188-92). Although her relations with Andrée are in the MSS,[1] the passage in which, contradicting herself, she assures Marcel that she hardly looks at her friend, whereas she had once told him that '"Andrée est ravissante"', was added to the MS (III 398a); so was Marcel's memory in La Fugitive of her offer to swear on her mother's grave that she had had no relations with

---

1 See below, pp. 273-74.

Andrée, and his discovery that her story about the airfield was 'inventé de toutes pièces': this is the passage describing Albertine's lies as 'si inattendus que j'avais peine à les assimiler à ma pensée' (III 611-12a). And all the sequences about the two rings that Albertine maintains have come respectively from her aunt and her own purchases, but which turn out, through the eager detective-work of Françoise, to be gifts from the same unknown person, were inserted into the MS (III 63c; III 165a; III 462-65a; III 641a).[1]

Last, new lies and prevarications emerge in open interrogation. The tortuously undignified four-page scene in Sodome et Gomorrhe in which Marcel catches Albertine out whilst she, squirming, tries to get away to someone momentarily transformed into 'une dame qui recevait, paraît-il, tous les jours' at Infreville was inserted in a layer glued to the typescript (II 798-802a, II 800a), and added also, to the MS of La Prisonnière, was the corresponding paragraph in which Albertine, blurting out angry words, entirely forgets this fiction (III 109d). Both Albertine's affirmation that Gilberte is not 'du genre de femmes'

---

1 See also III 67 n.1: III 1068b, added on the third typescript. (The final discovery, in a rough version, was originally to take place earlier, before Albertine's departure (at about the equivalent of III 81), but Proust noted in the margin of the page that he might place it elsewhere. See under III 462-65a. This is the passage referred to in III 81 Pl.n.1.)

disliked by Marcel, and her subsequent admission that Gilberte had kissed her and asked her if she liked women, were late (III 23b, c, d; III 376a).[1] Proust also added to the MS of <u>La Prisonnière</u> Albertine's remark that she has never had a single drawing-lesson, whereupon Marcel reminds her that she had once used just such a lesson as an excuse: this is the occasion on which Albertine, blushing, answers that she had formerly lied a great deal to Marcel, but, when pressed, gives a most implausibly harmless example (III 180-81a). The strange circumstances of the journey to Balbec with the chauffeur, and Albertine's too-hasty revelation that it never took place, form part of long additions to the third typescript (III 131-36a, p. 136; III 333-39a, pp. 333-35); and this confession is followed, in the same addition, by Albertine's insistence that she did not after all have close ties with Mlle Vinteuil and her friend, but had only wished to give herself prestige: 'Quand je vous mens, c'est toujours par amitié pour vous'! (III 333-39a, p. 336). This possibility of innocence is again stressed with the addition (apparently earlier, on the MS) of both Marcel's conviction that Albertine is lying about Mlle Vinteuil and her friend, and his reflection (accompanied by varying emotions) that her honesty has at least been enough to make her confess that she would have liked to see them again (III 396-97a;

1 (There seems to be some confusion in Proust's mind here, since in the latter addition Marcel states that Albertine <u>had</u> said Gilberte was of 'mauvais genre'.)

III 509a). Finally, Proust worked into the MS the interrogation during which Albertine, having said that very morning that she does not know Léa, reveals that she indeed does, and even made a three-week journey with her (III 349-51a).[1]

SUSPICIONS AND 'PROOFS' ABOUT ALBERTINE

At first sight, all these new lies give the impression that Proust was trying to make Albertine appear more guilty of infidelity than she originally was, and other insertions, not directly showing deceit but contributing to evidence of guilt, initially reinforce such an impression; but with the addition of discoveries absolving as well as condemning her, it becomes plainer that the principal intention is to generate more

---

1 The sequence about the Buttes-Chaumont is, oddly, divided between the MS (on clean paper: III 538, 543-44, 549, 608, 611) and additions (the second made on a rather old-looking page in the MS: III 19a,b; III 389a).
See also, for Albertine's duplicity, I 598c; I 869-951a, pp. 938-40; II 368-69a, p. 369; II 1097a; II 1114e; III 90-91a; III 91-94a, pp. 91-92; III 94-96a; III 100n.5: III 1073a,b; III 114b; III 170b; III 223-24a; III 359-60a, p. 360; III 384-85a; III 389-91a; III 507b; III 509-10a; III 615-17a (described by Proust as 'le plus capital de tout le livre' - see III 615n.1).
For other additions about lies, dissimulations, or contradictory or opaque replies to enquiries, see: I 767-79a, pp. 769-70, 773, 776; I 785d; II 161-64a, p. 163; II 908c; II 973-74a; II 1043a; II 1113b; III 204-7a, p. 204; III 213-14a, III 213a, III 222-23a, p. 223; III 266-72a, p. 271; III 280-82a, pp. 280-81; III 314-16a; III 315a; III 316d; III 441-42a; III 621a; III 750-51a; III 770-71a; III 813a; III 824-25a; III 841b,n.; III 1020-23a, p. 1022.

uncertainty around her actions, and to show the effect this has on Marcel.

The principal dichotomies Albertine presents now - is she faithful or not? and is she heterosexual or lesbian? - were in the MSS, but attached to far fewer subjects, and proportionately, in _Sodome et Gomorrhe_ and _La Prisonnière_, obtruding considerably less in the narration of events. The MS of _Sodome et Gomorrhe_, up to the last chapter, presented Andrée as almost the sole suspected partner in lesbian activities,[1] although Marcel did worry indistinctly about what Albertine might be doing when she was not with him, occasionally found her unavailable,[2] or realised with dismay that she had been looking at Bloch's sister and cousin in the Casino mirror.[3] The attention she paid to Saint-Loup, and Marcel's jealousy over it, were also in the MS;[4] but, until the revelation about Mlle Vinteuil and her friend (II 1114-31), this was all.

Subjects of jealousy in _La Prisonnière_ and _La Fugitive_ were similarly restricted. Andrée now appeared, for the most part, as Albertine's chaperone,[5] although Mme Bontemps revealed that Albertine might have returned from Balbec for the

---

1 See II 795-96, 803-5, 828, 830, 832-35, 841-42, without the additions.

2 See II 726, 729-34, 738, 787, 793-94, 797-98, 1015, 1017, without additions.

3 II 802-3.

4 II 856, 858-60, 864-65, 1021-22, without additions.

5 See III 19, 59, 61-62, 100-101, without additions; also III 469-70, 477-78.

sake of her friend, there was some suspicion,[1] and Andrée, after a denial, finally admitted she did have relations with Albertine.[2] The revelation about Mlle Vinteuil and her friend was exploited to some extent: Marcel realised that Albertine wanted to go to the Verdurins', found out, to his distress, that the couple were to come, and was surprised to be asked directly about this by Albertine;[3] he reverted inwardly to the problem throughout La Prisonnière and La Fugitive, only to be informed eventually by Andrée that Albertine had no relations with them, but was simply embarrassed about the proposed visit to the Verdurins' because marriage with Octave was being planned - this indeed, Andrée maintained, was the reason Albertine left him, and she had not been unfaithful at all whilst living with him.[4] As for other lesbian activities, the MS gave the news that it was Léa who was performing at the Trocadéro, told us

---

1 III 388-89, 392-93, 395-98, 404, 413, 509-10, 538, 543-45, 547-50, without additions.

2 III 548, 599, 601-3, 608-11, without additions; see also III 859.

3 (This is the only hint of infidelity in the early separation scene: III 332-33, without additions.)

4 III 87, 88, 90-91, 100-101, 106-7, 119, 222-25, 263, 265, 284, 288, 292-93, 295-96, 332-33, 367, 372-73, 393, 408, 413, 423, 431, 465, 500, 614-15, 617-23; also III 1030, without additions. (See also III 341-43, 348-49, 351-58, 360-63, without additions, for the MS version of the second part of the separation scene.)
Although Octave is in the MS here, his appearances earlier in the novel, in his 'je-suis-dans-les-choux' persona, are probably additions: I 869-951a, pp. 878-79, 883, 929-30; II 871a.

that she was the actress friend of the two girls of the Casino mirror episode, and touched on Marcel's anxiety about these three at regular intervals during La Prisonnière and La Fugitive;[1] if these are only suspicions, the harsher facts elicited from the shower-girl and the laundress in the course of Aimé's investigations were in the MSS too.[2] However, except for a few references back to the jealousy about Saint-Loup, some fruitless questioning of Gilberte in Le Temps retrouvé, and worries lest a friend like Bloch might fall in love with Albertine,[3] this, again, was all of substance that the early version comprised.[4] The basic problems and uncertainties were there and were well-explored, but in a more moderated manner than in the novel we

---

1 III 85, 119, 144, 148-49, 151, 152, 153-57, 225, 465, 485, 491, without additions.

2 III 84-87, 491-92, 512-21, 523-31, 533, 543-45, 611, without additions.

3 For Saint-Loup, see III 149, 305-6, 436, without additions; for Gilberte, III 706; and for Bloch, III 56, without additions. (As we knew already from the Pléiade edition notes (III 59nn.2,3) and from M. Suzuki ('Le "Je" Proustien', BSAMP, no. 9 (1959), p. 72), Bloch originally played more part here than at present.)

4 General suspicions, or Albertine's attempts to behave in such a way as to lull them, also appear in the MSS on III 28, 56-58, 177, 364, 384-86, 404-5, 472, 474-75, 489-90, 507-9, 550-51, 552-53, without additions.
Holland, sometimes specifically Amsterdam, is mentioned in the MS as a place to which Marcel does not want Albertine to go: III 385, 393, 413, 431. Bardèche (vol. II, pp. 31, 41n.1) provides the explanation for this; see also II 814d.

finally have, and covering a limited, if symmetrical, range; and more room was left for Albertine's possible innocence than at present, since the only real ground for suspicion was Andrée's avowals and Aimé's reports in _La Fugitive_.

Now, however, the very fact that Albertine becomes so much more a liar makes it less easy to exonerate her from shady activities; and her contradictions about people she has met or knows, the lie about the trip to the aviation-field, and the mysterious provenance of the two rings, seem to provide some support for Marcel's suspicions. The doubtful visit to the lady at Infreville, the drawing-lesson, and, above all, the non-existent trip to Balbec and the three-weeks' journey with Léa are even bolder indications, especially since during Albertine's three days at Auteuil rather than Balbec, she went out dressed as a man (III 333-39a, pp. 333-35). Again, some of these lies may be more innocent than they look, arising perhaps from the relationship with Octave or from Albertine's fear of Marcel's jealousy; but, whatever their final explanation, Proust also added a whole series of passages complementary to the new falsehoods, giving further examples of behaviour which could be seen as lesbian, while supplying at the same time a small minority of neutralising explanations.

On the side of either innocent or heterosexual motives, he inserted into _La Fugitive_ Andrée's comparatively sober claim that Albertine left Marcel out of uneasiness about the opinion of the little band (III 607-8a); and he stressed further the possible engagement to Octave with the addition of Françoise's dark hints that 'la pauvre captive (qui aimait les femmes) préférait un mariage avec quelqu'un qui ne semblait pas être moi' (III 96-99a, pp. 98-99). But even in this context, Proust added Marcel's later conclusion that, notwithstanding the fact that this marriage at first provides a quite different set of worries, it is not, after all, incompatible with interpretations of lesbianism, 'le goût pour les femmes n'empêchant pas de se marier' (III 614-15a). Albertine's heterosexuality might again seem to be implied by her staring at the Rivebelle waiter, an incident added to the _Sodome et Gomorrhe_ MS (II 1015-16a); and other MS insertions accentuate further Marcel's jealousy of Saint-Loup (II 1100-1101a; II 1101-1108a, pp. 1101-2, 1108; II 1108a).[1] But this very jealousy now takes on a new dimension. Charlus's talk of the spread of bisexuality does already, in the MS of _La Prisonnière_, undermine Marcel's assumption that Albertine's behaviour with Saint-Loup excludes lesbianism (III 305-8); but all those passages in _Sodome et Gomorrhe_ stressing Marcel's naīvety in believing 'qu'un goût en exclut forcément un autre' (II 875e) were added only to the typescript,[2] and the important definition of Marcel's anguish at the end of _Sodome et Gomorrhe_, starting 'Qu'était, à côté de la souffrance que je ressentais, la jalousie que j'avais pu

---

1 Also II 1101a, added to the typescript.

2 The others are II 865a; II 883-84a, p. 883; see also II 854a.

éprouver le jour où Saint-Loup avait rencontré Albertine avec moi [...]?', was an insertion in the MS (II 1120a).[1]

All the other additions play without qualification on Albertine's possible lesbianism. Proust not only made more mention of the suspicions about Mlle Vinteuil and her friend[2] (these probably needed development anyway: the MS account of Marcel's feelings at the Verdurin soirée was not very convincing), he also gave Léa a more prominent rôle: as well as the journey already cited (III 349-51a), he inserts Mme de Cambremer's story about meeting a certain Lina, Linette, Lisette or Lia with Albertine (II 1097a), and the latter's confession that after one performance of Léa's she and her friends watched the actress dress (III 356-57a,n.).[3] Whereas the only MS episode directly involving Albertine with Bloch's sister and cousin was that in the Casino, when she gazed at them in the mirror, Proust now describes the amorous stroll on which, emitting 'des gloussements, des rires, des cris indécents', they pass Albertine, Bloch, and Marcel, who is 'torturé en pensant que ce langage particulier et atroce s'adressait peut-

---

1 Taken up in two other additions too: III 385a; III 546a.

2 II 1114f; II 1121d; III 94a; III 128-31a, p. 131; III 222-23a; III 224a; III 225a; III 241-42a; III 245a; III 252-53a; III 253a; III 280a; III 293a; III 295-96a; III 333b; III 356-57a,n.; III 361-62a; III 396-97a; III 539-40a; III 547a; III 614-15a. See also I 869-951a, p. 883.

3 See also, for Léa and Albertine, I 869-951a, pp. 899-900, 903, 941-42; III 107a; III 119c; III 131-36a, pp. 132, 136; III 144-47a, pp. 144-46; III 149-51a, p. 151; III 150-51a.

être à Albertine' (II 850-51a); and, at the end of Sodome et Gomorrhe, the three occasions on which Marcel expresses his fear of them were all inserted into the MS (II 1121b; II 1124b; II 1124-25a, p. 1125).[1] Furthermore, although the cousin had briefly figured in the MS of La Prisonnière and was named as Esther (III 85), Proust added to this MS the entire series in which Marcel sends for her photograph, checks with Aimé, accuses Albertine, confronting her with the news that he has seen the photograph, and eventually finds out that Albertine had given her photograph to the young woman.[2] Where Andrée herself is concerned, Proust twice now makes the MS of Sodome et Gomorrhe refer specifically to 'games' or caresses between her and Albertine, where the first version had remained vague (II 804a, II 832b); and he inserts both the important seringa incident, worked into the typescripts of La Prisonnière, and the full explanation for it, which appears some 550 pages afterwards as a late layer addition to the MS of La Fugitive. Even this is characterised as 'tout cela dont je n'ai jamais su si c'était vrai' (III 55a,n.).[3] Finally, the questioning of Gilberte in Le Temps retrouvé, originally cursory and inconclusive (III 706 §1), is now further pursued, with the insertion of another conversation in which Gilberte denies

---

1 (Here they are both Bloch's cousins.)

2 III 86a; III 87b; III 111a; III 342a,b; III 364a; III 367n.2: III 1091a. Bloch's sister and cousin are themselves elaborated in SG, thus further justifying Marcel's worries: see below, p. 287.

3 The other additions are III 54-55a; III 55b; III 600-601a. See also, for Andrée, II 841a; but for Marcel's confidence in her, II 1125b; III 19b; III 19-20a; III 20a,b.

she had ever said Albertine was of 'mauvais genre' and Marcel, although doubting her honesty, thinks that Albertine might have pretended to more experience than she had, and had perhaps lived 'près de l'amie de Mlle Vinteuil et d'Andrée, séparée par une cloison étanche d'elles qui croyaient qu'elle "n'en était pas"' (III 707-8a; III 708a).[1]

Besides thus extending Albertine's relations with subjects already in the MS, Proust added some considerable passages, from Sodome et Gomorrhe on, introducing quite new suspects or ambiguous behaviour. Marcel's compulsion to check on Albertine 'pour voir s'il ne s'y faisait rien d'anormal' if she goes into a separate train-compartment with the other women was added to the MS of Sodome et Gomorrhe (II 1042a); so was the page that starts 'Mais bientôt la saison battit son plein' and goes on to describe Marcel's fears of the young women arriving and his attempts to persuade Albertine that the bad reputation of those of 'mauvais genre' 'n'était fondée sur rien' (II 840-41a). The incident which 'fixa davantage encore mes préoccupations du côté de Gomorrhe' was worked in partly on the MS and partly on the typescript of Sodome et Gomorrhe: Marcel now admires 'une belle jeune femme élancée et pâle', only to notice her directing towards Albertine 'les feux alternés et tournants de ses regards', and to establish her lesbianism, finally, by witnessing her behaviour with Bloch's cousin

1 For Gilberte, see also the lies mentioned above, pp. 270-71; and Ch. 5, pp. 211-12.

(II 851a, b; II 851-53a; II 852b).[1] This sequence comprises too the description of Albertine's coldness with her companions, perhaps belied, however, by her habit of turning round when some good-looking young woman gets out of a car and her pretence to Marcel that she is merely looking at a flag; and the passage immediately following, in which she reports her apparent rudeness to a woman of 'mauvais genre' ('exprès, par grossièreté, je l'ai presque frôlée en passant') was late too, given in a layer glued to the MS (II 853-54a).[2]

Additions to the base version of <u>La Prisonnière</u> continue in like manner. Two recollections of Albertine's behaviour at Balbec were inserted: in the first, Marcel remembers her staring at passing girls, then saying '"Si on les faisait venir? J'aimerais leur dire des injures"' (III 89-90a);[3] and the second, going back to a time before they knew each other, is his memory of her insolent laughter at him on the beach, 'non loin de telle dame avec qui j'étais fort mal et avec qui j'étais presque certain maintenant qu'elle avait eu des relations' (III 173-74a). Albertine's outburst of 'j'aime bien mieux que vous me laissiez une fois libre pour que j'aille me faire casser ..."', and Marcel's subsequent interpretation of this, are, of course, as new as the other disquieting activities implied in the long

---

1 See below, p. 287.

2 See also, for additions to <u>SG</u> about Marcel's suspicions or anxieties, II 732a; II 1036-37a.

3 See also III 89b.

addition to the 'separation' scene[1] (III 333-39a, pp. 337-39; III 339-41a). Marcel's meeting with Gisèle, in the course of which she observes that she has '*justement* quelque chose' to tell Albertine about 'de petites camarades à elle', was added, in a margin and layer, to the MS (III 177-80a); and the two-page mute by-play with the *pâtissière* was worked in as late as the third typescript (III 408-10a; III 409-10a). Marcel also now gives way to further suspicions or speculations after Albertine's death. Proust inserted into the MS of *La Fugitive* the sudden notion that Albertine, almost certainly outside the Balbec restaurant-window at night, 'sans doute levait là quelque fillette qu'elle rejoignait quelques minutes plus tard' (III 521a),[2] as well as the information that Saint-Loup had once thought of marrying Albertine because, Marcel concludes, he knew that 'elle était de Gomorrhe comme lui de Sodome' (III 679a; III 679-80a).[3]

However, the most pervasive new element in Marcel's doubts, or rather in his over-trusting beliefs, about Albertine's activities is her agreement with the chauffeur and her partnership with Morel. As was implied in the chapter on Morel,[4] all references to this oddly vague, darkly-hinted-at triangle are additions, from the insertion of such cryptic words as 'pour mon malheur' (II 995b) when Marcel's hiring of the chauffeur

---

1 These others are described above, p. 271.

2 See also III 479a; III 611a.

3 See here also III 706*n*.3: III 1120-21a.

4 Chapter 4, pp. 202-3.

in Sodome et Gomorrhe is mentioned, to the revelation that this chauffeur has indeed been conniving with Albertine (III 131-36a, pp. 133-34; III 333-39a, pp. 333-35),[1] and to the final allegation, the most extraordinary of all, that Albertine, together with Morel, would abduct young girls: 'Mais Albertine avait après d'affreux remords. [...] Elle espérait que vous la sauveriez' says Andrée (III 599-600a).[2]

BISEXUALITY AND INVERSION

Even these last additions about Albertine's lesbianism perhaps provide no firmer ground for conclusions than did the incidents already in the MS, often amounting to a chain of nervous deductions based merely on Albertine's stares; and no

---

1 Already noted; see p. 271.

2 The other additions about the chauffeur and Albertine are: II 1006-9a, p. 1006; II 1027b; II 1027-28a, p. 1028; III 17a; III 21-23a, p. 23; III 24a; III 126d, III 126-27a; III 131-36a, *passim*, III 134-35a; and about Morel and Albertine: II 1031-32a, p. 1032, II 1032a; III 373a. Further additions seeming to indict Albertine, or referring to Marcel's suspicions, are: II 733-34a; II 787a,c; II 788a,b; II 794d; II 796a; II 797a; II 803b; II 832-33a; II 834a; II 838-40a; II 842-45a, p. 842; II 1017-18a; II 1020-21a; III 28b; III 80-81a; III 81a; III 85a; III 85-86a; III 86b; III 86-87a; III 87a; III 88b; III 102b; III 348-49a; III 388a; III 389-91a; III 391-92a; III 397a; III 510-11a; III 515b; III 518a; III 524-25a; III 525a,b; III 617-18a,b.
For general discussions on this subject, or for additions about infidelities, 'proofs' of guilt or innocence, etc., not specifically Albertine's, but, for example, Rachel's, see: I 500-502a, p. 501; II 161-64a; II 281-83a; II 282a; III 905a,*n.*; III 916-17a.

doubt one reason for the increase of inaccurate reports in the novel, and for the new duplicity of some of the characters, was to cancel out to some extent the apparently overwhelming testimonies of Andrée, for example.[1] In spite of this uncertainty, and in spite of the fact that Albertine's incriminating blushes or obvious deceptions may mean no more than the dissimulation of a quite different truth, less disturbing but more embarrassing, the very enquiries about lesbianism, and the very suspicions of conspiratorial banding-together, create an atmosphere in which these considerations, constantly thrust under the reader's eyes, begin to weigh more and more heavily in the novel. Even if nothing is proved, something seems to be going on. And in the case of the other characters, the omniscient narrator shows without question that more figures in _A la recherche_ are indeed turning to bi-sexuality or overt homosexuality: the least one can say is that Proust wishes to bring a fundamental ambiguity into greater prominence.

It has already been shown that although Saint-Loup's change to homosexuality and his relationship with Morel were in the MS, Proust elaborated the liaison;[2] besides this, however, he added a number of more general references to Saint-Loup's

---

1 Andrée herself is not only made a liar (see above, p. 266), but also acquires unpleasant character-traits which might equally account for her stories: see above, Ch. 2, p. 76 _n_.3; Ch. 5, p. 221.

2 See above, Ch. 1, pp. 53, 55; Ch. 4, pp. 183, 202.

inversion, such as the rumour (and the subsequent confirmation) that each member of the group of four to which he belongs is homosexual (II 403-5a),[1] the growing resemblance of his manner to his mother's and Charlus's (III 703-4a), and the assertion that 'le petit Saint-Loup est "comme ça"', made by the 'sous-maîtresse' at Maineville, who is 'persuadée qu'en notre siècle la perversité des moeurs le disputait à l'absurdité calomniatrice des cancans' - thus proving an unlikely commentator on two of the new themes discussed in this chapter (III 662-64a, p. 662). Saint-Loup's preference for conversation about military strategy rather than homosexuality was inserted into the MS of <u>Le Temps retrouvé</u> ('pour le genre de choses auxquelles tu fais allusion, je m'y connais autant qu'en sanscrit') (III 705b); the friend of his who had kept Morel at the same time as he himself is an added character (III 956b,<u>n</u>.); and late too is Gilberte's naïve comment about their daughter: 'je crois tout de même qu'étant donné ses goûts, [...] il aurait préféré un garçon' (III 1028b).[2]

Charlus himself becomes the hero of further escapades, or acquires hitherto unspecified penchants. The development of Morel of course brings both the baron and his homosexuality to

---

1 Referred to above, pp. 261, 264<u>n</u>.1; in the <u>CG</u> addition already cited (above, pp. 221-22, 255) Bloch too proclaims a 'mal si épouvantable' of Saint-Loup that 'tout le monde en fut révolté' (II 228a).

2 See also, for Saint-Loup, III 670-71a; III 678a; III 679a; III 679-80a; III 680-81a; III 680a; III 681-82a; III 682a; III 683-84a; III 685a; III 686a; III 737b,<u>n</u>.; III 743-44a; III 746-47a, p. 747; III 818a; III 841b,<u>n</u>.; III 847a. For earlier added hints, see I 729a; II 182-83a; II 695a.

the fore: probably the most interesting elaborations here on Charlus's own state of mind are the two additions in one of which it is said that he is not jealous of Morel's success with women (III 216-19a, p. 217), but in the other that Léa's letter to Morel has thrown him into a state of confusion (III 214-16a, III 215a).[1] Apart from these, however, Proust worked in too the dinner with Mme de Chevregny's footman, related only in two late insertions in Sodome et Gomorrhe (II 986-87a; II 987-93a); the second of these includes the letter to Aimé,[2] whose rôle throughout the novel as an object of interest to Charlus is also new (I 766b; I 767d, f; II 169a). The baron's arrest for inversion was not in the original Temps retrouvé (III 852-53a); as for his attitude to bisexuality, in the MS he was simply deploring it as a recent trend (III 306-8), but now Proust gives him a need for 'du nouveau' that leads him to spend the night with a woman,

> de la même façon qu'un homme normal peut une fois dans sa vie avoir voulu coucher avec un garçon, par une curiosité semblable, inverse, et dans les deux cas également malsaine (III 210-11a).

---

1 See above, Ch. 4, p. 201; also, e.g., pp. 188-90 for Charlus's new feelings for Morel.
The disorientation produced in Charlus by Léa's letter has been most perceptively discussed by Leo Bersani, who finds central parallels for it in many other areas of the novel (Marcel Proust: The Fictions of Life and of Art, pp. 72-75, and the first part of the chapter 'The Anguish and Inspiration of Jealousy', pp. 56-72).

2 (See too the rather later II 990-91a; II 991a,b; II 992a; II 993a.)

Léa too is given more connections than those she already had with Albertine and with Bloch's sister and cousin: besides adding the acquaintance with Morel,[1] Proust inserted into the MS of Le Temps retrouvé the revelation that it was she who was walking down the Champs-Élysées, dressed as a man, with Gilberte (III 694-95a; III 695-96a; III 695b,*n.*).[2] Bloch's sister now behaves scandalously in the Grand-Hôtel (II 842-45a, p. 842), and his cousin manoeuvres with the 'belle jeune femme élancée et pâle', both of them carrying off, in front of the 'mari berné', an unquestioned pretence of a former school friendship (II 851-53a, pp. 852-53, II 852b). And Proust slipped in more disparate references than these. The disclosure in Sodome et Gomorrhe that a complaisant high society will 'bouleverser l'aménagement d'un château' to let two sisters sleep together was added to the MS, but in its first form talked of a brother and sister: even incest, then, is to support the theme of lesbianism (II 715-16a; II 716a). The homosexuals at the Verdurin soirée with whom Charlus exchanges 'propos furtifs' ('deux ducs, un général éminent, un grand écrivain, un grand médecin, un grand avocat') were not there in the MS version (III 243-44a, III 243b, III 244a); and not among the original guests at the prince de Guermantes's soirée was the diplomatic mission

1 See principally Ch. 4, pp. 201-2.

2 (The relevant passage in A l'ombre is of course an addition: I 621-35a, pp. 623-25a.)

composed entirely of inverts, but at one period headed by a heterosexual, soon to be replaced, however, by 'une Excellence nouvelle qui assura l'homogénéité de l'ensemble' (II 674-75a). The _Temps retrouvé_ addition describing Marcel's further enquiries of Gilberte about Albertine[1] not only speculates on Gilberte's bisexuality, suggesting that this may have accounted for Saint-Loup's marrying her; it offers that conclusion comprising, as well as Gilberte, the girls of the 'petite bande', in all of whom

> il y a une telle diversité, un tel cumul de goûts alternants si même ils ne sont pas simultanés, qu'elles passent aisément d'une liaison avec une femme à un grand amour pour un homme, si bien que définir le goût réel et dominant reste difficile
> (III 707-8a; III 708b).

Several other characters, mainly aristocrats, now betray or openly manifest homosexuality. The prince de Guermantes, although said by Charlus to be an invert in the MS of _La Prisonnière_ (III 306-7),[2] is given, besides the attraction to Morel,[3] the acquaintance with Mme de Chevregny's footman (II 987-93a, pp. 987-88).[4] The nature of the prince de Foix's small group is defined only in the third Gallimard galleys (II 403-5a, pp. 403, 405),[5] and the relevant facts in _Le Temps retrouvé_

---

1 See above, pp. 279-80.

2 III 306-8 are on very clean paper in the MS, and _might_ be of late composition (n.a.fr. 16718:15-19).

3 See Ch. 4, p. 202.

4 See also II 1044-45a; III 780-81a.

5 Referred to above, p. 285.

about the prince's father, who shares these tastes and is indeed rumoured to have paid attention to his own son, are late too (III 827-28a). The prince Von's proposal that Marcel should go home with him to hear explanations about the prince de Foix appears also for the first time in the third Gallimard galleys (II 509a; II 510a, b, c), and is the only indication in the whole novel of his homosexuality. The vicomte de Courvoisier (III 704-5a, III 824a) and M. d'Argencourt (III 852-53a) turn out to be inverts in additions to Le Temps retrouvé;[1] and although Legrandin's homosexuality was revealed in the MS of La Fugitive (III 665-67), it is a new passage which describes Françoise's belief that the protection he and others accord to young men is 'une coutume que son universalité rendait respectable' (III 700-701a).

More substantially, the reader will remember that one of the changes wrought in Morel was to make him, from 'simply' inverted, now bisexual.[2] This apart, all the references to Vaugoubert's homosexuality, and his eager questioning of Charlus, were late.[3] Proust inserted too the dumb-show in which the duc

1 See III 272-73a for an earlier addition about d'Argencourt in this context.

2 See Ch. 4, pp. 200-202.

3 II 642-47a; II 664-66a and indented additions; II 666-68a, p. 666; II 674-75a; II 676a; II 774d; III 45-47a. (See Ch.1, p. 44, for descriptions of some early SG versions.) Vaugoubert appears as Charlus's childhood friend in the MS, but not necessarily as an invert (III 246).

de Châtellerault knocks Poullein with his elbow (II 493d); he substituted the same Châtellerault for Charlus in a sequence already added in which the baron had been kicking Bloch under the table (II 505b);[1] and he incorporated into _Sodome et Gomorrhe_ not only Jupien's portrait of the duc (II 610-13a, pp. 611-12) but also the tale of his encounter with the usher who, on discovering his benefactor's identity, proudly announces him with more exalted nomenclature than he is entitled to (II 633-34a; II 636-37a; II 637a).[2] And, as I have mentioned, the invert Nissim Bernard, who keeps a young clerk and who is subjected to bewildering confrontations with the tomato-faced twins, pursues his career entirely outside the main body of all the base versions: even the reference to him in the heading for the second chapter of _Sodome et Gomorrhe II_ was added after all the others (II 782b). At what date he made his début is uncertain, since he appears in additions to _A l'ombre_ and _Le Temps retrouvé_,[3] which this study cannot date; but he does seem to belong for the most part to the post-1918

---

1 (He forgets to change accordingly an addition on the next page referring to M. de Guermantes's blushes: II 506b.)

2 Châtellerault's inversion is however mentioned by Charlus _in_ the MS, at roughly the same place as the prince de Guermantes's (III 308).

3 I 767-79a, pp. 773-75; III 737b, _n._; III 943-44a.

period.[1]

If Proust is spreading inversion, he introduces too a topsy-turvy heterosexuality, now making Nissim Bernard's clerk, the lift-boy and Morel all turn away from homosexuality in insertions into Le Temps retrouvé:

> Si un mouvement singulier avait conduit à l'inversion - et cela dans toutes les classes - des êtres comme Saint-Loup qui en étaient le plus éloignés, un mouvement en sens inverse avait détaché de ces pratiques ceux chez qui elles étaient le plus habituelles [...] (III 780-81a).[2]

---

1 Although the passage in which it emerges that he was not lying after all was, as I have said (above, p. 266), added to the 1914 galleys (II 276-77a), the other mention of him in Le Côté de Guermantes was made after the completion of the first Gallimard galleys (II 289-90a), and all the references but one in Sodome et Gomorrhe were added to or after the typescript (II 842-45a; II 843a; II 845-50a, p. 845; II 848a; II 850-51a, p. 850; II 854-55a and all indented additions; II 855b; II 858c. The MS addition, only a brief reference, is II 1101-8a, p. 1101). Finally, his loan to Morel appears only in the first TS of La Prisonnière (III 51-54a, pp. 53-54).
There is a long passage in the proofs of Sodome et Gomorrhe which indicates that Nissim Bernard might originally have been intended for a rather more important part: it describes his oriental tastes and shows him winding his way through the subterranean passages of the Grand-Hôtel (n.a.fr. 16766:298-300). Proust finally reduced this to the briefer paragraph 'Il aimait d'ailleurs tout le labyrinthe de couloirs [...] on le voyait en explorer furtivement les détours' (II 842-45a, p. 845). This penetration into the mysteries of the Grand-Hôtel had also been mentioned, with Charlus as the hero, in an addition to the end of a 'paperole' on n.a.fr. 16711: 43 (see II 772-75a). Eventually excised too, it ran thus (the 'y' is the Grand-Hôtel):

> Certes M. de Charlus me disais-je aurait pu s'y plaire mieux que l'année où je l'y avais connu, en quoi je me trompait (sic). Je le voyais s'attardant (?) dans tous ces retraits correspondant aux "coins intérieurs" du Temple Juif, et à tel ou tel petit sanctuaire où il était aisé de ne pas être vu.

2 Also III 781a. The addition about the clerk is III 737b,n.

However, more striking than these, or indeed than many of the other elaborations on homosexuality, is a group of additions about the co-existence of marriage, and happy family life, with inversion. The absurd juxtapositions Proust lovingly unfolds make for rather grim, even heavy-handed, comedy.[1] Charlus did, it is true, assert in the MS that if he had had a daughter to marry, he would have given her a homosexual husband 'si j'avais voulu être assuré qu'elle ne fût pas malheureuse' (III 306), and had made a veiled remark to Mme de Parme that 'Ce sont les meilleurs maris' (III 665);[2] but Proust himself went on to illustrate these generalisations with definite partnerships and with his own comments.

Saint-Loup's inversion could always have been thought to be incongruous with his marriage: Proust now, however, makes this incongruity quite specific, adding, for example, almost all of the sequences in which Robert, instead of contenting himself with inversion, makes Gilberte unhappy over supposed mistresses: 'Les homosexuels seraient les meilleurs maris du monde s'ils ne jouaient pas la comédie d'aimer les femmes' (III 683-84a, p. 683; III 678a; III 704-5a).[3] That Sodome et Gomorrhe description of the passing-on of traits from uncle to nephew (here Charlus to Saint-Loup) which refers to the conviction of 'les Messieurs

---

1 An aside in a similar key of humour, that telling the reader that elegant guests of the Verdurins' tend to mistake the Maineville brothel for a hotel, was also late, added to the typescript of SG (II 1075-76a).

2 Slightly rewritten by Proust; see III 665a.

3 (Mentioned in the MS on III 677-78, 698.) For other additions about Saint-Loup, see III 662-64a, p. 662; III 680-81a, III 681a.

de Charlus' that they are 'les seuls bons maris' and ends 'De tels mariages ne sont pas rares, et sont souvent ce qu'on appelle heureux', is late too (II 695a);[1] and so is Françoise's claim that if she had a marriageable daughter, 'je la donnerais au baron les yeux fermés', praise she has equally given Jupien (II 630a). Not only has the vicomte de Courvoisier become an invert: he and his wife are 'cités comme le meilleur ménage de Paris' (III 704-5a). The Action Libérale député, a regular client at Jupien's, who has had to change his times this once in order to attend his daughter's wedding, and who shows marital concern for his wife (III 816a), is an added character.[2] The information that Aimé never refuses the advances of 'une étrangère ou un étranger', for he has a wife and children and 'le travail doit passer avant tout', was a still further elaboration on the late description of Charlus's letter to him (II 990-91a).[3] Finally, the new group of the prince de Foix comprises a fifth homosexual member, who is restrained by religious scruples until he is married and the father of a family, 'implorant à Lourdes que le prochain enfant fût un garçon ou une fille, et dans l'intervalle se jetant sur les

1 See I 751a; II 953-54a, p. 954, for Charlus's own marriage.

2 He appears only once more, to be re-elected after the war: III 853-54a, p. 854.

3 See also II 842-45a, p. 845, where Aimé's rôle in Nissim Bernard's arrangements is not 'des plus limpides'.

militaires' (II 403-5a, p. 405).[1]

It seems possible, judging from Bardèche's research and Feuillerat's reconstructions, that Saint-Loup was not at first to become an invert;[2] the elaboration of this theme may, then, have been more gradual than that of some others, starting in the rough Cahiers and ending with the additions I have just described.

---

1 Another homosexual marriage takes place in II 674-75a, p.675. For other additions about homosexuality or bisexuality, see I 727b; II 104c; II 118a; II 243c; II 290-91a; II 290a; II 604a-f; II 620-23a; II 620-21a; II 621a; II 623b; II 659-61a, p. 659; II 838-40a, p. 840; II 852a; II 903b; II 953-54a, II 954a; III 242-43a; III 297c,*n.* (compare with III 307, *in* MS); III 298a,b; III 303a; III 303*n*.2: III 1087a; III 304a,b,c; III 306a; III 830-31a.
The phrase 'en être', whose new use in Léa's letter confuses Charlus (III 214-16a; III 215a), is in the MS on, e.g., III 527, but its present prominent emphasis by Proust is late: see II 934c; II 941a; II 969c; II 1021-22a; II 1044-45a, p. 1045; III 707-8a, p. 708; III 768-69a; III 864-65a. 'De la confrérie' is twice used in similar contexts: II 1051b, and II 910a, where it replaces 'en être' in a first version.

2 See Feuillerat, pp. 50, 82, 98, 228; none of his deductions is conclusive, however. Bardèche too is not altogether clear on this point, saying on the one hand that Saint-Loup *was* to change in the early versions, on the other that he did not become Morel's lover (vol. II, pp. 258-59); and whilst in one of the drafts he reproduces of the last matinée, there is no sign of Saint-Loup's inversion (Bardèche, vol. II, pp. 408, 410), in another there is, perhaps, a hint of obscure behaviour (vol. II, p. 407). See also Bardèche, vol. II, pp. 100, 139, 349, for vague indications that this change was always planned (it is not wholly apparent, however, whether the MSS are being referred to).

Whatever their chronology, the developments described in this chapter could be seen as antithetical to the end of the novel in the form it had always had. The wider reference to bisexuality, with its implications of confused identity or uncertainly-oriented desires, heightens the narrator's resolution in Le Temps retrouvé, his affirmation of the permanence of his self (III 1047), and his recognition of what it is he really wants to do. Forgetfulness helps the propagation of rumour,[1] whereas, for the narrator, memory finally becomes a keystone. Lying, as much a linguistic abuse as cliché, provokes consideration of the links between a different kind of 'fiction' or invention - the novel - and truth. Furthermore, Marcel's last experiences symbolise the discovery of, and belief in, a knowledge that is now firm;[2] this knowledge is more triumphant when it is attained after a futile exploration, or practice, of labyrinthine deceits.

Proust did add to Le Temps retrouvé sections which directly meditate on these themes elaborated elsewhere. As I said in Chapter 1,[3] he now stresses the usefulness to the writer of suffering in love, inserting, notably, the sour praise of 'la jalousie si utile':

---

1 See above, pp. 257-58.

2 This has been emphasised by, e.g., R. Fernandez, A la gloire de Proust, pp. 189-91; E.R. Curtius, Marcel Proust (Paris, 1928), pp. 23-25, 96.

3 p. 58.

> nous sentons que la vie est un peu plus compliquée qu'on ne dit, et même les circonstances. Et il y a une nécessité pressante à montrer cette complexité [...] tout se compose bien, grâce à la présence suscitée par la jalousie de la belle fille dont déjà nous ne sommes plus jaloux et que nous n'aimons plus (III 916-17a).[1]

The opposition of the lover's and his mistress's lies (as well as private clichés) to 'la vérité ressentie' was added to the MS:

> [...] toute notre indignation contre ses mensonges si naturels, si semblables à ceux que nous pratiquons nous-même, [...] ramener tout cela à la vérité ressentie [...], c'est abolir tout ce à quoi nous tenions le plus [...] (III 890-91a);

so was the paradox of the writer who, in his work, rejects everything that is not truth, but in his life ruins himself for lies (III 909-10a). Finally, that long late passage very near the end of the novel, which transforms attitudes also described in a previous chapter of this study,[2] begins with an affirmation of the worth of life, now that

> elle me semblait pouvoir être éclaircie, elle qu'on vit dans les ténèbres, ramenée au vrai de ce qu'elle était, en somme réalisée dans un livre!
> (III 1032-35a, p. 1032).[3]

---

1 See also III 902a; III 903-4a; III 904-5a; III 905-7a and indented additions; III 907a; III 907c,*n.*; III 908a,b,c,d; III 908-9a; III 910a.

2 See above, Ch. 5, pp. 252, 253.

3 See also, for additions to *TR* bearing on those cited in this chapter, III 896a,b; III 904a; III 1035a.

7 Decline and Illness

Besides building up an atmosphere of confusion, or at least widely suggesting covert and ill-defined behaviour, Proust worked into his novel pictures of a more tangible disintegration. Many of the 'fin d'un monde, fin du monde' scenes in _A la recherche du temps perdu_ were added to the base versions only during the last few years of Proust's life. The decline of the Faubourg Saint-Germain is not, of course, necessarily deplored; Proust often presents such shifts as an inevitable social evolution, or as another illustration of the unexpected mutability eventually shown to the observer by time. None the less, equally often the reader is left with the feeling that some cohesive structure is dispersing, or has collapsed; and, evidently, a similar, but even stronger, impression is created by the enormously increased references to illness and old age, which unequivocally play on the destruction of what was formerly solid and robust. 'Not only do [Proust's] hero and most of his other characters pass into mortal declines, but their world itself seems to be coming to an end'.[1]

---

1 E. Wilson, _Axel's Castle_ (London and Glasgow, 1964), p. 153.

CHANGES IN SOCIETY

Proust was always to make the penetration of the upper classes by the lower, or by the bourgeoisie, crucial in his novel: quite apart from Swann's extraordinary social success, Jupien's niece and others, Bardèche tells us, were from an early stage to rise in the world;[1] and the MSS of the last volumes showed Bloch, Legrandin and Odette ensconced, via different openings, in the Faubourg Saint-Germain.[2]

In spite of this, many important stages on the road to the social apotheoses of, say, Mme Verdurin and Odette, were not in the base versions, as Chapter 1 indicated;[3] and other interesting factors in social change had still to be fully considered. For example, the single most important political phenomenon which Proust examines, in his revision, developing its rôle as a catalyst in society, is the Dreyfus Affair.

Several general explanations of the effect the Affair has on the composition of the salons, or of corporate attitudes to it, are late. The 'social kaleidoscope' is now twice, in _A l'ombre_ and _Le Côté de Guermantes_, said to be about to tumble Jews down again as a result of the Dreyfus Affair, when they had in fact been achieving some measure of acceptance in

---

1 Bardèche, vol. II, pp. 258, 306-7; see also Painter, vol. II, p. 322.

2 See above, Ch. 1, p. 60 ; also, e.g., III 672, 967-68 without the additions.

3 See, e.g., pp. 23, 62.

elegant circles (I 516-23a, pp. 516-18; II 190a).[1] Proust inserted into _La Prisonnière_ the half-whimsical commentary on M. de Cambremer's grossly exaggerated ideas about the Affair ('On n'accusera pas l'affaire Dreyfus d'avoir prémédité d'aussi noirs desseins à l'encontre du Monde. Mais là certainement elle a brisé les cadres') (III 230-38a, p. 235); and, in asides added to _Le Temps retrouvé_, he points out the sameness of reactions to the war and to the Affair (III 732-33a), describes the forgiveness shown towards former Dreyfusards, now that the Affair is no longer new and '_shocking_' (III 727a, b), and brings out forgetfulness of it, or simply ignorance, in the younger people (III 957-58a).

As well as these general considerations, Proust inserted into _A la recherche_ individual failures or successes arising from the Affair. The MS of _Sodome et Gomorrhe_ had already mentioned the gratitude that anti-Dreyfusards in high society felt towards Odette for being '"bien pensante"', a double merit in someone with a Jewish husband (II 744, 747 without additions); but Proust elaborated this, embroidering Swann's impolite veto on introductions to anti-Dreyfusists ('"Mais voyons, Odette, vous êtes folle' etc.), and making its results more tangible ('les cartes cornées pleuvaient chez Odette') (II 747c, d, e, f).

---

1 These additions were, possibly, made at a comparatively early stage, since the _Côté de Guermantes_ passage was inserted on the 1914 galleys; so were two important ones shortly to be mentioned (II 252-53a, about Odette; II 238b, about Mme de Guermantes).

And Odette's professed nationalism is now responsible for her entry into 'quelques-unes des ligues de femmes du monde antisémites' (II 252-53a). Again, the Dreyfusism of the little clan had, in the MS of Sodome et Gomorrhe, been held to retard Mme Verdurin's acceptance by high society (II 744), but the further aside that her 'évolution timide' towards this high society has been 'ralentie par l'affaire Dreyfus, accélérée par la musique "nouvelle"', was added only later (II 870a), and so was the Patronne's wish, in spite of her sincere Dreyfusism, to find nevertheless 'dans la prépondérance de son salon dreyfusiste une récompense mondaine' - a wish doomed at present to failure, given that Dreyfusism 'triomphait politiquement, mais non pas mondainement' (II 885-86a). However, mitigating this, Proust inserted both the visit paid to Mme Verdurin by the prince de Guermantes, who is attracted by the Dreyfusism of the salon (II 1044-45a, p. 1044), and the two-sided effect of the Affair, seen in La Prisonnière not simply as a social hindrance but as a help, having brought writers into the clan (III 230-38a, pp. 235-36). As for the involvement of the Faubourg Saint-Germain itself, the occasion in Le Côté de Guermantes on which Charlus deplores the Dreyfus Affair is late: 'Toute cette affaire Dreyfus [...] n'a qu'un inconvénient: c'est qu'elle détruit la société' (II 287-90a, p. 290); and Proust at three junctures gives Mme de Guermantes similar observations or attitudes, adding, for example, in the margin of the 1914 galleys, the paragraph in which she says of Marie-Aynard's salon that

> C'était charmant autrefois. Maintenant on y trouve toutes les personnes qu'on a passé sa vie à éviter, sous prétexte qu'elles sont contre Dreyfus, et d'autres dont on n'a pas idée qui c'est (II 238b).[1]

This reconsideration of the Dreyfus Affair is none the less one aspect only of Proust's growing interest in social mobility. He went on to elaborate the rise of Gilberte and other Combray 'offshoots', to add new graphs of Odette's and Mme Verdurin's advance, to make Charlus's social descent and the reasons for it more prominent, and to insert into Le Temps retrouvé important discussions of the decline of the Faubourg Saint-Germain.

The 'bal costumé' did not, for example, originally contain the remarks on Marcel's erroneous impression that he has been the only Combray native to make a way upwards - erroneous since, on looking around, he sees that all kinds of other fountains 'du bassin de Combray' have shot up too: once Swann himself, now Legrandin, Gilberte and Bloch (III 968-69a; III 969a). Gilberte, indeed, is made to go still higher than she was at first to do: the three asides 'et bientôt après, comme on le verra, duchesse de Guermantes', 'cette duchesse de Guermantes', and 'puis la duchesse de Guermantes', were all added above the line (albeit looking like afterthoughts rather

1 The other two are III 230-38a, p. 235; III 576-77a. See also, for the Dreyfus Affair, II 400-401a; II 458-59a, p. 458; III 39c.

than true additions on the last two occasions) (III 669a; III 670a, b); and there does not appear to be any reference to this eventual transformation actually in the MS. However, it was to her mother and Mme Verdurin that Proust paid the most attention in his revision. He had already, in the MS of *Sodome et Gomorrhe*, ascribed Odette's rise partly to her patronage of literary men, partly to Gilberte's newly-inherited fortune, and had recounted the 'vrai coup de théâtre' of Mme de Marsantes's and the comtesse Molé's entry into her box one day (II 744-49). But all post-1914 are the three long passages in *A l'ombre* in which Proust writes that even if Odette is, temporarily at least, quite outside high society, she nevertheless has a slight acquaintance with one or two aristocrats, she has remained in relations with Mme Verdurin, and she will one day frequent the aristocracy (I 516-23a; I 599-603a; I 638-40a). Most significantly, she was not at first to be present at Mme de Villeparisis's matinée in *Le Côté de Guermantes*;[1] almost all of the additions putting her there were made, at a relatively early stage, on the 1914 galleys (II 252-53a; II 263-64a; II 267-68a; II 269b; II 270a, b, d; II 271-73a; II 273a, b). And Proust worked into *Le Temps retrouvé* Mme Verdurin's unsuccessful advances to Odette (III 732a) and the soirée at which the

---

1 Mentioned in Ch. 1, p. 31 , and by Feuillerat (pp. 106-7), who remarks elsewhere too on Odette's new social position (pp. 35-36) and makes accurate conjectures about social changes at the end of the novel (pp. 242-44).

former *cocotte*, insulted and nearly senile, at last receives, through Gilberte, a flock of duchesses and the most unattainable marquise (III 951-52a).[1]

The addition to *A l'ombre* describing the Patronne's visits to the Swann household shows her, too, beginning advances towards high society, although by routes unknown to Odette (I 599-603a, pp. 600-601). It is in insertions into *Sodome et Gomorrhe* that the Verdurins are said to be moving slowly in the direction of 'le monde', which for its part is 'tout préparé à aller vers eux', since the salon passes for a Temple of Music: and those brilliant men who, like the prince de Guermantes,[2] have come to Balbec without their wives, 'ce qui facilitait tout', now 'faisaient des avances et d'ennuyeux devenaient exquis' (II 869-71a, II 870b, c; II 1044-45a, p. 1044).[3] I have already mentioned the long sequence inserted into the MS of *La Prisonnière* in which Proust qualifies Mme Verdurin's feeling that 'elle avait déjà bien des fois manqué le coche' with the information that the Dreyfus Affair has in fact helped her (III 230-38a, pp. 235-36); but no doubt the most outstanding feature of his additions about the Patronne is the one to which attention was drawn in Chapter 1[4] - the fact that her rise to princesse de Guermantes is discussed for the first time in a layer glued to

---

1 See also, for Odette, II 744-45a.

2 His brief visit was mentioned above, p. 300.

3 See also II 870a, referred to above, p. 300.

4 pp. 60-61, 65.

the MS of <u>Le Temps retrouvé</u> (III 953-56a, pp. 954-56), even though, rather puzzlingly, Mme de Guermantes's reference to it, some sixty pages later, is in the MS (III 1012).[1]

Charlus's decline was also emphasised, in two additions to the MS of <u>Le Temps retrouvé</u> explaining (with some repetition) that his liking for the lower classes has precedents related by Saint-Simon ('Peut-être fatigue de vieillard, ou extension de la sensualité aux relations les plus banales, le baron ne vivait plus qu'avec des "inférieurs"') (III 830a, III 832a). The strong implication in <u>La Prisonnière</u> that Charlus's love for Morel is ruining his social situation forms part of a long margin and layer addition to the MS (III 216-19a, p. 218), and a passage written into the <u>Temps retrouvé</u> MS in margins now specifies that although the 'public' believes his present social isolation is caused by his bad reputation, in reality it stems from his deliberate aloofness or irascibility (III 764-65a). The most interesting insertion on this subject is, however, that of the lines in <u>La Prisonnière</u> putting reproaches into the mouth of the reader; added to the first typescript, it was, presumably, composed in the last year of Proust's life:

---

1 Gilberte's opinion of the new princess also appears in an addition: III 984-85a. See too, for the Verdurins, II 886a; II 897-99a, p. 899; II 928-29a, p. 928; III 729-30a; III 957-58a; III 995-99a, p. 995.

> Mais, malheureux romancier, pense le lecteur, vous tombez d'une invraisemblance dans une autre. On vous a passé la première [...].[1] Mais la seconde invraisemblance est trop forte.
>
> Comment, M. de Charlus vainement attendu tous les jours de l'année par tant d'ambassadeurs et de duchesses [...], tout le temps qu'il dérobe à ces grandes dames, à ces grands seigneurs, le passait chez la nièce d'un giletier! D'abord, raison suprême, Morel était là. N'y eût-il pas été, je ne vois aucune invraisemblance, ou bien alors vous jugez comme eût fait un commis d'Aimé [...]
> (III 49n.2-51a).

All these author's interventions into the novel are late; the other one written on a similarly gently mocking note - the 'conversation' in Sodome et Gomorrhe in which the reader addresses the author with deprecating remarks on his (the author's) lack of memory and deplores the digressive nature of his interruptions (II 650-52a) - could be taken, like the La Prisonnière insertion, as a protest from this average reader about what seems to him to be an implausible deterioration of normal standards: a young man's memory, the plot of a novel, social strata.[2]

Finally, several of the passages added to the 'bal costumé' meditate on the erosion of the Faubourg Saint-Germain. The generalisation that 'ce qui caractérisait le plus cette société, c'était sa prodigieuse aptitude au déclassement' comes

---

1 (The rise of Jupien's niece.)

2 The author's appeal to the reader to help out his memory in La P again emerges from a commentary on social mobility: III 230-38a, p. 235. See also III 47-49a, p. 48. M. Suzuki comments on the late authorial intervention in La P in 'Le comique chez Marcel Proust (II)', BSAMP, no. 12 (1962), pp. 585-86.

in the margin of the MS (III 957b,n.); and the rest of the additions tend to fall into two divisions. In the first are the now constant emphases on the ignorance and forgetfulness of society about its own origins (resembling the forgetfulness of the Dreyfus Affair); these run usually as follows:

> Cette ignorance n'était pas que du monde, mais de la politique, de tout. Car la mémoire durait moins que la vie chez les individus, et d'ailleurs, de très jeunes, qui n'avaient jamais eu les souvenirs abolis chez les autres, [...] les débuts étant oubliés ou ignorés, ils prenaient les gens au point d'élévation ou de chute où ils se trouvaient, croyant qu'il en avait toujours été ainsi, que Mme Swann et la princesse de Guermantes et Bloch avaient toujours eu la plus grande situation [...] Des ministres tarés et d'anciennes filles publiques étaient tenus pour des parangons de vertu
> (III 957-58a; III 958a).[1]

The second is a series of additions bringing out the actual changes that have taken place, and often stressing renewal as much as dilapidation: one good example of this series is the passage which, inserted almost at the very end of the novel, brings some individual histories to a conclusion and sets them in the perspective of the mutability working on so many other levels of the novel:

---

1 The other similar additions are: III 948-49a; III 957a,n., and III 957c; III 959-60a,n., p. 959; III 964-66a, III 964a, III 965a,b; III 976-78a, pp. 977-78; III 992-93a; III 1010a.

> Ainsi, dans le faubourg Saint-Germain, ces positions en apparence imprenables du duc et de la duchesse de Guermantes, du baron de Charlus, avaient perdu leur inviolabilité, comme toutes choses changent en ce monde, par l'action d'un principe intérieur auquel on n'avait pas pensé: chez M. de Charlus l'amour de Charlie qui l'avait rendu esclave des Verdurin, puis le ramollissement; chez Mme de Guermantes, un goût de nouveauté et d'art; chez M. de Guermantes un amour exclusif [...]. Ainsi change la figure des choses de ce monde; ainsi le centre des empires, et le cadastre des fortunes, et la charte des situations, tout ce qui semblait définitif est-il perpétuellement remanié, et les yeux d'un homme qui a vécu peuvent-ils contempler le changement le plus complet là où justement il lui paraissait le plus impossible (III 1018-19a).[1]

---

1 Other additions in this group are III 669b,n.; III 670-71a; III 929b; III 956n.1: III 1143a; III 1003-4a; III 1005-6a; III 1016a,n.
Proust also describes changes in society in I 740-48a, p. 746; II 211-12a, p. 212; II 866-68a; III 245b; III 293-94a; III 659a; III 729a; III 853-54a; III 853b; III 1019a; III 1024a; III 1026a,n.
The development of Bloch's bad manners towards an eventual discretion links with this theme and is brought out in some additions: see III 968a; III 969b; III 969-70a; III 970a.
For three additions about the Combray social attitudes of Marcel's mother, see II 986-87a, p. 986; II 1026-27a, II 1027a; III 658-59a.
There are, too, some late references to revolution or to political agitation. The depiction of the poor of Balbec looking through the restaurant window, discussed provocatively by H. March in The Two Worlds of Marcel Proust (pp. 183, 189-90), was added (I 681a; I 806-8a, p. 806); so was Marcel's speculation as to how the lift-boy would behave with him if there were a revolution (II 826-27a); and the Russian revolution is mentioned in a few additions, on the whole unfavourably (III 797-98a, p. 798; III 852a; III 853-54a, p. 854; III 982-83a). For other references to revolution, social agitation, etc., see I 453i; I 709a; II 27a; II 215a; II 242a; II 242-43a; III 32-33a, III 32c; III 630-39a, p. 632.
See also the note at the end of Ch. 5 giving details of Cottard's professional rise (p. 251n.1).

LACK OF WILLPOWER AND OF SELF-CONTROL

Even if these new developments about social change need not all be taken to denote decline, many other additions, in more moral or personal contexts, undoubtedly do.

Thus a number of Marcel's references in La Prisonnière and La Fugitive to his own lack of willpower are late ones, such as the comment on his plan to send Saint-Loup to Mme Bontemps: had he really known himself, the addition tells us, he would have seen all along that he would reach this 'déplorable' solution 'par manque de volonté' (III 436b). In other insertions on the subject - the majority, in fact - Proust takes as his focus the ebb of Marcel's willpower with Albertine compared to that he had used with Gilberte. I noted in a previous chapter all the late references to the pride left to Marcel, small though it is, from the days of Gilberte;[1] but those two long passages, in both La Prisonnière and La Fugitive, in which Marcel pinpoints the total collapse of this former strength were added to the MS (III 343-44a; III 429b), as were the exclamations in La Fugitive:

> Ah! combien mon amour pour Albertine, dont j'avais cru que je pourrais prévoir le destin d'après celui que j'avais eu pour Gilberte, s'était développé en parfait contraste avec ce dernier! Combien rester sans la voir m'était impossible!
>
> (III 447a).

---

1 Ch. 5, p.243.

The pride and willpower shown in the break with Gilberte were not, as we knew from Feuillerat, in the 1914 version of _A l'ombre_;[1] these additions on Albertine therefore counterbalance an important aspect of the expanded Gilberte affair - in fact, a crucial one: René Girard even sees the diminishing of the narrator's willpower as the central difference between the two relationships.[2] Furthermore, the effects of these additions need not be confined to the love-episodes: they are drawing out the overall pattern of the novel with their stress on a problem mooted in the 'drame du coucher' and restated by Marcel himself in the long additions just mentioned:

> [...] ce défaut de volonté que ma grand'mère et ma mère avaient redouté pour moi, à Combray, [...] avait été en s'aggravant d'une façon de plus en plus rapide [...]
> (part of III 343-44a)

> [...] à force de m'habituer à ne pas vouloir, qu'il s'agît de travail ou d'autre chose, j'étais devenu plus lâche [...]
> (part of III 429b).[3]

More obtrusive than these is a set of new passages demonstrating lack of self-control in the other characters.

---

1 Feuillerat, pp. 39, 119-22. See particularly I 607-15a, _passim_, for the willpower element in the separation from Gilberte.

2 In _Mensonge romantique et vérité romanesque_, p. 244. In a review of Painter's (vol. I) and Barker's biographies, J.M. Cocking tantalisingly hints too at differences here, but does not elaborate the point (_The Romanic Review_, LII (1961), pp. 309-315 (p. 312)).

3 See also III 94-96a, p. 95; III 112c.

This group, in which the phrase 'ne put s'empêcher' recurs again and again, is very often comic, as I implied in Chapter 2.[1] The additions sometimes amount to only a few inserted words, but are almost certainly all linked by a consistent intention on Proust's part. Thus, one addition likening the foolishly scandalous behaviour of certain young men to that of young women who then spend the rest of their lives trying to climb back up the slope 'qu'elles avaient trouvé si amusant de descendre' was altered further by Proust to end: 'qu'elles avaient trouvé si amusant, ou plutôt n'avaient pas pu s'empêcher de descendre' (II 620-23a, p. 623; II 623a). Where part of an insertion about Andrée originally read: 'Mon plaisir avait l'air de l'agacer prodigieusement', it now runs: 'Mes satisfactions lui causaient un agacement qu'elle ne pouvait cacher' (III 60a). Aimé's involuntary display of greed in <u>Sodome et Gomorrhe</u> was added only to the typescript: he

> ne pouvait s'empêcher, avec des yeux passionnés, curieux et gourmands, de regarder quel pourboire je donnais au chauffeur [...] l'argent qu'un autre recevait excitait en lui une curiosité incompressible et lui faisait venir l'eau à la bouche [...] (II 1024-25a).

That paragraph in which Swann, at the prince de Guermantes's soirée, 'ne put s'empêcher d'attacher sur le corsage de [Mme de Surgis] de longs regards de connaisseur dilatés et concupiscents' was added to the MS (II 705a), and so were the lines two pages later in which, shaking her hand in farewell, he once more stares 'dans les profondeurs du corsage',

---

1 See above, pp. 74, 81-82.

> presque sans dissimulation, qu'une vie déjà avancée lui en eût ôté soit la volonté morale par l'indifférence à l'opinion, ou le pouvoir physique par l'exaltation du désir et l'affaiblissement des ressorts qui aident à le cacher [...] (II 707c).[1]

It is Charlus, however, who is the chief exemplar. On a first level, Proust made numerous additions describing the baron's repeated self-betrayal, inserting into La Prisonnière the information that 'l'aggravation de son mal [...] le poussait perpétuellement à révéler, à insinuer, parfois tout simplement à inventer des détails compromettants' (III 213-14a), or, into Le Temps retrouvé, the news that, 'en proie presque chaque jour à des crises de dépression mentale, caractérisée non pas positivement par de la divagation, mais par la confession à haute voix', he is openly revealing both his Germanophilia and his inversion (III 864-65a). And many other late incidents illustrate these, and less overt, ways in which the baron compromises himself - by tone, gesture, or supposedly deliberate pleasantries about homosexuality, so much so that the 'fidèles' of the little clan slyly refer to his inversion in front of him.[2] But Charlus also joins the other characters in additions which show him succumbing with the same directly stated helplessness. Already in the MS of Sodome et Gomorrhe was the

---

1 See also II 708a.

2 See II 295a,b; II 715-16a; II 716-19a, pp. 718-19; II 908a,c; II 921a,b; II 966-67a; II 1042a,b,c; II 1044-45a; II 1045a; II 1099-1100a; II 1100b,d; III 47-49a, p. 49; III 208-10a,n., p. 210; III 212a; III 214a,b; III 221d; III 226a; III 258-59a, p. 259; III 290a; III 295b; III 296-97a; III 302a; III 303-4a; III 784-93a, p. 787; III 800-801a.

observation that 'il ne pouvait s'empêcher [...] de jeter sur les hommes de peine, les militaires, les jeunes gens en costume de tennis, un regard furtif' (II 1037); but now Proust, in an addition to the Sodome et Gomorrhe soirée, characterises Charlus's manner of looking at young men as

> un regard particulier, venu des profondeurs, et qui, même dans une soirée, ne pouvait s'empêcher d'aller naïvement aux jeunes gens, comme les regards d'un couturier qui décèlent sa profession par la façon immédiate qu'ils ont de s'attacher aux habits (II 697a).[1]

He works into Sodome et Gomorrhe the two occasions on which, charmed first by the overtones of defeatism in Morel's dislike of military service, then by the young man's plan to seduce an innocent girl, the baron 'ne put se retenir de pincer l'oreille au violoniste' (II 964a; II 1006-9a, p. 1008); and, to the brief La Prisonnière scene in which Charlus playfully touches the end of a valet's nose, Proust adds both the phrase 'hésita un instant, puis, ne pouvant plus se contenir', and the word 'irrésistiblement' (III 227b).[2]

If Charlus is the main representative, it is Mme Verdurin who becomes the most comic one in this new series, and who provokes the lengthiest commentary. Two of the three discussions of her inability to refrain from the 'revelations' to Morel were

---

1 This comparison with tailors is one Proust was fond of: see also II 697n.1, the first ending of this addition, but especially III 366-67a, III 366a, for an almost identical use, likening Françoise to a tailor who 'même ne peut s'empêcher de [...] palper' the material of one's clothing.

2 See also II 562b,c,d for similar behaviour with Marcel; and II 1053b; III 314b.

added to the third typescript of La Prisonnière, and may thus be among the last Proust ever wrote (they are the first and third mentioned just below). Not only did he insert the remarks about Mme Verdurin's forehead which were cited in Chapter 2, mentioning the need to utter 'un mot qu'il est non seulement abject, mais imprudent de répéter':

> C'est à ce besoin que, après quelques légers mouvements convulsifs du front sphérique et chagrin, céda la Patronne (III 314a);[1]

he also wrote in the aside telling us that

> Mme Verdurin, du reste, eût-elle, toutes réflexions faites, trouvé qu'il était plus sage d'ajourner les révélations à Morel qu'elle ne l'eût plus pu. Il y a certains désirs, parfois circonscrits à la bouche, qui, une fois qu'on les a laissés grandir, exigent d'être satisfaits, quelles que doivent être les conséquences; on ne peut plus résister à embrasser une épaule décolletée qu'on regarde depuis trop longtemps et sur laquelle les lèvres tombent comme l'oiseau sur le serpent [...] (III 309a).[2]

And the lines on the undesirable effect of Mme Verdurin's indiscretions, which will inevitably be passed on and eventually rebound on her, is the last addition in the trio: 'Elle le savait, mais ne pouvait retenir le mot qui lui brûlait la langue' (III 314b).[3]

---

1 See pp. 90-91.

2 This compulsive fascination is brought out elsewhere not merely in the case of Swann and Mme de Surgis, just cited, but also in that of Saniette, transfixed by the letter (II 1024a,b: see above, Ch. 5, pp. 209-10).

3 See also III 228-30a, p. 229, for Mme Verdurin. See III 517b for Albertine, and II 506a for Bloch. It is no doubt significant that, apart from those about Mme Verdurin, most of these additions were made to versions of Sodome et Gomorrhe.

DISSOLUTION

Many of the expansions described so far in this chapter are summed up in some miscellaneously-conceived apocalyptic additions, which, with wider application, pick up once more the trait of lack of willpower, and contribute to the atmosphere of dissolution and destruction in parts of _A la recherche_.

Proust, for example, goes further, in his new examination of boredom, than to associate it with a growing taste for cruel dramas in the Verdurins and in Mme de Guermantes;[1] he creates one character who is to display a cosmic boredom: Mme de Citri. This marquise makes her only appearance in a long addition to _Sodome et Gomorrhe_ which depicts her violent nihilism: she has 'un tel besoin de destruction que, lorsqu'elle eut à peu près renoncé au monde, les plaisirs qu'elle rechercha alors subirent l'un après l'autre son terrible pouvoir dissolvant', and soon 'ce qui fut ennuyeux, ce fut tout' - letter-writing, fine objects, paintings. In the end, 'ce fut la vie elle-même qu'elle vous déclara une chose rasante, sans qu'on sût bien où elle prenait son terme de comparaison' (II 687-88a).

As for the rest of the nobility, Proust added to the MS of _Sodome et Gomorrhe_ Cottard's characteristically unsubtle 'testimony' to their physical degeneration (II 933d); and Proust's own remarks

---

1 See above, Ch. 5, pp. 214, 227-28, 230.

on this degeneration, with, again, the assumption of a certain disbelief in the reader,[1] form part of a margin and layer addition to the third typescript of La Prisonnière. Some bizarre activities of Charlus's have just been narrated: but

> Avant de revenir à la boutique de Jupien, l'auteur tient à dire combien il serait contristé que le lecteur s'offusquât de peintures si étranges. D'une part (et ceci est le petit côté de la chose), on trouve que l'aristocratie semble proportionnellement, dans ce livre, plus accusée de dégénérescence que les autres classes sociales. Cela serait-il, qu'il n'y aurait pas lieu de s'en étonner. Les plus vieilles familles finissent par avouer, dans un nez rouge et bossu, dans un menton déformé, des signes spécifiques où chacun admire la "race". Mais parmi ces traits persistants et sans cesse aggravés, il y en a qui ne sont pas visibles, ce sont les tendances et les goûts
> (III 45-47a, pp. 46-47).[2]

And indeed, a few important passages bearing directly on Charlus himself are late ones: Proust added in the margin of the Temps retrouvé MS, only thirty pages before the end of the novel, the conclusion that both he and his brother, 'si différents dans leurs goûts, étaient arrivés à la déconsidération à cause d'une même paresse, d'un même manque de volonté' (III 1016a,n.); and he inserted into the MS of La Prisonnière both the comment that after his illness Charlus goes back down his slope 'avec une vitesse que nous verrons progressivement croissante' (III 322-24a, p. 324; III 324a), and the description of his secret life as 'une vie crapuleuse racontée par la déchéance morale'

---

1 See the discussion above, pp. 304-5.

2 For the hereditary building-up of 'faults', see here Ch. 2, p. 76.

which betrays itself, like a physical illness, on the face (III 207a).[1]

The boldest additions on this theme are those bracketing moral decline with violent physical destruction in the extended simile that compares war-time Paris to Pompeii. This simile is not in the MS of Le Temps retrouvé at all.[2] It gathers in, indeed, other post-1914 developments, since Charlus, having drawn the narrator's attention to what are perhaps 'les derniers jours de notre Pompéi', goes on to compare this possible destruction with that of Sodom and Gomorrha (III 802-7a, p.806; III 806a; III 806-7a); and another long addition, assimilating these days of air-raids and vice to the last days of Pompeii, finally describes those particular vices, resulting from 'manque de volonté', which have brought certain men to a 'mauvais lieu composite' (III 834-36a; III 835a).[3]

However, more apocalyptic than any is that part of the long insertion on Bergotte's death which likens his illness to the ultimate extinction of Earth; these lines may have come at an even later stage than the bulk of the addition:

---

1 For Charlus, see also III 838a.

2 (And the other two references to Pompeii in the novel may also be late, since the first comes in the long 'jeunes filles' passage (I 869-951a, p. 909), and the second in the section on the grandmother's death, for which I could not consult the early versions (II 318).)

3 For the other comparisons with Pompeii, see III 833b; III 837c,n.; and III 840b provides another comparison with Sodom and its destruction.

> Il allait ainsi se refroidissant progressivement, petite planète qui offrait une image anticipée de la grande quand, peu à peu, la chaleur se retirera de la terre, puis la vie. Alors la résurrection aura pris fin [...] (III 184a).[1]

EXHAUSTION, ILLNESS AND OLD AGE

Proust thus, in the addition on Bergotte, sets up a refraction between the end of the individual and the ending of a whole world; and some of the late passages about Charlus, for example, imply little difference between his moral, his physical and his social degeneration. This evocation of both personal and universal disintegration was reinforced by Proust in a large series of additions about exhaustion, or about the characters' illness, old age and (sometimes) death.

Exhaustion

Proust now, in a few margin additions on the first Gallimard galleys of Le Côté de Guermantes, shows an interest in tiredness as a subjective phenomenon, whose force is felt according to the attitude of the sufferer. He inserted both du Boulbon's advice to the grandmother - 'La fatigue est la réalisation organique d'une idée préconçue. Commencez par ne pas la penser' - (II 306-7a), and the 'insomnies nerveuses' of the Fronde historian, whose exhaustion is relieved when he temporarily forgets it

1 Two other additions about dissolution are III 694-95a, p. 695; III 772a.

(II 193b, II 215b).[1] No such saving grace, however, operates for the other characters. Proust added to the MS of Le Temps retrouvé the digression in which Charlus wonders how the soldiers will react if the war continues for years: 'Que feront les hommes au retour? la fatigue les aura-t-elle rompus ou affolés?' (III 796-97a); and, in another insertion, he attributed the new solemn pallor and majesty of the comte de ..., at least in part, to 'une fatigue qui allait jusqu'à l'envie de dormir' (III 938c). Late too are the passages about Françoise in which her neck is said to be 'courbé par la fatigue et l'obéissance' and in which her hatred of Albertine is put down to exhaustion from overwork: 'plus encore que d'égards, Françoise avait besoin de sommeil' (II 735a; III 96-99a, p. 99). It is Charlus's 'fatigue de vieillard' which, the narrator now speculates, leads him to relations with the lower classes;[2] and Proust tells the reader in an addition to La Prisonnière that the baron's illness makes him too exhausted to give due thought to the revenge he might enact on the Verdurins (III 322-24a).

The most interesting subject of these additions is Marcel himself. He had already closed the MS account of his 'second stage of indifference' for the dead Albertine with these words:

> La vérité et la vie sont bien ardues, et il me restait d'elles, sans qu'en somme je les connusse, une impression où la tristesse était peut-être encore dominée par la fatigue (III 623).

---

1 See also II 704b for the psychological effects of forgetting one's exhaustion.

2 This addition (III 830a) was mentioned above, p. 304.

But now not only does Proust write into Le Temps retrouvé that the life of those who need suffering to learn truths 'finit par être bien lassante' (III 908-9a), he more concretely adds to the pretended separation scene Marcel's constant reminders to Albertine of the late hour ('Et ainsi je semais d'allusions à la nuit déjà si avancée, à notre fatigue, les questions que je posais à Albertine') (III 357a); and he inserted into La Fugitive the statement that

> la même fatigue, la même lâcheté qui m'avaient fait me soumettre à Albertine quand elle était là, m'empêchaient de rien entreprendre depuis que je ne la voyais plus (III 492a).

The most direct and poignant addition is, however, that passage in Sodome et Gomorrhe about the 'splendide jeune fille' who boards the train at Saint-Pierre-des-Ifs: this appears for the first time in the typescript, in Proust's handwriting, and concludes with a reflection on the

> jour imprévu et triste comme une nuit d'hiver, où on ne cherche plus cette jeune fille-là, ni aucune autre, où trouver vous effraierait même. Car on ne se sent plus assez d'attraits pour plaire, ni de force pour aimer [...] on sent que c'est une trop grande entreprise pour le peu de forces qu'on garde. Le repos éternel a déjà mis des intervalles où l'on ne peut sortir, ni parler. [...] On ne peut plus assumer la fatigue de se mettre au pas de la jeunesse. Tant pis si le désir charnel redouble au lieu de s'amortir! [...] (II 883-84a).[1]

---

1 This impression of sad tiredness reappears in other additions not necessarily mentioning the word 'fatigue', but suggesting a weariness, and inability for the struggle, which leads to platonic love: II 159-60a; II 790a; II 837-38a; II 838a; III 818-19a; III 819a. See also II 733-34a, p. 733; II 859a; III 645a.
Other additions made partially or wholly to develop this theme are I 787-98a, p. 788; II 325-26a, p. 326; II 581a; II 603a; II 710a; II 980-86a, p. 986; III 102-6a, p. 104; III 141-43a, p. 143; III 183-84a; III 630-39a, p. 631.

Illness and old age

In a much larger group of additions than those on fatigue, various characters grow more infirm, succumb to new ailments, or, in a substantial number of insertions towards the end of the novel, are now visibly marked by their old age, whether or not this is coupled with bad health. The late comedy about doctors should be recalled here;[1] continuing on this lighter note, Proust made one of Nissim Bernard's characteristics hypochondria, as I mentioned in Chapter 2,[2] and, although Mme de Cambremer-Legrandin's possibly incurable illness is mentioned in the 1914 galleys (II 55), the two Sodome et Gomorrhe references to it in the comic context of her longings for fashion and high society were added to the MS (II 817a, II 820d).

More seriously, Proust also inserted, for example, that suggestive passage, in the section on the grandmother's death, comparing the attacks of an illness to a mistress's infidelities, and the doctor to the interrogated go-between: but really

> Celle que nous pressons, dont nous soupçonnons qu'elle est sur le point de nous trahir, c'est la vie elle-même, et malgré que nous ne la sentions plus la même, nous croyons encore en elle, nous demeurons en tous cas dans le doute jusqu'au jour qu'elle nous a enfin abandonnés (II 316-17a; also II 316a, II 317a).

Still in Marcel's family, the information that Léonie, against Françoise's advice, would not go to the doctor was added to the first Gallimard galleys of Le Côté de Guermantes (II 26j), and,

1 See Ch. 2, pp. 83-84.

2 p. 81. See II 842-45a, p. 845.

although Marcel's great-aunt had fallen gravely ill in the MS for the end of Sodome et Gomorrhe (II 1122), three emphases of this, and the fact that the illness is a fatal one, are late (II 1112c; II 1122b, c; III 14c). Both the discussion of Swann's death, and the account of Bergotte's last illness and death, seem to have been written after the composition of the main MS of La Prisonnière (III 199-201a; III 182-92a).[1] Details of the contradictory, even malicious, in any case useless, recommendations given to Bergotte by certain doctors are even further expansions of this latter addition; so is Proust's apparent affirmation of an instinctive common sense in matters of illness (III 182-83a; III 184-86a). And, these substantial pieces aside, the parenthesis in Le Côté de Guermantes telling us that Swann's illness 'était celle qui avait emporté sa mère et dont elle avait été atteinte précisément à l'âge qu'il avait' was added to the MS (II 578-79a), and the two paragraphs citing Bergotte's afflictions in a cheerless bulletin, and insisting on the strain to which his fame subjects him, appear only in the margin of the third Côté de Guermantes Gallimard galleys (II 325-26a).[2]

As might be expected, it is above all the last four or five hundred pages of the novel which were manipulated, in addition after addition, to extend the picture of inexorable mortality.

---

1 Including indented additions under III 182-92a. (The late insertion of both deaths was mentioned in Ch. 1, pp. 45, 46.)

2 See also, for Bergotte, II 743-44a; II 745b; II 971a; and for Swann, II 595a; II 691a; II 714a.

Even before the 'bal masqué', Proust was adding to his MSS, for example, the description of Norpois and Mme de Villeparisis in Venice, both versions of which stress the old age of the couple, especially Mme de Villeparisis's (III 630-39a; III 630n.1: III 1051-54a; III 1052-53a; III 1053b). The brief paragraph in La Fugitive in which Mme de Guermantes exclaims that she is afraid 'pauvre Babal et pauvre Gri-Gri' 'n'en aient pas pour longtemps, ni l'un ni l'autre' was inserted as a separate layer (III 588b), and so was the longer Temps retrouvé paragraph about the unsociable habits of Andrée's husband, the writer, who, 'déjà fort malade', chose to meet only new people whom his 'ardente imagination' could anticipate as attractively different, not wishing to risk, for those he knew, 'une fatigue dangereuse pour lui, peut-être mortelle' (III 731a). Charlus's stroke and temporary blindness were in the MS of Le Temps retrouvé (III 859-64), but there it was stated that 'Même sa mémoire était intacte' (III 861), whereas Proust now adds the speculation that he may indeed be suffering from forgetfulness as a result of the stroke (III 860-61a,n.), as well as his ingenious disguises of his aphasia (III 861a). Two further references to Charlus's blindness were inserted here (III 859b, III 864c), and so was the encounter with the embarrassed duchesse de Létourville - who has recently had a prolonged illness herself (III 862-63a). Not only this, but Charlus's list, recited 'avec une dureté presque triomphale', of the members of his family or social circle who have died, is late too (III 862a, b, c, d): it includes M. de Bréauté, said to be dying in the addition 300 pages previously.[1]

The reader will already have some idea of the expansions of the 'bal masqué' itself, both from the preliminary account of the MS version,[2] and from the discussion of the new sculpture imagery;[3] but I shall now outline the main revisions that make the characters older or more infirm than they had been.[4] Odette's eventual senility did not appear in the MS version (III 951-52a).[5] The parenthesis about Françoise, who, 'si vieille maintenant, [...] n'y voyait plus goutte', was added in a still further layer attached to a long glued-on sheet (III 1033d). The protracted and unflattering meditation on M. d'Argencourt's metamorphosis ('ce personnage ineffablement grimaçant, comique et blanc') was written in, in varying stages, only *aprés coup* (III 921-23a; III 921b; III 923-24a; III 924a, b; III 924-25a). Legrandin's pallor is new: 'on se disait que cette cause qui avait substitué au Legrandin coloré et rapide un pâle et triste fantôme de Legrandin, c'était la vieillesse' (III 934a,*n*.). The unusually urgent passage on Bloch's social

---

1 III 588b, mentioned just above.

2 See Ch. 1, pp. 59-63.

3 See Ch. 2, pp. 118-21.

4 W. Hachez's article, which tells us how old all the characters are in this scene, could be referred to here: 'La chronologie et l'âge des personnages de "A la Recherche du Temps perdu"', *BSAMP*, no. 6 (1956), pp. 198-207 (pp. 203, 206-7); see also the further discussion in *BSAMP* no. 11 (1961), pp. 392-98 (especially p. 397).

5 See above, pp. 302-3, and Ch. 1, p. 62.

success, with its double 'A quoi cela l'avançait-il? [...] A quoi cela l'avancerait-il?', and its picture of 'le visage presque effrayant, tout anxieux, d'un vieux Shylock attendant, tout grimé, dans la coulisse, le moment d'entrer en scène', is an added one (III 966-67a); there is no such sombre hint in the MS version.[1] The long description of M. de Guermantes's now ruined and craggy face, with its expression, 'bâtie par la maladie, de lutte contre la mort, de résistance, de difficulté à vivre', is also late: it is the one characterising old age as 'l'état le plus misérable pour les hommes et qui les précipite de leur faîte le plus semblablement aux rois des tragédies grecques' (III 1017-18a; III 1017-18b; III 1018a).[2] All the pages on La Berma's illness are added, from the tale of the aggravation of her fatal illness by her son-in-law, her daughter, and the doctor courting this young woman, to the last rather melodramatic picture: she is abandoned at a moment when she retires into her bedroom spitting blood (III 995-99a; III 1013-15a).[3] Finally, not only did Proust insert the considerable development defining the society of the matinée as a society of dying people, succumbing one after another, to the indifference

1 See above, Ch. 1, p. 62.

2 Discussed by A. Barnes (with some reference to an earlier addition on n.a.fr. 16760) in 'A propos d'un paragraphe du Temps retrouvé: Proust et le tragique', <u>BSAMP</u>, no. 23 (1973), pp. 1609-13.

3 These are prepared by III 856a. See also III 1003a, where Rachel maliciously attributes an unflattering age to La Berma.

or pleasure of the survivors (III 976-78a; III 977a); he added too, concentrated in layer and margin insertions over only about twelve pages of the MS (now sixteen or so in the Pléiade edition),[1] a very large number of the general commentaries on changes wrought by old age in anonymous or specially invented characters, and running typically thus:

> Certains hommes boitaient: on sentait bien que ce n'était pas par suite d'un accident de voiture, mais à cause d'une première attaque et parce qu'ils avaient déjà, comme on dit, un pied dans la tombe. Dans l'entrebaîllement de la leur, à demi paralysées, certaines femmes [...] ne pouvaient se redresser, infléchies qu'elles étaient, la tête basse, en une courbe qui était comme celle qu'elles occupaient actuellement entre la vie et la mort, avant la chute dernière. Rien ne pouvait lutter contre le mouvement de cette parabole qui les emportait et, dès qu'elles voulaient se lever, elles tremblaient et leurs doigts ne pouvaient rien retenir
> (III 938a).[2]

However, as with the additions on exhaustion, the most interesting subject of this elaboration is the narrator himself. Marcel was always, of course, delicate to the point of the unhealthy; the 1914 galleys had given details of his illness in A l'ombre, and of his need to avert a 'crise' by drinking alcohol in the train to Balbec (I 495-97; I 651). But in the reworking not only of Le Temps retrouvé but of the other volumes,

---

1 n.a.fr. 16727:19-31; III 934-51.

2 For the others (one or two mentioning characters already in the novel), see: III 934-35a,n.; III 935-36a; III 936a; III 936-37a; III 938b; III 939a; III 939-40a; III 940a,b; III 941a; III 941-42a; III 942-43a; III 943a,b; III 944-45a; III 945a,b; III 945-46a; III 945c; III 946a,n.; III 946-47a; III 947b; III 948a,c,d; III 949-50a; III 951a.

Proust makes the ill-health of his narrator a more salient feature, and increases the references to his age and his possibly imminent death.

For example, he added to the base version of Sodome et Gomorrhe this reply of the 'author' to the supposed reader's reproaches about his lack of memory:

> C'est très fâcheux en effet, Monsieur le lecteur. Et plus triste que vous croyez, quand on y sent l'annonce du temps où les noms et les mots disparaîtront de la zone claire de la pensée, et où il faudra, pour jamais, renoncer à se nommer à soi-même ceux qu'on a le mieux connus [...] (II 650-52a).[1]

This half-whimsical, half-serious attitude also marks the additions in which M. de Cambremer comments on Marcel's 'étouffements':[2] these choking-fits may not, here, be the direct centre of attention, but the fact that they are now mentioned, however modestly, at points where they were non-existent before, does reinforce the image of a poorly hero.[3] And more straightforward references to illnesses of Marcel's are worked in by Proust: where, at Balbec, the doctor was merely called in (to give general advice, presumably), now it is specified that this is 'pour un accès de fièvre que j'avais eu'(I 704a).[4] The

---

1 Already mentioned, p. 305.

2 See above for the complete list, Ch. 5, p. 218n.2.

3 For Marcel's difficulties with breathing, see also I 496c; II 226-27a,n.; II 969b; III 403b, III 415a. Interestingly, some additions attribute difficulties in breathing to other characters in situations where (usually) they are being buffeted about; for Saniette, see II 934d; III 225b; III 228b; and, on a comic level, the bathing simile for the princesse de Parme was greatly extended: II 457a; II 469a; II 479a; II 497a,b,c; II 499b,c.

4 See also I 704b.

observation that

> de plus en plus souffrant, j'étais tenté de surfaire les plaisirs les plus simples à cause des difficultés mêmes qu'il y avait pour moi à les atteindre

may be post-1914, occurring rather disconnectedly in a long late 'jeunes filles' passage in A l'ombre (I 787-98a, p. 787). Again, the grandmother's demand that Marcel should lie down for an hour before going out to dinner at Rivebelle is in the 1914 galleys, but the concluding clause is not: 'sieste que le médecin de Balbec m'ordonna bientôt d'étendre à tous les autres soirs' (I 798-99a, p. 798).

We have seen that Proust evoked, in some additions, the exhausting effects of suffering in love:[1] he inserted others actually stressing the physical dangers attendant on it. The lines in A l'ombre on the increased difficulties of making a courageous decision in love, the older one grows, are of course new, contributing to one of the post-1914 Gilberte sequences:

> Qu'on retire du plateau où est la fierté une petite quantité de volonté qu'on a eu la faiblesse de laisser s'user avec l'âge, qu'on ajoute dans le plateau où est le chagrin une souffrance physique acquise et à qui on a permis de s'aggraver,

and it is the 'cowardly' solution 'qui nous abaisse' at the age of fifty (I 581-92a, p. 586). This connection is reiterated in three important additions coming considerably later in the novel: they are those passages in, respectively, La Fugitive, La Prisonnière and Le Temps retrouvé in which the narrator brings out 'l'angoisse physique' of his suffering over Albertine, an anguish which 'mon coeur, plus mal portant que jadis, ne pouvait

---

1 See above, pp. 318-19.

plus tolérer' (III 429b), and writes that one day the heart will give way in the sorrows caused by love (III 224a; III 905-7a, III 906a). Furthermore, Proust inserted into La Prisonnière Marcel's sudden notion that he may be dying, in his worry over Albertine's possible departure: he has begun to react like his grandmother when she was in coma, so light, and sensitive to sound, is his anxious sleep: 'Étais-je donc entré, moi aussi, en agonie? était-ce l'approche de la mort?' (III 403d).[1]

Proust also significantly elaborated references in the last matinée to Marcel's own ill-health and age, and to his understanding of their meaning, adding the crucial passage now reproduced as a footnote:

> Et maintenant je comprenais ce que c'était que la vieillesse - la vieillesse qui de toutes les réalités est peut-être celle dont nous gardons le plus longtemps dans la vie une notion purement abstraite [...] (III 932a,n.).

The only revelations in the MS of Marcel's own advancing years were the difficulties others have in recognising him (III 923), the young Guermantes's 'Vous qui êtes un vieux Parisien' (III 927), the duchesse's description of him as 'mon plus vieil ami', and her remarks that he is 'toujours le même' and is old enough to have had sons at the front (III 927, 929-30). Proust now, however, adds the young Létourville's letter, signed 'votre

1 Cp. here too the passage on the sleeping Albertine, 'figure allégorique de quoi? de ma mort? de mon oeuvre?' (III 359-60a; cited above, Ch. 2, pp.117-18). See also III 445-46a; III 696a.

petit ami' (III 927-28a; III 928a), the conversations in which Marcel is told that influenza tends not to attack those 'de votre âge' and hears that he has been referred to as 'le père' (III 929a), his misplaced annoyance at the duchesse's calling herself an old woman and sadness at her 'vous êtes étonnant, vous restez toujours jeune' (III 929b, c, d), and his final realisation of the discrepancy between his own view of his age and the actual reality (III 930a) - although he still finds this difficult: 'Je n'avais pas un cheveu gris, ma moustache était noire. J'aurais voulu pouvoir leur demander à quoi se révélait l'évidence de la terrible chose' (III 931-32a, p. 932).[1] Where the writing of the book itself was in question, the MS did describe the narrator's apprehensiveness about an accident, external or internal, and discussed the illness which, causing him to 'mourir au monde, m'avait rendu service' (III 1035-44); but Proust develops Marcel's concern with a few harsh words about a 'catastrophe interne' at one point (III 1038b) and a substantial consideration at another (III 1035b, c), and he moves this concern towards some new possibilities and more specific dangers. The narrator now fears memory-loss (III 1037e), and refers to his near-fall downstairs and his feeling of being left quite without strength (III 1039-41a; III 1040a).[2] It is in an addition that he remarks that the idea of death has come to live with him permanently, little signs seeming to indicate, in spite of his unwillingness to believe them, that it is near (III 1042-43a); late too is the passage in which Marcel is now shown to be

1 See also III 932-34a, pp. 932-33.

2 Bergotte too stumbles downstairs - II 325-26a, p. 325.

sinking towards death himself:

> depuis le jour où mes jambes avaient tellement tremblé en descendant l'escalier, j'étais devenu indifférent à tout, je n'aspirais plus qu'au repos, en attendant le grand repos qui finirait par venir [...] (III 1041-42a).

Finally, Proust inserted the discussion (similar to that about the eventually lifeless Earth[1]) on the death of the narrator's works: 'Sans doute mes livres eux aussi, comme mon être de chair, finiraient un jour par mourir [...]' (III 1043a,*n*.).[2]

---

1 III 184a; referred to above, pp. 316-17.

2 For Marcel, see too I 481-83a; I 607-15a, p. 610; II 114b; II 798a; II 1019b; III 20a.
For other additions about illness, age and death, see I 488b; I 556-57a, p. 556; I 605-6a, p. 606; I 713-14a; I 869-951a, p. 943; II 10e; II 19b, II 66b; II 150c,d; II 151-52a, p. 152; II 219a; II 450a; II 581c; II 685-86a, p. 685; II 699-702a, p. 700; II 714-15a; II 716*n*.1: II 1184-85a, p. 1184; II 751-52a; II 751c; II 768a; II 770b; II 776a; II 861a; II 908-9a; II 1049b; III 212b; III 642a; III 665*n*.1: III 1116b; III 732a; III 849a; III 903b; III 928b; III 932-34a; III 933a,b; III 940*n*.1: III 1141a; III 973a; III 979-80a; III 987-88a; III 991b,*n*.; III 1020b; III 1046a,b; III 1047e; III 1047-48a; III 1048a,b,c,*n*.
Elstir becomes older in the additions: see below, Ch. 8, p.351.
A common picture in the insertions on old age, especially those in *TR*, is that of heredity at last taking over, or of some final form inside one waiting to emerge, as with the passage about the Shylock in Bloch (see above, p. 324). The similar lines on the 'mufle' and the 'prophète' in Swann were added to *SG* (II 690c); although Marcel's growing resemblance both to his father and to Léonie is in the MS (III 79), it is now much expanded (III 78-79a; III 78b; III 79a,b); and the character Mme X, who has come to look like a 'vieille Turque' as her mother had, is specially invented to make the point (III 941a. See also II 862-63a; II 942a; III 943-44a; III 951a; III 1015a; III 1031-32a; III 1032a,*n*.).
Proust also worked in a series of passages further illustrating the devotion or resemblance of Marcel's mother to her own dead mother: these cast a chill where they appear, and Proust himself points out on one occasion the idolatry implicit in her actions (II 769-70a, p.770. The others are II 807-8a; II 1019a; II 1121e; II 1122a,b,d; II 1128-29a; II 1129a,b; III 13-14a; III 16-17a; III 658-59a; III 660a,b; III 674a). See also the note in Ch. 2 about Mme de Sévigné, p. 86*n*.1.

The dramatic repercussions of these additions are evident. To emphasise disintegration, and the rapid change of forms once familiar to the narrator, is greatly to increase the urgency of his task if he is to salvage anything from the wreck. In spite of the two additions about the ultimate death of even the writer's works,[1] the reader nevertheless feels an opposition between all these passages and the actual creation of the novel. He knows that in spite of Marcel's anxiety, the book is there and written; aware of the structure of A la recherche, whether consciously or unconsciously, he has been experiencing something which is patterned rather than fluctuating, and is in a completed arrangement. Again, the narrator's discovery, at last, of some firm purpose and vigour, and his determination to make the most of what health he still has, contrast with his surroundings, at best fading, at worst collapsing.

If the end of A la recherche is seen not as a retreat from a reality that is becoming too shapeless and disturbing for satisfaction, but as some kind of rebirth,[2] the multiplication of references to illness and death must be counted as one of Proust's most powerful choices in these years. And, as with

---

1 See above, p. 330.

2 Amongst those who, in separate ways, emphasise such an interpretation (not by any means a universal tenet of Proust criticism) are G. Brée, Du Temps perdu au temps retrouvé, p.55; R. Girard, Mensonge romantique et vérité romanesque, e.g. pp. 310-12; and R. Fernandez, A la gloire de Proust, pp. 155-56, 168. Hans Meyerhoff offers interesting discussion around the subject in Time in Literature (Berkeley and Los Angeles, 1955), pp. 76-78.

the other expansions, Proust makes a few additions to Le Temps retrouvé specifically renewing, in different circumstances, the themes elaborated elsewhere. One of the late similes for the writing of the book describes the author as bearing it 'comme une fatigue' (III 1032-35a, p. 1032); the statement that 'à force de se renouveler' Marcel's fear of death 's'était naturellement changée en un calme confiant' is an insertion (III 1037d); and finally, the quotation from Hugo and the commentary on it are added:

> Victor Hugo dit:
> Il faut que l'herbe pousse et que les enfants meurent. Moi je dis que la loi cruelle de l'art est que les êtres meurent et que nous-mêmes mourions en épuisant toutes les souffrances, pour que pousse l'herbe non de l'oubli mais de la vie éternelle, l'herbe drue des oeuvres fécondes, sur laquelle les générations viendront faire gaîment, sans souci de ceux qui dorment en dessous, leur "déjeuner sur l'herbe" (III 1038a).[1]

---

1 This passage is included by V. Graham in what he calls the exceptional twenty or thirty 'non-logical' images of the novel (The Imagery of Proust, pp. 250-51).
See also, in TR, III 869a; III 902a.
M. Marc-Lipiansky interestingly remarks that in Jean Santeuil, by contrast with the mature novel, not only is death treated lightly, but that there is 'une vision optimiste' of old age (La Naissance du monde proustien dans Jean Santeuil, pp. 156, 158).

8 Vinteuil and Elstir

If most of the conspicuous post-1914 developments are not ones which elaborate the experiences of involuntary memory or the resolution to write a novel, there are, none the less, enlargements of the rôles of Vinteuil and, especially, Elstir, which do often refer indirectly to the other new movements in the novel, but now putting them in the context of a creativity that either straightforwardly succeeds in rising above the 'negative' features added elsewhere, or else synthesises them in the actual work of art.

VINTEUIL

Though less substantial than those about Elstir, the expansions worked in around Vinteuil are already most interesting. It seems, oddly, that in the original version of the novel there was to be very little mention of his music after _Du Côté de chez Swann_; until the end of _Sodome et Gomorrhe_, only four of the present references to him occurred in the base documents - then merely _en passant_ (I 536; II 584; II 894;

II 1114).[1] He did start to appear on a larger scale in the MS of La Prisonnière (III 56 on), and it could be that since he was initially Vington, a naturalist,[2] Proust started to incorporate the change into his main drafts at a relatively late stage. (This would be confirmed by Henri Bonnet's important article 'Esquisse pour une "Prisonnière"', which dates a rough version of the Vinteuil Septet at about 1915.[3])

Any significant discussions between the end of Du Côté de chez Swann and the beginning of La Prisonnière are, therefore, late, such as both the Sodome et Gomorrhe description of Vinteuil's growing prestige (added to the MS: II 869-71a, p.870), and the Côté de Guermantes characterisation of his 'transparent' manner of playing the piano[4] (inserted on the 1914 galleys: II 47a). Nor did the 1914 A l'ombre galleys contain the five-page sequence involving Vinteuil. This is the scene which shows

---

1 Even the first of these is part of an addition to the 1911-12 typescript: I 536-37a. However, there was a more substantial passage in the MS of Sodome et Gomorrhe, eventually excised, in which Marcel played the Sonata, compared it to his feelings for Albertine, and thought of Swann's reactions to it. Vinteuil's other works, so Marcel believed, 'étaient restées dans ce néant' of the mind alone; and he could not imagine them (n.a.fr. 16710:67-70; at about the equivalent of II 739).

2 We first knew this from P. Kolb: 'An Enigmatic Proustian Metaphor', The Romanic Review, LIV (1963), pp. 187-97 (p. 192); see also G. Brée, 'Les Manuscrits de Marcel Proust' (p. 186).

3 In Le Figaro Littéraire, 1-7 février 1971, pp. 10-12 (see particularly the last paragraph, p. 12).

4 (Juxtaposed with, and compared to, La Berma's delivery.)

Odette playing part of the Sonata, and which, reflecting generally on the listener's progress towards knowledge and love of a given piece of music, talks of the gradual 'education' that a masterpiece has to give its own public; late too are those concluding comments of Swann's which make it clear that what he is 'reading into' the Sonata derives less from his appreciation of the music itself than from his own remembered associations with it (I 526-36a, pp. 529-34).[1]

Even in La Prisonnière, however, where Vinteuil was much more prominent in the MS, there were still important changes to be wrought. For example, the musician's first principal appearance in the volume as it now stands is on the occasion of Marcel's thoughts about his music and Wagner's (III 158-162); but in the MS it was only Wagner who was the subject of these reflections. On revision, Proust altered Marcel's playing of Wagner with the insertion of the phrase 'et ouvris au hasard la Sonate de Vinteuil' (III 158a), and slipped in, as a joining measure, the resemblance between a phrase of Vinteuil's and one of Wagner's - a resemblance now held responsible for Marcel's eventually going on to pick up some of Tristan (III 158-59a;

---

1 These pages, and the rôle of Vinteuil's music in general in the novel, are the subject of an acute discussion by P. Costil in 'La construction musicale de la "Recherche du Temps perdu" (II)', BSAMP, no. 9 (1959), pp. 83-110. See also his article no. I, of the same name, in BSAMP, no. 8 (1958), pp. 469-89 (pp. 476-83), for remarks on the genesis of this passage.
Other added references to Vinteuil before La P occur in I 869-951a, pp. 877-78; II 906a; II 948b (see II 1114).

III 159a, b). And Proust interpolated at this point three quite new elements. In the first addition of any length, he harks back to the A l'ombre discussion of aspects of a musical work that strike us afresh at a late stage of familiarity with it;[1] more fundamental, he now shows Marcel considering his old ambition to be an artist, and wondering if he has given up something more real than life (III 158d). Third, where the MS merely observed that Wagner's 'tristesse du poète' was, unfortunately, perhaps attenuated by 'l'allégresse du fabricateur', and compared this technical ability to the soaring of the aeroplane which, marvellous though it is, prevents one appreciating 'le silence des espaces',[2] Proust added to this a distinct note of worry, inserting in the margin of the MS Marcel's admission that he is 'troublé par cette habileté vulcanienne':

> Serait-ce elle qui donnerait chez les grands artistes l'illusion d'une originalité foncière, irréductible, en apparence reflet d'une réalité plus qu'humaine, en fait produit d'un labeur industrieux? Si l'art n'est que cela, il n'est pas plus réel que la vie, et je n'avais pas tant de regrets à avoir [...]
> (III 161-62a).

Thus, whereas the MS was here largely a static exploration of, and homage to, certain characteristics of Wagner's work,[3] the final version leaves this section open on an unresolved question

---

1 See I 526-36a, pp. 529-31.

2 III 161-62, without additions.

3 Even though this description can be taken as a partial self-description by Proust: see, e.g., R. Vigneron, 'Structure de Swann: Balzac, Wagner et Proust', The French Review, XIX (1946), pp. 370-84 (pp. 378-80, 382-83).

about individuality and technique, re-introduces the temporary failure of Marcel's vocation, but at the same time draws in the name of the composer who will help to answer these problems. The passage, initially a rather disjointed appreciation, is now firmly linked with Marcel's own development, and, with the posing of the puzzle, given a narrative impetus it previously lacked.

Set in such a perspective, the MS account of the Septet, even unexpanded, would have been more forceful when it came. This first version started, as now, with Marcel's recognition of the Septet as Vinteuil's, and gave the 'prose-poem' descriptions of both it and the Sonata (III 249-50, etc.); it stressed the fundamental sameness of the two compositions, insisting that it was 'une même prière' which, for all artists, both united the individual's works and showed the qualitative differences between separate visions (III 255, 257-58); and it brought out strongly the motif of joy and happiness that finally triumphed over the more sorrowful strain (III 250-52, 260-61), culminating with Marcel's insight that there existed something else, 'réalisable par l'art sans doute', than the 'néant' of all other pleasures, and his acceptance of the fact that 'si ma vie me semblait si vaine, du moins n'avait-elle pas tout accompli' (III 261, 263).

When Proust reworked this, not only did he emphasise some ideas already expressed; he entirely renovated certain parts of the description. He had mentioned in the MS that Vinteuil's 'habituelle spéculation' was 'débarrassée des formes analytiques du raisonnement' (III 256), but he now inserts the page-long interlude between movements during which Marcel, rendered indifferent to the conversation around him, thinks of the intoxication of 'ce retour à l'inanalysé' and wonders if Music might not have had the potential to be 'la communication des âmes', had it not been for the invention of language, the formation of words, and the analysis of ideas (III 258-59a). Although, too, the MS had compared the Sonata and the Septet in 'prose-poem' terms - saying that the Septet was 'rougeoyant' whilst the Sonata was 'blanche', and that a phrase from the Sonata later appearing in the Septet was 'baignée dans le brouillard violet qui s'élevait, surtout dans la dernière période de l'oeuvre de Vinteuil' (III 250, 255, 259) -, there was no specific underpinning of these impressions with suggestions as to a possible emotional development; whereas when Proust revised the section, he added the phrase 'l'une si calme et timide, presque détachée et comme philosophique, l'autre si pressante, anxieuse, implorante' (III 255c). The reiteration of this, two pages further on, is also late: in the Septet, a layer insertion tells us, 'les phrases interrogatives s'y faisaient plus pressantes, plus inquiètes, les réponses plus mystérieuses'; Proust goes so far this time as to refer to an 'âcreté' which 'pouvait choquer', and even observes that the most intelligent of the public recognised Vinteuil's vision to be now more in harmony with the 'souvenir de la patrie intérieure', since 'l'on déclara plus tard les dernières oeuvres de

Vinteuil les plus profondes' (III 257a). And Proust consolidated this quite new element with the further claim that

> A côté de ce Septuor, certaines phrases de la Sonate, que seules le public connaissait, apparaissaient comme tellement banales qu'on ne pouvait pas comprendre comment elles avaient pu exciter tant d'admiration

and the statement that had Vinteuil left, on his death, only what he had been able to complete, no real idea, 'en exceptant certaines parties de la Sonate', could ever have been gained of his true greatness (III 263-64a).

However, the most consistent elaboration is that about the proof of personal individuality afforded by the work of great artists. This was, as I said, central in the MS version, which laid stress on Vinteuil's unconsciously unique, yet steadily persisting, accent (III 255-58); but Proust brought it into still sharper relief, unequivocally answering the question Marcel had asked himself in the addition some 100 pages previously.[1] He not only added the lines on the particular universes of Elstir and Vinteuil, 'un univers insoupçonné, fragmenté' (III 255a, b); on two separate occasions in the description of the Septet, he now asserts that it is fruitless to focus either on similarities between musicians - such as, no doubt, that discovered by Marcel, the same afternoon, between Vinteuil and Wagner - or on 'cette originalité acquise' which had also struck him, for, if one trusts to direct impression, one senses that, 'en dépit des conclusions qui semblent se dégager de la science, l'individuel

---

1 See above, pp. 336-37.

existait' (III 255-56a; III 256-57a). And Proust inserted, as a separate addition on an already written layer, Marcel's brief inner debate towards the end of the evening as to whether 'le monde des différences' exists ('Le septuor de Vinteuil avait semblé me dire que oui. Mais où?') (III 277a).

The only other considerable revision that Proust made in the Verdurin soirée description of the Septet, but that a vital one, was to take a reference already in the MS to the 'joie supra-terrestre' of one of the musical motifs (III 261), and now compare this elation to Marcel's impressions in front of the Martinville steeples and the three trees, cited in the addition as 'les amorces pour la construction d'une vie véritable' (III 261a).[1] This link (made once in the MS, but not at so crucial a moment[2]) was renewed by Proust in his reworking of Le Temps retrouvé, since the two main references to the composer here are late: the first, the reader will recall, comes in the very middle of the involuntary memory of Saint Mark's, when this and similar experiences are said in an addition to resemble 'tant d'autres sensations dont j'ai parlé et que les dernières oeuvres de Vinteuil m'avaient paru synthétiser' (III 866c); and in the second, Vinteuil's music is held up as a criterion of victory,

---

1 The other additions to the La P concert do not bring anything substantially new to the description, often consisting of only a few words: they are: III 249a; III 250a,b,c; III 252b; III 252-53a, p. 253; III 254a,b; III 260a.

2 III 374-75. Even here, Proust elaborated it: see III 374a,b,c, and particularly III 374n.2: III 1091-92a.

to support Marcel's declaration that, not letting himself be trapped yet again, he will strive to reach

> ce que, toujours déçu comme je l'avais été en présence des lieux et des êtres, j'avais (bien qu'une fois la pièce pour concert de Vinteuil eût semblé me dire le contraire) cru irréalisable [...] (III 877a, b).[1]

These are the most important additions about Vinteuil.[2] To summarise, Proust's principal motives in making them were, then, to explore the process of gradual knowledge of a musical composition (I 526-36a, pp. 530-31; III 158d); to specify the differences between the Sonata and the later Septet (III 255c, III 257a, III 263-64a); to connect on two further occasions, and now unmistakably, Vinteuil's music with Marcel's more joyful experiences and revelations (III 261a; III 866c; III 877a, b); to stress the problems of the technical on the one hand, the qualities of the unanalytical on the other (III 161-62a; III 258-59a), and thence to affirm the particularity of the artist's vision, which, though unprovable, can nevertheless be strongly felt (III 255a, b; III 255-56a; III 256-57a; III 277a).

It was structural good sense to juxtapose Vinteuil's music with Marcel's involuntary memories, and own strivings for art, at such points of climax as the concert and the entry into the last matinée; and it is curious that the link should, on the

---

1 See also III 877-78a.

2 Others about him or mentioning him are: III 216-19a, p. 219; III 222b; III 225b; III 240-41a; III 274-75a, p. 274; III 305a; III 333-39a, p. 336; III 373a,b; III 376a; III 501-3a; III 559-60a; III 1030c.

whole, have come so late, since Maurois tells us of a self-'reminder' of Proust's in one of the Carnets to the effect that he might make precisely this association.[1] Indeed, the absence of such a link might have seemed an odd gap, although the reader would probably always have assumed the connection at these moments, even without direction from the narrator. Working at a less obvious level of structural reinforcement, the other expansions equally appear to echo, or 'answer', added parts of the novel. The stress on the unpredictable in a piece of music we believe to be familiar[2] harmonises with the new volte-faces, or relative views, described in more personal relationships elsewhere; the additions on technique in music may be amplifying those about Morel's virtuosity, especially given the close proximity, at only a few lines' distance, of Marcel's worries about technique and the violinist's inability to command himself (III 162-64a).[3]

More provocative, in their way, are the insertions contrasting the Sonata and the Septet.[4] It is not implausible that Proust may here be setting into his very novel a subdued comment on its own development.[5] It is possible to feel that there is,

---

1 A la recherche de Marcel Proust, p. 162: this Carnet is probably post-1914, since it refers to Albertine.

2 (See above, pp. 335, 336.)

3 See above, Ch. 4, p. 192.

4 (See above, pp. 338-39.)

5 Fernandez, however, takes the Sonata to resemble in this respect Les Plaisirs et les jours (A la gloire de Proust, p. 182).

in many of the additions described in this study, a note of 'âcreté' which 'pouvait choquer' (III 257a); with the expansion of the Albertine affair, the narrative does become 'pressante, anxieuse, implorante' (III 255c) in a way that Du Côté de chez Swann is not. To accept this as one interpretation would, of course, entail applying to the 1912-13 writings Proust's more unfavourable comments on the Sonata, and his statement that Vinteuil's 'dernières oeuvres' were 'les plus profondes' (III 257a);[1] this is a matter which would need to be discussed elsewhere, if justice were to be done to it.[2]

However, it is the additions about the individuality of the artist which most deserve close attention, particularly since they are paralleled by the late incorporation into Le Temps retrouvé of that central discussion of style as 'une

---

1 It is especially interesting that in this particular addition Proust made a slip and wrote 'Bergotte' for 'Vinteuil': see III 257n.3.

2 Critics who have had access to the MSS have remarked that there is a more sombre, stormy, almost a heavier note in Proust's later work that was not originally there; see not only Feuillerat (whose judgements in this sphere are sometimes suspect, of course), pp. 131-32, 262, but also P. Clarac's brief observation, cited above, Ch. 2, p. 105n.1, and Bardèche, vol. II, pp. 208, 249-50, 260. (Here Bardèche asserts that in 1916 and 1918 there was 'une transformation profonde chez Proust [...] un changement sensible de sa personnalité'.)
J. Milly even reports, on not very well-grounded evidence, that Proust's ideas on style had changed since DCS, and he no longer found this earlier writing so 'suitable': Proust et le style (Paris, 1970), pp. 134-35. See the short discussion above in Ch. 2, pp. 104-6.

question non de technique mais de vision', and as the demonstration of the 'différence qualitative qu'il y a dans la façon dont nous apparaît le monde, différence qui, s'il n'y avait pas l'art, resterait le secret éternel de chacun' (III 895-96a).[1] The elaborations around the figure of Vinteuil, proclaiming the uniqueness of each personality and pointing to art as the only adequate expression of this, defend one tenet of _A la recherche_ as it was always to be; but they also imply, perhaps, a commentary on another of Proust's expansions, that of the characters' language. Although there is individuality of a kind in their means of expression too, their stereotypes or strained 'newness' can be set against Vinteuil's ability to find what is most specific in himself, then to convey this truthfully and originally. Finally, the 'coming home' imagery used in _La Prisonnière_ ('patrie perdue', III 257a), and the unity posited for this 'artistic personality' (III 256-57a), oppose still more sharply the searching outside himself to which the narrator gives himself up during this volume and the next; they suggest an alternative to the discrepancies between Marcel's volatile 'moi's', changing from one moment to the next at this point of the novel especially, but also for almost its whole course.

---

1 This passage is one of those additions of evidently early inspiration, if not insertion: cp. the interview given to _Le Temps_ in 1913, reproduced in _Textes retrouvés_, recueillis et présentés par P. Kolb et L.B. Price (Urbana, Chicago and London, 1968), pp. 215-20 (pp. 218-19).

ELSTIR

Strangely enough, Elstir does not appear at all in the body of the 1913 galleys of A l'ombre.[1] However, at the appropriate place in the uncorrected copy of these galleys, a cross is marked and 'v.C' written in pencil - possibly the C of Jean Santeuil;[2] and at the end of the corrected 1913 galleys Proust, apparently rather arbitrarily, made some rough additions referring to Elstir, which then appear in the text of the 1914 galleys.[3]

At any rate, he is firmly in the 1914 galleys (from galley 63, p. v, to 65, p. i), and it is this version of Marcel's meeting with the painter, and of his visit to the studio, that has been described by Feuillerat.[4] (Incidentally, it took place much nearer the end of the volume than now, since the 1914 stay in Balbec finished only eleven galley pages later.[5]) I shall briefly recall what Marcel was originally to gain from this encounter; its most important features are in any case in the

---

1 n.a.fr. 16753: see table, I 825b on. He is, however, in the pre-1914 TS of CG: see, e.g., II 28, 125-26.

2 n.a.fr. 16754:94vi. See here Bardèche, vol. I, pp. 171-72, for a stage in the Cahiers between C and Elstir.

3 (Details are given below, p. 349.)

4 pp. 54-65.

5 On galley 66, p. iv.

final version, but diluted amongst other, later, elements.[1]

In the early version, then, Marcel and Saint-Loup contrived to approach Elstir at Rivebelle,[2] and he invited Marcel to his studio.[3] A discussion of Elstir's solitary life[4] moved straight into the beginning of the visit to him, and into the rejuvenation he effected in Marcel's vision of the Balbec church, indeed of Balbec in general; and this was to be the main subject of the pages that followed.

> Le plus grand charme qu'eut pour moi cette visite que je fis à l'atelier d'Elstir, ce fut d'ouvrir un champ nouveau aux désirs que j'avais apportés à Balbec et auxquels la réalité si différente n'avait guère répondu. Sans doute pour ce qui était par exemple, de l'église de Balbec la conversation d'Elstir, les paroles qu'il me dit furent aussi efficaces que ses tableaux pour me faire oublier ma déception et à me faire souhaiter de revenir devant la vieille façade.
> - Comment vous avez été déçu [...]
> (n.a.fr. 16761:63viii).[5]

The sequence now pursued roughly as it does in the present text, with Elstir's finely observant description of the Balbec church. However, after Marcel's discovery that the church does indeed

---

1 A glance at the A l'ombre tables, from I 825b, will show the sections from the 1914 version that remain, still approximately the same, in the present text: they are those marked: Not in 16753 [...]; in 16761 [...].

2 See I 825b; I 825-26a.

3 See I 826-28a, p. 827.

4 See I 826-28a, p. 828.

5 See I 840-42a, p. 840, for the continuation. (Punctuation, here and in other quotations, is as it appears on the galleys.)

have parts that make it 'presque persane' (I 842), the 1914 version diverged again from the one we now have. The narrator went on to say how greatly he was inspired by Elstir's words, which made him long to revisit the church: 'Un homme d'un grand goût venait de jeter en moi les fondements de nouveaux désirs' (n.a.fr. 16761:64iii). He himself, he told us, was later to become such a man of taste; when his faculty of admiration had dried up, he would have acquired a historian's or scholar's approach, 'me consolant de ne pas recevoir la même impression poétique que j'avais eue jadis à Combray devant les pierres tombales pareilles aux alvéoles d'un miel durci, doré et doux' (n.a.fr. 16761:64iii).

More than Elstir's conversation, however, his paintings changed the form of Marcel's dreams, 'avaient dirigé constamment mes désirs sur ce qu'ils avaient dédaigné jusque-là'. For example, at Balbec

> je m'étais toujours devant la mer, efforcé d'expulser du champ de ma vision les baigneuses du premier plan, les yachts de plaisance aux voiles trop blanches comme un costume de plage en coutil blanc, tout ce qui m'empêchait de me persuader que je contemplais le flot immémorial qui déroulait déjà cette même vie mystérieuse avant l'apparition de l'espèce humaine jusqu'à ce que j'eusse vu dans l'atelier d'Elstir une marine de lui ou (sic) une jeune femme en robe de barège, dans un yacht échenillant le long de ses drisses au soleil et au vent, ses flammes multicolores, mit dans mon imagination le "double" spirituel d'une robe de barège et du grand pavoi d'un yacht, qui réchauffa, y couva un désir insatiable d'en voir le plus tôt possible comme si cela ne m'était jamais arrivé [...]
> (n.a.fr. 16761:64iii-iv).

All in all, 'Elstir me rendit moins exclusif' (n.a.fr. 16761:64v).

The 1914 version next moved into an explanation of the statement that when Elstir was creating, he had the courage to forget everything he knew and take the physical world as it appeared, recreating his first impression.[1] For him, ancient monuments and modern buildings were on the same footing, a levelling-out which had earned him reproaches; but the 'unité profonde' of his work derived from his transcribing only what he had personally felt. These paintings all taught Marcel to look affectionately on objects to which he had previously paid no attention - such as an open oyster, a knife on a table-cloth, a 'table desservie' (n.a.fr. 16761:64vii); and he wished now to visit local places whose charm Elstir had pointed out to him. 'C'est ainsi qu'il introduisait en tout des différences, des qualités esthétiques qui m'enflammaient [...]' (n.a.fr. 16761: 64viii). Finally, the artist gave Marcel two paintings he had just completed, one showing the curious night-time effect of gas-lights on the beach during a firework-display, the other of Balbec beach 'irisée comme un arc-en-ciel par le prisme qu'y émiettaient d'innombrables méduses, transparentes comme de grandes girandoles mauves, bleuâtres et rosées'. And the narrator left Elstir in a state of exaltation which remained sterile, since he used it up running back and forth in the train and repeating to himself 'Quel être adorable! quel homme de génie' (n.a.fr. 16761:65i).

---

1 Now more briefly at the beginning of I 840-42a.

Apart from this episode, there were, very near the end of the original Balbec stay, the curious hasty passages already mentioned, those first occurring as additions on the corrected 1913 galleys and then appearing in the 1914 ones.[1] These concluded the 'message' of the early Elstir. They not only took up the substance of that passage in the present text in which Marcel '[restait] maintenant volontiers à table pendant qu'on desservait' (I 869-951a, p. 869); going back to the other objects in the 1914 paintings, they also described the narrator's new enthusiasm for fireworks, regattas and jellyfish, of which last he said:

> De dégoût je n'en ressentis[2] aucun, car le sentiment esthétique nous fait franchir les limites qu'impose (<u>sic</u>) à nos goûts les préférences [ou les répu][3] du corps (n.a.fr. 16753:95ii).

This draft, the principal section of which occupied about twelve galley pages, thus did bring out what is to be so important in the second Elstir - the fact that he forgets what he knows and paints only what he sees -[4] but it was, for the moment, largely to support the main purpose of the encounter, which was to break down a certain aesthetic snobbery in Marcel and make him appreciate more 'ordinary' things that he had not, until then, deigned to notice - whilst still implying a rather too great dependence on Elstir's choice of object. As is by

---

1 See above, p. 345.

2 'sentis' in n.a.fr. 16761:65vi.

3 Words in brackets crossed out.

4 See above, p. 348.

now clear, the burden of this, divided up and slightly rewritten, is in the present text. Proust retained not merely the new pleasure in the clearing-away of the table,[1] but transported almost exactly into the final version the 1914 description of Marcel's yearning to see a 'robe de barège' and the 'grand pavoi d'un yacht'[2] (I 869-951a, p. 902). The 1914 version gave too his desire to go to Carquethuit since seeing it in a painting of Elstir's (I 854-55a): at present, however, this desire is demonstrated even more forcibly to spring from Marcel's misunderstanding of what it is that he finds attractive about the aforesaid painting (I 842-54a, p. 854). And the novel we now have also describes Marcel's attempt to ignore the distasteful buildings in Elstir's residential area (I 828-40a, pp. 833-34), and, later, his wish that the artist might paint certain flowers so that his genius could reveal what he, Marcel, had vainly looked for in them (I 842-54a, p. 847) - thus taking up still further the central points of the 1914 version.[3]

---

1 Mentioned just above: it is now also prepared by I 694-96a, pp. 694-95, which describe Marcel's attempts to ignore the table at the end of the meal.

2 See above, p. 347.

3 Besides these, various other elements were kept by Proust, such as, evidently, the description of the Balbec church (see above, pp. 346-47). Some 1914 lines on the Creuniers appear, expanded but recognisable, in the present text (I 869-951a, p. 925), and Elstir's presentation of a gift to Marcel, now in the final version (I 855-66a, p. 860), was in the 1914 one too, although the early Elstir was more generous than the later, giving Marcel not a sketch, but two paintings! (n.a.fr. 16761:64viii-65i: see above, p. 348). See too the present I 869-951a, pp. 897-98.

In one sense, Proust did not, then, make any surprising changes to the lesson Elstir teaches Marcel, since, although it was subdued, the need to rely on impression, not intelligence, in art was stated,[1] and there were already comments on the aesthetic potential of hitherto rejected subjects, and on the value of the artist's vision rather than of its objects. However, Proust did go on to give a particular significance to parts of this lesson; and he incorporated into the episode features that are quite new.

First of all, three brief additions make Elstir older (giving him a greying beard) (I 825c), tell us that he is to become famous only a few years later (I 826a), and describe the amour-propre that may at first accompany the voluntary solitude of the artist, given the difficulty of an immediate break with one's former self (I 828a). And the actual visit to the studio is now expanded so that it falls into three main blocks, each of several pages long.[2]

The first describes in much more detail than the 1914 version what Marcel sees of Elstir's work. This is of course well-known, but to summarise rapidly: what initially strikes Marcel is the power of creativity in Elstir's work - the new form and dignity he gives to the 'chaos que sont toutes choses que nous voyons' by continuing their existence in his painting.

---

1 See above, p.348.

2 (These three blocks mingle with passages, presumably late, about the 'jeunes filles', who will be mentioned here only in so far as they affect Marcel's talk with Elstir.)

There is now some information about Elstir's first and second manners (the mythological and Japanese, of no great interest to Marcel); and Proust pursues with the much-discussed description of the metaphorical nature of Elstir's work and his re-creation of things by taking away their names, which correspond to a notion of the intelligence 'étrangère à nos impressions véritables'.[1] This late block includes the further comments on the way in which the intelligence makes demarcations that had not at first been seen; it contrasts this simplification with Elstir's success in reproducing the multiplicity of the impression itself. Post-1914 too are the lines on the coalescing of land and sea in his paintings, and on the pioneer interest in uses of perspective and chiaroscuro that had led him to paint 'de véritables mirages', and to exploit light and shifting angles in such a way as to make, for example, a river seem dislocated and broken, a town 'bouleversée', the mass of its houses 'confuse' as they lie along the 'fleuve écrasé et décousu', and a pathway, 'cette partie à demi humaine de la nature', vanish and reappear by turns (I 828-40a, pp. 828, 830, 833-40).

---

1 See here J. Autret on Ruskin's influence, in _L'influence de Ruskin sur la vie, les idées et l'oeuvre de Marcel Proust_ (Geneva, 1955), pp. 41, 84;M.E.Chernowitz, _Proust and Painting_ (New York, 1944), e.g. pp. 111-13, 156, 167-72. Chernowitz gives some discussion of Feuillerat's discoveries about the first and second Elstir (pp. 100-107); so too does J.M. Cocking, in _French 19th Century Painting and Literature_ (pp. 316-17).
L. Bersani puts this aspect of Elstir's work into a wider perspective than the purely sensory, in _Marcel Proust: The Fictions of Life and of Art_, p. 158.

The elements of the next substantial addition are more disparate. This is the twelve-page sequence in which Elstir advises Marcel that it is important to know one's dreams through and through rather than to turn away from them, at the risk, otherwise, of suffering, and of becoming the plaything of a multitude of appearances for not having understood them - counsels followed instantly and doubtless symbolically by the rapid arrival and departure of Albertine. This addition recounts, second, Marcel's unearthing of the portrait of Miss Sacripant, his hesitation over the sex of the model, and his feeling that the painter, going beyond concerns of morality or immorality,

> s'était au contraire attaché à ces traits d'ambiguïté comme à un élément esthétique qui valait d'être mis en relief et qu'il avait tout fait pour souligner.

And the description, the reader will recall, closes on the enigmatic nature of this being, the painting suggesting sometimes a mannish girl, sometimes 'un jeune efféminé vicieux et songeur', only for each impression successively to fade away. Less obtrusively, Proust also added here the consideration of the kind of inspiration an artist needs as he grows old, and the danger of idolatry of the subjects that once gave him his masterpieces (I 842-54a).

The last considerable insertion about Elstir is that in which Marcel guesses that Miss Sacripant is Odette. Into this Proust incorporated the long aside asserting that even if the portrait had been painted later than it was, Elstir's vision would have been enough to 'disorganise' the face Odette subsequently 'built up' for herself, since artistic genius can dissociate given combinations and re-order them; nor will the artist spare the aging woman. The insertion winds to an end with the further disclosure that Elstir was M. Biche (an identification therefore not originally to be made in the 1914 Balbec stay), and his unembarrassed avowal of it; and late too, of course, are his displeasure on seeing the disappointment on Marcel's face, his overcoming of this momentary hostility, and his preference not for the 'paroles qui auraient pu venger son amour-propre', but for those 'qui pouvaient m'instruire', which inspires the culminating speech that opens

> "Il n'y a pas d'homme si sage qu'il soit [...] qui n'ait à telle époque de sa jeunesse prononcé des paroles, ou même mené une vie, dont le souvenir lui soit désagréable et qu'il souhaiterait être aboli

and ends:

> On ne reçoit pas la sagesse, il faut la découvrir soi-même après un trajet que personne ne peut faire pour nous, ne peut nous épargner, car elle est un point de vue sur les choses. Les vies que vous admirez, les attitudes que vous trouvez nobles [...] représentent un combat et une victoire [...] l'image de ce que nous avons été dans une période première [...] ne doit pas être reniée pourtant, car elle est un témoignage que nous avons vraiment vécu, que c'est selon les lois de la vie et de l'esprit que nous avons, des éléments communs de la vie, [...] extrait quelque chose qui les dépasse."

To this Marcel makes no reply, absorbed in his misfortune at losing the chance to meet the girls of the little band! (I 855-66a, pp. 860-64).

These are the main additions about the painter, although

others continue to mention him into <u>Le Temps retrouvé</u>. Of these, the <u>Sodome et Gomorrhe</u> description of the 'rural' sea is one of the more central in the narrator's own progress (II 783-84a). This passage, as I have mentioned, was in fact not added but transferred, since it originally appeared in <u>A l'ombre</u>;[1] but what <u>is</u> new is the reference to Elstir, whose influence is now held to be largely responsible for Marcel's capacity to perceive natural ambiguities.[2]

What differences, then, does one notice in the 'second' Elstir? First of all, as in the case of Vinteuil, there are now references to the stages of Elstir's style,[3] as well as to age - both Elstir's and his models' - and to the passing of time.[4] This reflects both growing preoccupations inside Proust's novel, especially those discussed in the last chapter,[5] and, no doubt, biographical considerations outside it.

---

1 See above, Ch. 1, p. 27; Ch. 2, p.105<u>n</u>.3.

2 For mention of Elstir in the MS for <u>CG</u> on, see, e.g., II 418-22 without additions. Additions referring to him, other than those discussed so far, are: I 825f; I 827a,b,c,d; II 45-46a; II 419b; II 420-21a; II 420a,b; II 421a,b; II 461a,b; II 500a,b; II 501a,b,c,d; II 502-3a, p. 502; II 568b; II 573a; III 71a; III 167b; III 168a; III 440a; III 714a,b, III 720a,<u>n</u>. (these give, and comment on, the revelation through the Goncourt diary that M. Tiche (<u>sic</u>) is Elstir; but as we have seen, this had already been added to <u>A l'ombre</u>). Odette as Miss Sacripant is, as I said in Ch. 4 (p.177, and <u>n</u>.2), mentioned <u>in</u> the MS of <u>La P</u> (III 299), and, as the subject of a portrait by Elstir, in the MS of <u>La F</u> (III 440).

3 See above, pp. 338-39 for Vinteuil and p. 352 for Elstir.

4 Above, pp. 351, 353-54.

5 pp. 320-30.

Second, the most striking aspect of the sequences just cited is, I think, their new emphasis on the way in which Elstir catches distortion and ambiguity, from the natural to the sexual (in the figure of Miss Sacripant). It need hardly be repeated at this point that, although fundamental in _Du Côté de chez Swann_ too, precisely some of Proust's most sustained efforts during the post-1914 period were to add identical effects to his own work. If Elstir reveals the multiplicity of impression, this is what Proust too adds to Marcel's confusion in front of the many-faceted Albertine, showing even further his inability to reduce _his_ impression into clear-cut units, much as he would like to.[1] Elstir paints mirages and tricks of perspective, such that objects seem dislocated, 'bouleversé', 'écrasé et décousu', and disappear and reappear inconsistently, different each time. Again, one cannot but think not only of Albertine's new lies, but also of Morel, and of the volte-faces worked into the novel;[2] and an even stronger idea of the topsy-turvy or the upset is introduced in the image of the overturned town with its confusion of houses. Miss Sacripant, like so many of the latterly changed characters, could be either a man or a woman.[3] In other words, Elstir is now painting what Proust is writing. And if the revision brings out still further that Elstir creates by removing sharp distinctions from things and taking them out of the jurisdiction of the intelli-

1 See above, Ch. 6, pp. 267-83.

2 See above, Ch. 4, e.g. pp. 199-200; Ch. 2, pp. 76-79.

3 See above, Ch. 6, pp. 283-94.

gence, Proust is here not only commenting on some of the other insertions, contrary as Elstir's practice is to that of the younger Marcel, whose interests lie in etymology and military strategy,[1] and similar as it is to that of the narrator, who in the later additions does not even give himself a proper name;[2] he is reinforcing the aim of the novel as it had always been, since the author Marcel follows the aesthetic of both the 1914 and the post-1914 Elstir by re-creating, in his writing, the immediacy of experience, not its categorisation by the logical faculties.[3]

The seriously moral side now attributed to Elstir is no less important. If he delights in suggesting equivocal appearances, he nevertheless tells Marcel that, in another sense, the artist must not be dominated by his own self-created

---

1 See Ch. 2, pp. 91-96.

2 This has been known for some time, from M. Suzuki ('Le "Je" Proustien', BSAMP, no. 9 (1959), pp. 72-74): the name 'Marcel' appears in MS additions (III 75a, III 113-16a, p. 115, III 157a), but is made the subject of doubt only in TS ones (III 75b; III 115a).

3 See too the addition about the 'inanalysé' in music (above, pp. 337 - 38); and also some of the additions on drunkenness, sleep and dreams, etc., which describe Marcel's more blurred impressions (Ch. 2, pp. 99-104).
It is most interesting that the crucial development in La Fugitive of Marcel's ideas about Habit is late too: he now sees it not merely as suppressing the originality of perceptions, but as so ingrained in us that to be deprived of it is actually agonising: 'je voyais soudain un nouveau visage de l'Habitude', etc. (III 420a).

illusions or confusions: 'Il importe qu'on connaisse entièrement ses rêves', since otherwise 'vous serez le jouet de mille apparences parce que vous n'en aurez pas compris la nature' (I 842-54a, p. 843[1]). Elstir, it is stressed, is no longer subject to amour-propre, either in his devotion to his art, or in his reactions to Marcel's disappointment on learning that he was the foolish M. Biche;[2] and his positing of a calm self-acceptance which goes beyond feelings of shame and embarrassment, together with the remarks on the attainment of wisdom, which one must find oneself after a journey 'que personne ne peut faire pour nous [...] car elle est un point de vue sur les choses [...] un combat et une victoire' should not be treated as a disjointed homily from Proust.[3] This 'message' is inseparable from the discovery of a permanent self and an at last stable view of life, and from the decision to write about the errors that led up to the discovery, which the last part of <u>Le Temps retrouvé</u> represents. Unlike the imitative use of cliché, this achievement has to be a personal effort, and unlike the sudden succumbing to disorienting blows, it has to signify a firm yet flexible 'point de vue sur les choses'.

---

1 Cited above, p. 353.

2 See above, pp. 351, 354.

3 Feuillerat is condescending about it: see his p. 59.

Conclusion

This study has not, clearly, covered all the late passages: as I suggested in the introduction,[1] this would have been both difficult and unsatisfactory, since the more important ones could not then have been treated in such detail. For example, of the longer additions mentioned in Chapter 1, there has been no further reference to those about the inheritance of Léonie's fortune and about the narrator's gift of her furniture to the brothel; the discussion has left aside the sections on Marcel's entranced state at the Swanns', on Odette's 'cocotte' taste for flowers, and on Saint-Loup's intellectual nature, as well as some of the changes to Bergotte and the meeting with the princesse Mathilde.[2] Again, the elaboration of the money element in _La Fugitive_, the letters of congratulation on Marcel's article, and his depression about the marriages, have not been mentioned after Chapter 1;[3] neither have the _Côté de Guermantes_ additions on the Iénas and their furniture, or on the Courvoisiers, for instance.[4] The story of Odette's amorous career and the

1 Above, p. 2.

2 See above, pp. 22-23, 25.

3 See above, pp. 50, 52, 53.

4 See above, pp. 34-35.

sequence about Rachel's apparently flirtatious glances at Marcel, although substantial interpolations into the last matinée, seemed to me not to link with other expansions firmly enough to warrant, in the scope of this book, a separate, close description.[1] I have, therefore, taken here the major additions, those most obviously representing a central development or an extended new preoccupation.

Proust, then, in the 1914-22 period, gave his characters numerous set expressions, paid special attention to Morel, and endowed other figures with interfering, callous, or self-pitying traits; he made Charlus prouder and more insolent; he increased greatly references to rumour and to lying, and brought bisexuality and inversion into a position so prominent as to be, by conventional standards, exaggerated; he wished particularly to chart and to discuss the process of social change, and he stressed a new effect of time and gave the novel a firmer narrative impetus by introducing so many scenes depicting illness or old age. He took up some of his own added themes, and even perhaps made reference to his own development as a novelist, in the growth of Vinteuil and Elstir; and throughout the revision of the novel, he was always concerned with the comic or metaphorical potential of a given episode, with the dramatic surprises which the work could be further adapted to hold, and with the subtle retrospective balance *Le Temps retrouvé* must continue to be. These expansions should not be

---

1 . See above, p. 62.

forced into a unity they do not necessarily have, but it seems, for example, that the notion of the inchoate or the distorted particularly preoccupied Proust in these years, as indicated by the new etymologies, some of the incorrect language, the discussion on Morel's character, the further lies, the conflicting evidence about Albertine, the additions on drunkenness, sleep, and dreams, and the strong emphasis on Elstir's skill in re-creating similar effects.

Further conclusions about the discoveries outlined in this book could form the subject-matter of another. It is evident that Feuillerat's view must give way to a more complex one. Other questions remain, however. Readers of *A la recherche du temps perdu* may want to consider what external influences may have led Proust to develop the novel in the directions he did, or whether all the additions are equally successful. Perhaps the most interesting task ahead is, as I implied in Chapter 2,[1] an examination of the new passages in the contexts in which they appear, based on a recognition that many of them strengthen the pattern of the novel in an unobtrusive manner,[2] rather than making it awkward or seemingly digressive. The fact that Morel now knows Albertine actually tightens the structure of the work.

---

1 pp. 73, 122-23.

2 J.M. Cocking draws attention to this aspect in a general discussion of the expansions, part of 'The Coherence of *Le Temps retrouvé*', in *Marcel Proust: A Critical Panorama*, edited by L.B. Price, pp. 82-101 (p. 84).

The introduction of the relatively chaste, 'unfertilised', Vaugoubert, and of his mannish wife, illustrates the strangeness and hermaphroditism of the orchid sequence much more appositely than Charlus on his own at the soirée could have done (II 642-47a, pp. 645-47); and the rumours, now appearing so preponderantly on social occasions in Le Côté de Guermantes and Sodome et Gomorrhe, not only give the Faubourg Saint-Germain a further dimension of empty malice, they also quietly prepare the reader for the ambiguous reports of the 'Albertine volumes'. The addition to the bluffing separation scene in which Marcel is said to allude constantly to 'la nuit déjà si avancée', to 'notre fatigue', gives the impression, an important one in the Albertine affair, of a nadir of darkness and incapacity, especially when it is shortly followed by the description of Albertine as an allegorical figure 'de quoi? de ma mort? de mon oeuvre?' (III 357a; III 359-60a): this is Proust controlling his novel - making it tauter, not more diffuse.

This type of study could, in fact, eventually prove a more fruitful approach to the expansion of the novel than that adopted here.[1] The method used in this book makes it appear that Proust 'thought out' a widespread trait, then 'put it in', and while, as I said in the introduction and in Chapter 2,[2]

---

1 Pierre Costil, e.g., adopts such an approach in 'La construction musicale de la "Recherche du Temps perdu"' (I and II), BSAMP, nos. 8, pp. 469-89, and 9, pp. 83-110; so, to a lesser extent, does A. Pugh, who in his thesis goes through the novel volume by volume, not subject by subject.

2 Above, pp. 5, 122-23.

this seems to be the case in some instances, the process is unlikely to have been as mechanical as my grouping has implied. This is particularly true of the new moral aspects, where some of the changes - those to Saniette, for example - doubtless sprang as much from the demands of the character taking greater definition in Proust's imagination as from any more abstract interest.

Select Bibliography for Parts I and II

1. - WORKS BY PROUST

A la recherche du temps perdu, Bibliothèque de la Pléiade (3 vols., [Paris], 1954)

Chroniques (Paris, 1927)

Contre Sainte-Beuve, précédé de Pastiches et mélanges et suivi de Essais et articles, Bibliothèque de la Pléiade ([Paris], 1971)

Contre Sainte-Beuve, suivi de Nouveaux Mélanges, edited by B. de Fallois (Paris, 1954)

Jean Santeuil, précédé de Les Plaisirs et les jours, Bibliothèque de la Pléiade ([Paris], 1971)

Textes retrouvés, recueillis et présentés par P. Kolb et L.B. Price (Urbana, Chicago and London, 1968)

Translations:

RUSKIN, J. La Bible d'Amiens (Paris, 1947)

RUSKIN, J. Sésame et les lys (Paris, 1935)

2. - CORRESPONDENCE

(Some books and articles under sections 3 and 5 include letters of Proust's.)

BIBESCO, princesse — *Au Bal avec Marcel Proust* (Paris, 1928)

______ — *Le Voyageur voilé: Marcel Proust* (Geneva, 1949)

BISSON, L.A. — 'Deux Inédits de Marcel Proust', *French Studies*, II (1948), pp. 341-47.

BOYLESVE, R. & PROUST, M. — *Quelques échanges et témoignages* (Paris, 1931)

DAUDET, Lucien — *Autour de soixante lettres de Marcel Proust* (Paris, 1929)

DREYFUS, R. — *Souvenirs sur Marcel Proust* (Paris, 1926)

GREGH, F. — *Mon Amitié avec Marcel Proust* (Paris, 1958)

MORAND, P. — *Le Visiteur du Soir* (Geneva, 1949)

PASQUALI, C. — *Proust, Primoli, La Moda* (Rome, 1961)

PROUST, M. — *A un ami* (Paris, 1948)

______ — *Correspondance: Tome I: 1880-1895*, texte établi, présenté et annoté par P. Kolb ([Paris], 1970)

______ — *Correspondance avec sa mère*, présentée et annotée par P. Kolb (Paris, 1953)

______ — *Correspondance générale* (6 vols., Paris, 1930-36)

______ — *Choix de lettres*, présentées et datées par P. Kolb (Paris, 1965)

PROUST, M. 'Lettres' (between Gide and Proust), Nouvelle Revue Française, XXXI (1928), pp. 609-15.

_____ Lettres à la N R F (Paris, 1932)

_____ Lettres à Madame C. (publ. J.B. Janin, 1946)

_____ Lettres à Reynaldo Hahn, présentées, datées et annotées par P. Kolb (Paris, 1956)

_____ Lettres à une amie (Manchester, 1942)

_____ Lettres retrouvées, présentées et annotées par P. Kolb ([Paris], 1966)

_____ Marcel Proust et Jacques Rivière: Correspondance 1914-1922, présentée et annotée par P. Kolb (Paris, 1955)

_____ Marcel Proust: Lettres inédites, présentées par Camille Vettard (Bagnères-de-Bigorre, 1926)

_____ 'Quatre lettres à son frère Robert', Nouvelle Revue Française, 18e année, no. 209 (1970), pp. 744-50.

_____ Quelques lettres de Marcel Proust à Jeanne, Simone, Gaston de Caillavet, Robert de Flers, Bertrand de Fénelon ([Paris], 1929)

ROBERT, L. de Comment débuta Marcel Proust, re-edition ([Paris], 1969)

3. - WORKS ON PROUST

ABRAHAM, P. — *Proust: Recherches sur la création intellectuelle* (Paris, 1930)

AUTRET, J. — *L'Influence de Ruskin sur la vie, les idées et l'oeuvre de Marcel Proust* (Geneva, 1955)

BARDÈCHE, M. — *Marcel Proust romancier* (2 vols., Paris, 1971)

BARKER, R.H. — *Marcel Proust: A Biography* (New York, 1962)

BECKETT, S. — *Proust* (London, 1931)

BELL, C. — *Proust* (London, 1928)

BELL, W.S. — *Proust's Nocturnal Muse* (New York and London, 1962)

BERSANI, L. — *Marcel Proust: The Fictions of Life and of Art* (New York, 1965)

BIBESCO, princesse — *La Duchesse de Guermantes: Laure de Sade Comtesse de Chevigné* (Paris, 1950)

BONNET, H. — *Le Progrès spirituel dans l'oeuvre de Marcel Proust* (2 vols., Paris, 1946 & 1949)

_____ — *Marcel Proust de 1907 à 1914*, new edition (Paris, 1971)

BRÉE, G. — *Du Temps perdu au temps retrouvé* (Paris, 1950)

_____ — *The World of Marcel Proust* (London, 1967)

BRIAND, C. — *Le Secret de Marcel Proust* (Paris, 1950)

BUTOR, M. — *Les Oeuvres d'art imaginaires chez Proust* (London, 1964)

CATTAUI, G. — L'Amitié de Proust (Paris, 1935)

CAZEAUX, J. — L'Écriture de Proust ou l'art du vitrail ([Paris], 1971)

CHANTAL, R. de — Marcel Proust critique littéraire (2 vols., Montreal, 1967)

CHERNOWITZ, M.E. — Proust and Painting (New York, 1944)

CLERMONT-TONNERRE, E. de — Robert de Montesquiou et Marcel Proust (Paris, 1925)

COCKING, J.M. — Proust (London, 1956)

CURTIUS, E.R. — Marcel Proust (Paris, 1928)

DANDIEU, A. — Marcel Proust: Sa révélation psychologique (Paris, 1930)

DAUDET, C. — Répertoire des personnages de "A la recherche du temps perdu" (Paris, 1927)

DELATTRE, F. — Bergson et Proust: Accords et dissonances (publ. Albin Michel, 1948)

DELEUZE, G. — Proust et les signes (Paris, 1970)

FARDWELL, F.V. — Landscape in the Works of Marcel Proust (Washington, D.C., 1948)

FERNANDEZ, R. — A la gloire de Proust (Paris, 1944)

FERRÉ, A. — Géographie de Marcel Proust (Paris, 1939)

FEUILLERAT, A. — Comment Marcel Proust a composé son roman (New Haven, 1934)

GALLIMARD (publ.) — Hommage à Marcel Proust (Paris, 1927)

_____ — Morceaux Choisis de Marcel Proust (Paris, 1928)

_____ — Études Proustiennes I & II, publiées sous la direction de Jacques Bersani, Michel Raimond et Jean-Yves Tadié ([Paris], 1973 & 1975)

GRAHAM, V.E. — The Imagery of Proust (Oxford, 1966)

GRAMONT, E. de [i.e. E. de Clermont-Tonnerre] — Marcel Proust (Paris, 1948)

HIER, F. — La Musique dans l'oeuvre de Marcel Proust (New York, 1933)

JACKSON, E.R. — L'Évolution de la mémoire involontaire dans l'oeuvre de Marcel Proust (Paris, 1966)

KING, A. — Proust (Edinburgh and London, 1968)

KOLB, P. — La Correspondance de Marcel Proust: Chronologie et commentaire critique (Urbana, 1949)

LEON, D. — Introduction to Proust: His Life, His Circle and His Work (London, 1940)

LOURIA, Y. — La Convergence stylistique chez Proust (Geneva and Paris, 1957)

MANSFIELD, L. — Le Comique de Marcel Proust (and Proust et Baudelaire) (Paris, 1953)

MARCH, H. — The Two Worlds of Marcel Proust (London, 1948)

MARC-LIPIANSKY, M. — La Naissance du monde proustien dans Jean Santeuil (Paris, 1974)

MASSIS, H. — Le Drame de Marcel Proust (Paris, 1937)

MAURIAC, F. — Du Côté de chez Proust (Paris, 1947)

MAUROIS, A. — A la recherche de Marcel Proust, re-edition ([Paris], 1970)

MILLY, J. — Proust et le style (Paris, 1970)

MINOGUE, V. — Proust: Du Côté de chez Swann (London, 1973)

MONNIN-HORNUNG, J. — Proust et la peinture (Geneva and Lille, 1951)

MOSS, H. — The Magic Lantern of Marcel Proust (London, 1963)

MOUTON, J. *Le Style de Marcel Proust* (Paris, 1948)

_____ *Proust*, Les écrivains devant Dieu, no. 19 (publ. Desclée de Brouwer, 1968)

MULLER, M. *Les Voix narratives dans la Recherche du temps perdu* (Geneva, 1965)

PAINTER, G.D. *Marcel Proust: A Biography* (2 vols., London, 1959 & 1965)

PICON, G. *Lecture de Proust* (Paris, 1963)

PIERRE-QUINT, L. *Marcel Proust: Sa vie, son oeuvre* (Paris, 1925)

_____ *Après Le Temps retrouvé: Le Comique et le mystère chez Proust* (Paris, 1928)

_____ *Comment travaillait Proust* (Paris, 1928)

_____ *Comment parut "Du Côté de chez Swann"* (Paris, 1930)

PIROUÉ, G. *Par les chemins de Marcel Proust* (Neuchâtel, 1955)

_____ *Proust et la musique du devenir* (Paris, 1960)

POMMIER, J. *La Mystique de Marcel Proust* (Geneva, 1968)

POULET, G. *L'Espace proustien* ([Paris], 1963)

PRICE, L.B. (ed.) *Marcel Proust: A Critical Panorama* (Urbana, Chicago and London, 1973)

PUGH, A.R. 'The Composition of Marcel Proust's *A la Recherche du Temps Perdu*' (unpublished Ph.D. thesis, University of Cambridge, 1959)

RAPHAEL, N.P. *Introduction à la correspondance de Marcel Proust. Répertoire de la correspondance de Proust* (Leiden, 1938)

REMACLE, M. — _L'Élément poétique dans A la recherche du temps perdu de Marcel Proust_ (Brussels, 1954)

REVEL, J.-F. — _Sur Proust_, re-edition (Paris, 1970)

RICHARD, J.-P. — _Proust et le monde sensible_ (Paris, 1974)

RIVANE, G. — _Influence de l'asthme sur l'oeuvre de Marcel Proust_ (Paris, 1945)

ROGERS, B.G. — _Proust's Narrative Techniques_ (Geneva, 1965)

SCOTT MONCRIEFF, C.K. (collected by) — _Marcel Proust: An English Tribute_ (London, 1923)

SEILLIÈRE, E. — _Marcel Proust_ (Paris, 1931)

SHATTUCK, R. — _Proust's Binoculars_ (London, 1964)

——— — _Proust_ (London, 1974)

TADIÉ, J. Y. — _Proust et le roman_ (Paris, 1971)

TAUMAN, L. — _Marcel Proust: Une Vie et une synthèse_ (Paris, 1949)

VALLÉE, C. — _La Féerie de Marcel Proust_ (Paris, 1958)

ZÉPHIR, J.J. — _La Personnalité humaine dans l'oeuvre de Marcel Proust_ (Paris, 1959)

4. - BOOKS WITH A CHAPTER, OR PARTS, ON PROUST

BARNES, A. 'Proust et les patins de Goethe', in *The Artist and the Writer in France*, edited by Francis Haskell, Anthony Levi and Robert Shackleton (Oxford, 1974), pp. 163-72.

BARTHES, R. 'Proust et les noms', in *To Honor Roman Jakobson* (3 vols., The Hague and Paris, 1967), vol. I, pp. 150-58.

BENDA, J. *La France byzantine, ou le triomphe de la littérature pure* ([Paris], 1945)

BENJAMIN, W. *Illuminations* (London, 1970)

COCKING, J.M. 'Proust and painting', in *French 19th Century Painting and Literature*, edited by Ulrich Finke (Manchester, 1972), pp. 305-24.

GENETTE, G. *Figures* (Paris, 1966)

_____ *Figures II* (Paris, 1969)

_____ *Figures III* (Paris, 1972)

GIRARD, R. *Mensonge romantique et vérité romanesque* (Paris, 1961)

KRUTCH, J.W. *Five Masters: Boccaccio, Cervantes, Richardson, Stendhal, Proust* (London, 1931)

LEMAITRE, G. *Four French Novelists: Marcel Proust, André Gide, Jean Giraudoux, Paul Morand* (New York, 1938)

MAGNY, C.-E. *Histoire du roman français depuis 1918* (Paris, 1950)

MEYERHOFF, H. *Time in Literature* (Berkeley and Los Angeles, 1955)

PEYRE, H. *French Novelists of Today* (New York, 1967)

POULET, G. _Études sur le temps humain_ (Paris, 1949)

ROUSSET, J. _Forme et Signification_ (Paris, 1962)

SARTRE, J.-P. _Situations, II_ ([Paris], 1948)

SHATTUCK, R. _The Banquet Years_, revised edition (London, 1969)

SPITZER, L. _Études de Style_ ([Paris], 1970)

WILSON, E. _Axel's Castle_ (London and Glasgow, 1964)

5. - ARTICLES ON PROUST

AMOSSY, R. & ROSEN, E. 'La dame aux catleyas: fonction du pastiche et de la parodie dans "A la recherche du temps perdu"', _Littérature_, no. 14 (1974), pp. 55-64.

ANON. 'Chronique des bibliothèques françaises: Département des manuscrits: Acquisition des manuscrits de Marcel Proust', _Bulletin des Bibliothèques de France_, no. 7 (1962), pp. 380-81.

BANCROFT, D. 'Cocteau's Creative Crisis, 1925-1929: Bremond, Chirico and Proust', _The French Review_, XLV (1971), pp. 9-19.

BARNES, A. 'Le retour des thèmes dans la _Recherche du Temps perdu_ et l'art de Proust', _Australian Journal of French Studies_, VI (1969), pp. 26-54.

_____ 'Le Jardin de Marcel Proust: pour le cinquantenaire des "Jeunes Filles en Fleurs"', _The Modern Language Review_, LXIV (1969), pp. 546-54.

BELLEMIN-NOËL, J. '"Psychanalyser" le rêve de Swann?', _Poétique_, no. 8 (1971), pp. 447-69.

BEZNOS, M.J. 'Aspects of Time According to the Theories of Relativity in Marcel Proust's _A la recherche du Temps perdu_', _The Ohio University Review_, X (1968), pp. 74-102.

BLACK, C.J., Jr. 'Albertine as an Allegorical Figure of Time', _The Romanic Review_, LIV (1963), pp. 171-86.

BOREL, J. 'Notes sur l'imparfait proustien', _Critique_, XXVII (1971), pp. 1060-84.

BRÉE, G. 'Marcel Proust et Maurice Barrès', _The Romanic Review_, XL (1949), pp. 93-105.

BRÉE, G. 'New trends in Proust criticism', Symposium, V (1951), pp. 62-71.

——— 'The Enchanted World of Marcel Proust', The American Society Legion of Honour Magazine, XXXIII (1962), pp. 9-27.

——— 'Les Manuscrits de Marcel Proust', The French Review, XXXVII (1963), pp. 182-87.

——— 'Marcel Proust: Changing Perspectives', Australian Journal of French Studies, I (1964), pp. 104-113.

——— 'Le "Moi Oeuvrant" de Proust', The Modern Language Review, LXI (1966), pp. 610-18.

——— 'Proust's Combray Church: Illiers or Vermeer?', Proceedings of the American Philosophical Society, CXII (1968), pp. 5-7.

——— '"Vision" et création selon Proust', Australian Journal of French Studies, VI (1969), pp. 180-86.

CLERC, J.-M. 'De Rousseau à Proust: Les intermittences du bonheur dans la littérature', L'Information Littéraire, 20e année (1968), pp. 202-208.

COCKING, J.M. Reviews of G. Painter's (vol. I) and R. Barker's biographies, The Romanic Review, LII (1961), pp. 309-315.

——— 'Literature in Proust's life and thought', Forum for Modern Language Studies, V (1969), pp. 286-91.

COHN, R.G. 'Proust and Mallarmé', French Studies, XXIV (1970), pp. 262-75.

DOBBS, A.-C. 'Rousseau et Proust: "Ouvertures" des Confessions et d'A la recherche du temps perdu', L'Esprit Créateur, IX (1969), pp. 165-74.

DUNCAN, J.A. 'Imaginary Artists in "A la recherche du temps perdu"', The Modern Language Review, LXIV (1969), pp. 555-64.

FERRÉ, A. 'Quelques fautes de ponctuation dans les éditions de Marcel Proust', Revue d'Histoire Littéraire de la France, 54e année (1954), pp. 213-18.

FINN, M.R. 'Proust and Dumas fils: Odette and La Dame aux camélias', French Review, XLVII (1974), pp. 528-42.

GRAHAM, V. 'Proust's etymologies', French Studies, XXIX (1975), pp. 300-312.

GRAY, S.E. 'Phenomenology, Structuralism and Marcel Proust', L'Esprit Créateur, VIII (1968), pp. 58-74.

GUICHARD, L. 'Proust avait-il lu Tourgueneff?', Revue des Sciences Humaines, XXXV (1970), p. 105.

GUTWIRTH, M. 'Swann and the Duchess', The French Review, XXXVIII (1964), pp. 143-51.

_____ 'La bible de Combray', Revue des Sciences Humaines, XXXVI (1971), pp. 417-27.

HODSON, W.L. 'Proust's Methods of Character Presentation in "Les Plaisirs et les Jours" and "Jean Santeuil"', The Modern Language Review, LVII (1962), pp. 41-46.

JACKSON, E.R. 'The Crystallisation of "A la recherche du temps perdu" 1908-1909', The French Review, XXXVIII (1964), pp. 157-66.

JONES, P. 'Knowledge and Illusion in A la Recherche du Temps Perdu', Forum for Modern Language Studies, V (1969), pp. 303-22.

KELLMAN, S.G. 'Imagining the Novel Dead: Recent Variations on a Theme by Proust', Modern Language Quarterly, XXXV (1974), pp. 45-55.

KNODEL, A.J. 'Marcel Proust et Saint-John Perse: le fossé infranchissable', La Revue de Paris, 76e année (1969), pp. 80-92.

KOLB, P. 'Le Marquis de Norpois: Encore les "clefs" de Proust', Mercure de France, 1 mai 1951, pp. 178-81.

_____ 'Le "mystère" des gravures anglaises recherchées par Proust', Mercure de France, 1 août 1956, pp. 750-55.

_____ 'Proust's Portrait of Jaurès in Jean Santeuil', French Studies, XV (1961), pp. 338-49.

_____ 'An Enigmatic Proustian Metaphor', The Romanic Review, LIV (1963), pp. 187-97.

_____ Review of V. Graham's The Imagery of Proust, Modern Language Quarterly, XXIX (1968), pp. 116-20.

KOSTIS, N. 'Albertine: Characterisation through Image and Symbol', Publications of the Modern Language Association of America, LXXXIV (1969), pp. 125-35.

LAPP, J.C. 'The Jealous window-watcher in Zola and Proust', French Studies, XXIX (1975), pp. 166-76.

LAYTON, M.J. 'Deux transformations métaphoriques de Proust', Littérature, no. 14 (1974), pp. 49-54.

LERNER, M.G. 'Édouard Rod and Marcel Proust', French Studies, XXV (1971), pp. 162-68.

LINN, J.G. 'Notes on Proust's Manipulation of Chronology', The Romanic Review, LII (1961), pp. 210-225.

MARTIN-CHAUFFIER, L. 'Proust and the Double "I" of Two Characters', Partisan Review, XVI (1949), pp. 1011-26.

MARTINOIR, F.N. de — 'Du temps des essences à l'illusion volontaire ou la fonction des robes et des salons dans l'univers imaginaire de Marcel Proust', Revue des Sciences Humaines, XXXVI (1971), pp. 405-15.

MATORÉ, G. & MECZ, I. — 'Le thème de la communication dans "La recherche du temps perdu": le volet et le rideau', Journal de Psychologie Normale et Pathologique, LXVIe année (1969), pp. 15-34.

MEIN, M. — 'Fromentin, a Precursor of Proust', Forum for Modern Language Studies, VII (1971), pp. 221-36.

_____ — 'Proust and Balzac', Australian Journal of French Studies, IX (1972), pp. 3-22.

_____ — '"Le moi oeuvrant" : the Enigma of a Proustian Theme', Forum for Modern Language Studies, VIII (1972), pp. 215-29.

MILLY, J. — 'Sur quelques noms proustiens', Littérature, no. 14 (1974), pp. 65-82.

MOULINE, L. — 'La mer et la vision proustienne dans les ébauches du "Temps perdu"', Revue des Sciences Humaines, XXXV (1970), pp. 93-103.

MULLER, M. — '"Sodome I" ou la naturalisation de Charlus', Poétique, no. 8 (1971), pp. 470-78.

MURRAY, J. — 'Proust's Views on Perception as a Metaphoric Framework', The French Review, XLII (1969), pp. 380-94.

O'BRIEN, J. — 'An Aspect of Proust's Baron de Charlus', The Romanic Review, LV (1964), pp. 38-41.

PASCO, A.H. — 'Albertine's Equivocal Eyes', Australian Journal of French Studies, V (1968), pp. 257-62.

PASCO, A.H. 'Blue and the Ideal of A la recherche du temps perdu', Romanische Forschungen, LXXXV (1973), pp. 119-138.

REDDICK, B. 'The "La Berma" Passages in Proust's A la recherche du temps perdu: The Theatre of Experience', The French Review, XLII (1969), pp. 683-92.

ROBERTSON, J. 'The Relationship between the Hero and Françoise in A la Recherche du Temps Perdu', French Studies, XXV (1971), pp. 437-41.

RODITI, E. 'Proust Recaptured', The Kenyon Review, XXX (1968), pp. 23-39.

ROWLAND, M. 'Contre Sainte-Beuve and Character-Presentation in A la recherche du temps perdu', Romance Notes, VIII (1967), pp. 183-87.

SAVAGE, C.H. 'Nostalgia in Alain-Fournier and Proust', The French Review, XXXVIII (1964), pp. 167-72.

SIMONS, M.A. 'Les Regards dans A la recherche du temps perdu', The French Review, XLI (1968), pp. 498-504.

SLATER, M. '"L'Inconnu": A Fragment of "Jean Santeuil"', The Modern Language Review, LXV (1970), pp. 778-84.

SOUCY, R. 'Bad Readers in the World of Proust', The French Review, XLIV (1971), pp. 677-86.

TAYLOR, R. 'The adult world and childhood in Combray', French Studies, XXII (1968), pp. 26-36.

TUKEY, A. 'Notes on Involuntary Memory in Proust', The French Review, XLII (1969), pp. 395-402.

VIARD, J. 'Péguy et Proust ou la foi dans les Lettres', Nouvelle Revue Française, no. 244 (1973), pp. 66-75.

VIGNERON, R. 'Genèse de Swann', Revue d'Histoire de la Philosophie, 5e année (1937), pp. 67-115.

_____ 'Marcel Proust ou l'Angoisse créatrice', Modern Philology, XLII (1945), pp. 212-30.

_____ 'Structure de Swann: Balzac, Wagner et Proust', The French Review, XIX (1946), pp. 370-84.

VINCENOT, C. 'Les procédés littéraires de Marcel Proust et la Représentation du Monde chez l'enfant', Revue des Sciences Humaines, XXXIII (1968), pp. 5-28.

WEBER, S.M. 'Le Madrépore', Poétique, no. 13 (1973), pp. 28-54.

ZANTS, E. 'Proust and the New Novel in France', Publications of the Modern Language Association of America, LXXXVIII (1973), pp. 25-33.

Special numbers on Proust:

Adam International Review, Year XXV, no. 260 (1957).

L'Arc, no. 47 (1971?).

Bulletin de la Société des Amis de Marcel Proust et des Amis de Combray, nos. 1-25 (1950-75).

Cahiers de l'Association Internationale des Études Françaises, no. 12 (1960), pp. 189-301.

L'Esprit Créateur, V, no. 1 (1965).

L'Esprit Créateur, XI, no. 1 (1971).

Europe, 48e année, nos. 496-497 (1970).

Europe, 49e année, nos. 502-503 (1971).

Le Figaro Littéraire, 1-7 février 1971.

Nouvelle Revue Française, novembre 1971.

Proust Research Association Newsletter, nos. 1-14 (March 1969-Fall 1975).

Revue d'Histoire Littéraire de la France, 71e année, nos. 5-6 (1971).

Index

UNIVERSITY LIBRARY
NOTTINGHAM